W9-CDT-131

PCMCIA System Architecture
16-Bit PC Cards

Second Edition

MINDSHARE, INC.
DON ANDERSON

Addison-Wesley Publishing Company
Reading, Massachusetts • Menlo Park, California • New York
Don Mills, Ontario • Wokingham, England • Amsterdam
Bonn • Sydney • Singapore • Tokyo • Madrid • San Juan
Paris • Seoul • Milan • Mexico City • Taipei

Library of Congress Cataloging-in-Publication Data

ISBN: 0-201-40991-7

Sponsoring Editor: Keith Wollman
Production Coordinator: Deborah McKenna
Cover design: Barbara T. Atkinson
Set in 10 point Palatino by MindShare, Inc.

1 2 3 4 5 6 7 8 9 -MA- 9998979695
First printing, July 1995

For Doris and Darrel Anderson, my mother and father.

Contents

Part One
Introduction to PCMCIA

Chapter 1: The Problem

Chapter 2: The PCMCIA Solution

PCMCIA System Architecture

Chapter 3: Tying the Pieces Together

Part Two
Socket and Host Bus Adapter Design

Chapter 4: The Physical Specifications

Chapter 5: The Memory-Only Socket Interface

Contents

Chapter 6: The Memory or I/O Interface

Chapter 7: The DMA Interface

PCMCIA System Architecture

Chapter 8: The ATA Interface

Chapter 9: The AIMS Interface

Chapter 10: The PC Card Host Bus Adapter

Contents

Part Three
PC Card Design

Chapter 11: The Card Information Structure (CIS)

Chapter 12: Function Configuration Registers

Chapter 13: An SRAM Card Example

Chapter 14: A Flash Card Example

Contents

Chapter 15: A FAX/Modem Example

Chapter 16: An ATA PC Card Example

Chapter 17: A Multiple Function PC Card Example

Part Four
PCMCIA Software

Chapter 18: The Configuration Process

Contents

Chapter 19: Socket Services

Chapter 20: Card Services

Chapter 21: Client Drivers

Contents

Chapter 22: Booting from PC Cards

Chapter 23: Execute In Place (XIP)

Part Five
ExCA (QuickSwap)

Chapter 24: ExCA (QuickSwap)

PCMCIA System Architecture

Part Six
An Example HBA

Chapter 25: An Example HBA—The CL-PD6722

Appendices

Figures

Tables

PCMIA System Architecture

Tables

Special Recognition

Special thanks to Tom Shanley, my best friend, business partner and hiking companion, who keeps me on the right path.

Acknowledgments

I extend my appreciation and gratitude to the developers at IBM and Intel who provided valuable information and insight during the development of this book and training course. Special thanks to those at the IBM Toronto site who struggled with me during the early stages. Thanks also to those at Cirrus Logic who answered many questions and provided valuable information. Finally, I would like to thank Maxtor for providing information on their ATA drive.

Thanks to those at Norand in Cedar Rapids for their efforts in catching many errors in the manuscript and suggesting improvements to both text and illustrations.

The MindShare Architecture Series

The series of books by MindShare on system architecture includes; *ISA System Architecture, EISA System Architecture, 80486 System Architecture, PCI System Architecture, Pentium™ Processor System Architecture, PCMCIA System Architecture, PowerPC™ System Architecture, Plug and Play System Architecture,* and *CardBus System Architecture,* all published by Addison-Wesley.

Rather than duplicating common information in each book, the series uses a building-block approach. *ISA System Architecture* is the core book upon which the others build. The figure below illustrates the relationship of the books to each other.

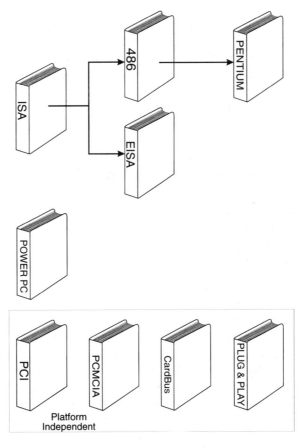

Architecture Series Organization

Organization of This Book

PCMCIA System Architecture is organized into six parts consisting of twenty-five chapters. A brief description of each chapter follows:

Part One — Introduction to PCMCIA

Chapter 1:   The Problem. This chapter focuses on the industry needs that led to the emergence of PCMCIA and the development of PC Card Standard.

Chapter 2:   The PCMCIA Solution. This chapter discusses the emergence of PCMCIA, traces its evolution and introduces terminology and key concepts behind PCMCIA. Key features of the latest release of the 16-bit PCMCIA standard (called the PC Card Standard) are also introduced.

Chapter 3:   Tying the Pieces Together. This chapter explains the relationships between the various hardware and software elements employed in a typical PC Card environment. The elements discussed include: the PCMCIA Host Bus Adapter (HBA); the PC Card socket; the PC Card; socket services; card services; and enablers.

Part Two — Socket and Host Bus Adapter Design

Chapter 4:   The Physical Specifications. This chapter focuses on the various physical packages defined by PCMCIA for PC Cards and the related environmental specifications. The chapter also describes the standard socket and low-voltage socket types.

Chapter 5:   The Memory-Only Socket Interface. This chapter details the memory-only electrical interface between the PC Card and socket. Each pin is defined and it relationship to the PC Card and the HBA is discussed. The memory-only interface is the interface initially seen by 16-bit PC Cards when they are first inserted into a socket. This permits the memory-mapped CIS to be accessed to determine the PC Card type and interface requirements. If the card is designed for an interface type other than memory-only, then the HBA and PC Card are configured to communicate via one of the other interfaces defined by the PC Card Standard (discussed in the following chapters). Also discusses the timing of socket accesses to PC Cards of differing speeds, including transfers with attribute memory and common memory.

Chapter 6:   The Memory or I/O Interface. This chapter details the memory or I/O socket interface. The memory-only interface is converted into a memory or I/O interface by software after it detects that an I/O PC Card has been installed into the socket interface. Pins that are added or redefined by the memory or I/O interface are discussed along with their relationship to the I/O card function. Some of the memory-only pins are replaced with I/O specific pins when the interface is redefined for I/O. This chapter describes how the functions associated with the replaced memory-only pins are handled.

Chapter 7:   The DMA Interface. This chapter defines the DMA compliant electrical interface, permitting I/O Cards to use PC compatible DMA transfers. The DMA interface allows I/O devices that use DMA to take advantage of existing compatible software when performing data transfers.

Chapter 8:   The ATA Interface. This chapter discusses the PC Card ATA interface. An PC Card ATA interface provides a PC compatible hardware and programming interface that simplifies the job of implemented hard drive solutions in the PCMCIA environment. This chapter defines the various ways that a PC Card ATA can be mapped in the system along with the electrical interfaces that are used. Differences between the PC compatible ATA implementation versus the PC Card ATA interface are also discussed.

Chapter 9:   The AIMS Interface. This chapter focuses on the optional Auto-Indexing Mass Storage (AIMS) interface. The transfer mechanism is described, along with the registers that must be programmed to initiate the transfer.

Chapter 10: The PC Card Host Bus Adapter. This chapter discusses the role of the PCMCIA Host Bus Adapter. Individual Host Bus Adapter functions are discussed. A functional block diagram of an HBA adapter is provided along with detailed explanations of each function.

Part Three — PC Card Design

Chapter 11: The Card Information Structure (CIS). This chapter discusses layer one of the metaformat, commonly referred to as the card information structure, or CIS. The chapter details the role of the CIS in the PC Card configuration process. Tuples are also introduced and their format and structure are described. The basic structure of the CIS's configuration table required by I/O cards is also described.

Chapter 12: Function Configuration Registers. This chapter discusses the configuration registers and provides a complete description of each register specified by the PC Card standard. Configuration register implementations for both single and multiple function cards are covered.

Chapter 13: An SRAM Card Example. This chapter describes a sample SRAM card implementation, including a functional block diagram of the SRAM card along with a sample CIS.

Chapter 14: A Flash Card Example. This chapter describes a flash card implementation, including a functional block diagram of the card, a sample CIS, and configuration registers implemented by the card.

Chapter 15: A FAX/Modem Example. This chapter describes an example FAX/Modem implementation, including a functional block diagram, sample CIS, and related configuration registers.

Chapter 16: An ATA PC Card Example. This chapter describes an example PC Card ATA drive implementation, including a functional block diagram, a sample CIS, and configuration registers implemented by the card.

Chapter 17: A Multiple Function PC Card Example. This chapter discusses the multiple function PC Card strategy and the mechanisms for achieving it. It also includes a functional block diagram of a multiple function PC Card, a sample multi-function CIS, related configuration registers, and multi-function interrupt handling.

Part Four — PCMCIA Software

Chapter 18: The Configuration Process. This chapter provides an overview of the PCMCIA software environment and the configuration process. The primary role and interaction between each piece of software is established. This chapter also introduces the common software solutions provided along with the most popular suppliers.

Chapter 19: Socket Services. This chapter discusses the role of socket services. It also describes the initialization of socket services and explains the basic purpose of the functions commonly supported in the PC environment.

Chapter 20: Card Services. This chapter focuses on the role of card services in the PCMCIA environment. This chapter review each of the functions defined by the PC Card specification that apply to 16-bit PC Cards, along with related return codes. The call back mechanism is also described and the event and call back codes are defined.

Chapter 21: Client Drivers This chapter discusses the three basic types of enablers: point enablers, device-specific enablers, and super enablers. The chapter also discusses the jobs performed by generic memory enablers (and MTDs) and I/O device enablers.

Chapter 22: Booting from PC Cards. This chapter discusses the problems associated with loading the operating system from a PC Card. It also defines mechanisms used to determine whether a given PC Card is a bootable device, and the firmware support required to support PC Card booting.

Chapter 23: Execute In Place (XIP). This chapter discusses the Execute-In-Place mechanism defined by PCMCIA that allows code to be executed directly from the card rather than copying files to and executing from system memory.

Part Five — ExCA (QuickSwap)

Chapter 24: ExCA (QuickSwap). This chapter introduces the ExCA (QuickSwap) specification that defines a required set of hardware and software support, intended to improve PC Card interoperability across platforms based on Intel x86 architecture.

Part Six — An Example HBA

Chapter 25: An Example HBA–The CL-PD6722. This chapter provides an overview of a sample PCMCIA host bus adapter (The Cirrus Logic CL-PD6722) used in Intel x86 implementations for either an original PC or ISA compatible host bus.

Appendices

SRAM CIS Example

Flash CIS Example

FAX/Modem CIS Example

ATA Disk CIS Example

Metaformat Layers 2, 3, and 4

References

Who Should Read This Book

This book is intended for use by hardware and software designers and support personnel. Due to the clear and concise explanatory methods used to describe each subject, personnel outside of the design field may also find the text useful.

Prerequisite Knowledge

We highly recommend that you have a thorough knowledge of PCs, including hardware and software interaction prior to reading this book. Several Mind-Share publications provide all of the background necessary for a complete understanding of the subject matter covered in this book. Much of the background information can be obtained from the *ISA System Architecture* book.

Documentation Conventions

This section defines the typographical conventions used throughout this book.

Hex Notation

All hex numbers are followed by an "h". Examples:

9A4Eh

0100h

Binary Notation

All binary numbers are followed by a "b". Examples:

0001 0101b

01b

Decimal Notation

When required for clarity, decimal numbers are followed by a "d". Examples:

256d

128d

Signal Name Representation

Each signal that assumes the logic low state when asserted is followed by a pound sign (#). As an example, a PC Card modem asserts the IREQ# signal to a logic low state when signaling an interrupt request to the system.

Signals that are not followed by a pound sign are asserted when they assume the logic high state. As an example, a PCMCIA Card asserts READY to logic high state, indicating that it is ready to be accessed.

Identification of Bit Fields (logical groups of bits or signals)

All bit fields are designated as follows:

[X:Y],

where "X" is the most-significant bit and "Y" is the least-significant bit of the field. As an example, the PCMCIA socket supports address lines A[25:0], where A25 is the most-significant and A0 the least-significant bit of the address.

CardBus

An enhanced version of PCMCIA is also defined by the PC Card standard. The new high-speed CardBus cards incorporate 32-bit data transfers and bus mastering capability. See MindShare's *CardBus System Architecture* book published by Addison-Wesley for details regarding the CardBus implementation.

We Want Your Feedback

MindShare values your comments and suggestions. You can contact us via mail, phone, fax, or internet email.

E-Mail/Phone/FAX

Email: mindshar@interserv.com

Phone: (214) 231-2216

Fax: (214) 783-4715

Mailing Address

Our mailing address is:

MindShare, Inc.

2202 Buttercup Drive

Richardson, Texas 75082

Part One

Introduction to PCMCIA

Chapter 1

This Chapter

This chapter focuses on the industry needs that led to the emergence of PCMCIA and the development of PC Card Standard.

The Next Chapter

The next chapter introduces the PCMCIA solution and reviews the evolution of the PCMCIA Standard.

The Mobile Computing Environment

The growth of the microcomputer industry in the 1980s and the popularity of the PC led to the proliferation of laptop, notebook and sub-notebook computers. Manufacturers strived to deliver desktop performance in smaller and lighter portable systems, powered by batteries. This fueled the need for lighter, smaller, and less power hungry peripheral devices. A major focus of this effort revolved around the relatively large, heavy, power hungry floppy drive subsystem.

In addition to being small, lighter, and more power efficient, the alternative system had to provide many of the same characteristics of the floppy disk; it had to include removable media that was transportable to other systems, and had to be immediately accessible when installed into the system for reading and writing files. Early interest revolved primarily around the use of battery-backed memory cards implemented as a virtual floppy drive subsystem. Memory cards were physically small, could store large amounts of data, and consumed relatively little system power when compared to the floppy drive. Furthermore, the emergence of Flash memory promised to provide an economical memory card solution that required no battery back-up.

Small Form-Factor I/O Expansion Devices

The mobile computer environment also had a need for small and power efficient I/O expansion devices. The small PCMCIA form-factor drew attention as a possible solution for I/O expansion devices. The initial PCMCIA designs supported only memory cards however, the need to expand PCMCIA to include I/O device support was clear.

Chapter 2

The Previous Chapter

The previous chapter focused on the industry needs that led to the emergence of PCMCIA and the development of PC Card Standard.

This Chapter

This chapter discusses the emergence of PCMCIA, traces its evolution and introduces terminology and key concepts behind PCMCIA. Key features of the latest release of the 16-bit PCMCIA standard (called the PC Card Standard) are also introduced.

The Next Chapter

The next chapter explains the relationships between the various hardware and software elements employed in a typical PC Card environment. The elements discussed include: the PCMCIA Host Bus Adapter (HBA); the PC Card socket; the PC Card; socket services; card services; and client drivers.

The Virtual Floppy Drive Subsystem

Solid state memory cards can provide an alternative to the mechanical floppy and floppy drive. In other words, memory cards can be implemented as a virtual floppy drive subsystem. Such a solution must permit standard PC software to access the memory cards as if they were floppy disks. This necessitates translation of PC compatible software calls used to access an ordinary floppy disk into commands that access files stored within the memory card. To ensure compatibility with existing PC software a standardized software protocol was required to ensure compatible operation of the memory cards.

Memory cards implemented as virtual floppy disks must also have the ability to be inserted and removed from the system at any time as is done with floppy disks. When a card is installed, software must be able to access the files stored on the memory card or write new files to it. How was this to be done? Several key questions come to mind: How would the insertion of a memory card be detected? Were memory cards to be accessed via an I/O port as done with the floppy drive interface, or mapped into the processor's memory address space? What system resources would be required? What software would be responsible for the various aspects of recognizing, configuring, and accessing the memory cards? These questions and others clearly pointed to the need for hardware and software standards that could be implemented by system manufacturers to ensure interoperability of memory cards between IBM compatible systems.

The Lack of a Standard Memory Card Design

Numerous memory card manufacturers produced cards with differing physical and electrical properties, making compatibility a major obstacle in fulfilling industry needs. A standard physical package, electrical interface and connector were needed to ensure compatibility of memory cards.

Emergence of PCMCIA

Several manufacturers met in the summer of 1988 to investigate the possibility of forming a standards organization to deal with memory card standards and interoperability issues. A year later the Personal Computer Memory Card International Association (PCMCIA) was founded, and the first PCMCIA Standard (Release 1.0) was introduced in September 1990. This standard specified the design of memory cards (commonly called PC Cards) and a socket interface to be implemented as virtual disk drives.

PCMCIA was formed to promote the standardization and interchangeability of PC Cards. Initially, its primary focus was defining PC Card standards for IBM PC-compatible (DOS-based) systems. The long-term goal is to allow a variety of computer types and non-computer products to freely interchange PC cards. With these goals in mind the PCMCIA defined standards for PC Cards.

The Japanese Electronics Industry Development Association (JEIDA) began working on memory card standardization issues in 1985. In 1989 PCMCIA adopted JEIDA's 68-pin connector as its socket interface. To serve the goals of compatibility and interoperability JEIDA and PCMCIA began working jointly to ensure compatibility between their standards. In 1990 PCMCIA announced its first standard (release 1.0) and JEIDA released its fourth standard (release 4.0). As newer versions of the standards are released, JEIDA and PCMCIA continue to work closely to support each other's standards.

Support for I/O-based PC Cards Added

The mobile computing environment also needed standardized small form-factor I/O devices that could be added to mobile systems as expansion devices. PCMCIA's release 2.0 added support for I/O devices that could be inserted into a PCMCIA socket. Like memory cards, these devices are designed to be automatically detected by the system when installed and automatically configured. This gives PC Cards the ability to be inserted into a PCMCIA socket after the system has already been powered up and is operational.

The PC Card Standard

The PCMCIA standard defines the following major items:

- Physical design of the PC Card
- Physical design of the connector (socket)
- Electrical interface to PC Cards
- Software architecture

The PC Card standard has been designed with flexibility in mind, allowing PC Card socket implementations to be adapted for a wide variety of systems. Major features of today's PCMCIA standard include items listed in table 2-1.

PC Cards come in a wide range of memory and I/O devices. Memory devices include RAM, FLASH memory and various types of ROM. I/O devices include voice, data and FAX modems; network interface cards; wireless communications (such as, Global Positioning Systems (GPS), pagers and networks); AT Attachment (ATA) Hard Drives (also called IDE drives); small computer system interface (SCSI) adapters; and many others.

Three sizes of PC Cards are specified by the physical standard. Each type of card has the same electrical interface and planar dimensions, but the thickness varies to accommodate designs that require more physical space. Generally, type I cards (3.3mm thick) are used for memory devices of various kinds, type II cards (5.0mm thick) for modems, LANs, etc., and type III cards (10.5mm thick) for devices such as ATA hard drives.

Table 2-1. PCMCIA Feature Summary

Feature	Description
Small Form-Factor: Three Physical Device Types Defined	PCMCIA cards have a standard length and width of 85.6mm (3.370") X 54.0mm (2.126"). The card type determines the card's thickness — Type 1 = 3.3mm (0.130"); Type 2 = 5.0mm (0.197"); Type 3 = 10.5mm (0.413").
Host Bus Independence	PCMCIA sockets can be connected to a wide variety of host buses. Sockets are connected to the host systems via host bus adapters designed for a particular bus interface.
Three Address Spaces	PCMCIA supports common memory address space (standard memory addresses), attribute memory space (for automatic configuration) and I/O address space.
64 MB of Address Space	Twenty-six address lines provide address space up to 64 MB for each address space.
16-bit Data Path*	Sixteen data lines permit word transfers to/from PC Cards.
I/O Device Support	I/O devices as well as memory devices can be implemented in the credit card form-factor.
Direct Memory Access (DMA) Support	The PC Card standard incorporated DMA support so that standard PC expansion devices that use DMA can be supported in PC Card implementations and take advantage of the existing software.
Multifunction PC Cards Support	The PC Card standard directly supports PC Cards that include multiple memory or I/O functions or both.
Automatic Configuration	When installed, PC Cards are configured automatically without the need for user intervention.
Software Transparency	Software written for standard host bus devices can be used when accessing the same device that is implemented in a PC Card. Once the PC Card is installed and configured it typically behaves like any other host device.
Easy to Implement Configuration Software	PCMCIA provides a standard software interface, simplifying the design and implementation of device-drivers required to configuration PC Cards.
Low Voltage Support	The PC Card standard supports 5 volt, 3.3 volt and what PCMCIA refers to as X.X voltage (an arbitrary low voltage to be specified sometime in the future).

Table 2-1 PCMCIA Feature Summary (continued)

Feature	Description
Support for Several Different File Systems on a Single Card	PC Cards provide a means for specifying support for a variety of different data-recording formats and data organizations.
Execution of Code Directly from Memory Card	PCMCIA memory cards, typically implemented as virtual disks, can be accessed directly for code, without copying it to main memory. This support requires a software protocol called XIP (execute-in-place).

* The PC Card standard also defines a 32-bit PC Card and socket interface called CardBus.

Summary of PCMCIA Releases

Since the first PCMCIA standard was released, many revisions and enhancements have been made. Table 2-2 highlights the chronology of releases, providing a perspective of the pace of change that has occurred in a relatively short period of time. The most recent release (February 1995) is called the PC Card standard, consisting of a 12 volume set listed in table 2-3.

Table 2-2. Evolution of the PCMCIA Specification

Specification	Version	Release Dates
Card Standard	1.0	November, 1990
	1.01	September, 1991
	2.0	November, 1992
	2.1	July, 1993
Socket Services	A.0	June, 1991
	1.00	August, 1991
	1.01	September, 1991
	2.0	November, 1992
	2.1	July, 1993
Card Services	1.0 (draft)	December, 1991
	2.0	November, 1992
	2.1	July, 1993
ATA Interface	1.0	July, 1992
	1.01	November, 1992

Table 2-2. Evolution of the PCMCIA Specification (continued)

Specification	Version	Release Dates
Auto-Indexing Mass Storage (AIMS)	1.0	July, 1992
	1.01	November, 1992
Card Extensions	1.0	November, 1992

Table 2-3. List of Individual Volumes Included in the PC Card Standard

Volume Name	Description of Contents
Overview and Glossary	This volume introduces each volume and provides a glossary of terms.
Electrical Specification	The electrical specification provides definition of the socket interface pins, signaling environment, and transfer timing and control.
Physical Specification	The physical specification describes the card and socket dimensions, mechanical specifications, and environmental storage and operational parameters that must be met.
Metaformat Specification	This specification describes a four layer model that encompasses the basic compatibility layer that all PC Cards must implement. The compatibility layer describes a variety of PC Card characteristics and capabilities needed to configure the card. The subsequent layers define a memory card's method of recording data and describe its organization. This information provides software with the information it needs to manage access to a variety of PC memory cards in a compatible fashion.
Card Services Specification	This specification defines function calls used by a PC Card's client driver to configure and control access to it's PC Card.
Socket Services Specification	This specification defines function calls used principally by Card Services to access a particular HBA. These functions are comparable to BIOS functions provided in IBM compatible PCs.

Table 2-3. List of Individual Volumes Included in the PC Card Standard (continued)

Volume Name	Description of Contents
Media Storage Formats Specification	This specification describes how data is formatted on many PC Cards that are used as virtual disks. This information can be used to help provide exchangeability of PC memory cards between different host systems.
PC Card ATA Specification	The ATA specification describes the electrical and programming interface required by PC Cards implemented as ATA devices.
XIP Specification	XIP describes the programming interface required by applications that support execution directly from the PC Card file, rather than having to copy the executable file to system memory and executing from there.
Guidelines	This volume provides guidelines for the implementation of a variety of PC Card types.
PCMCIA Extensions	The PCMCIA extensions document features that are not supported by JEIDA, but which are offered as optional capabilities by PCMCIA.
JEIDA Extensions	The JEIDA extension document features that are not supported by PCMCIA, but which are offered as optional capabilities by JEIDA.

Chapter 3

The Previous Chapter

The previous chapter discussed the emergence of PCMCIA, traced its evolution and introduced terminology and the key concepts behind PCMCIA.

This Chapter

This chapter explains the relationships between the various hardware and software elements employed in a typical PC Card environment. The elements discussed include: the PCMCIA Host Bus Adapter (HBA); the PC Card socket; the PC Card; socket services; card services; and enablers.

The Next Chapter

The next chapter focuses on the various physical packages defined by PCMCIA for PC Cards and the related environmental specifications. The chapter also defines the socket interface types.

Overview

This section introduces key PCMCIA terms and discusses the relationship of the major hardware and software elements typically implemented in PCMCIA host system and PC Card designs. Later chapters detail each of these major elements and discuss specific implementations. The PCMCIA solution typically consists of:

Hardware

- The 16-Bit PC Card
- PCMCIA Socket
- The PCMCIA Host Bus Adapter (HBA)

Software

- Socket Services
- Card Services
- PC Card Enablers

The PCMCIA hardware consists of the PC Card, card socket and the host bus adapter (HBA). The HBA bridges the host expansion bus (e.g. ISA, EISA, Micro Channel, or PCI) to the PC Card socket or sockets.

The PCMCIA software architecture consists primarily of a PC Card's enablers, card services and socket services. These software layers exist to support PCMCIA's automatic configuration and "" capability. The term hot insertion is frequently used to refer to the ability of PC Cards to be inserted into a socket when power is applied to the PC. The system automatically detects and configures the PC Card allowing the system to treat it as a floppy disk. That is, once a PC memory card is inserted into a socket, the user can read files or write files just as if a floppy disk had been inserted into a floppy drive. From the user's perspective, the ability to format the memory card (virtual disk), perform chkdsk commands and read and write files is the same as with a floppy drive. The only perceptible difference is the lightning speed at which these operations occur when compared to the speed of the same operations performed with a floppy drive. This is due to the much faster access to solid state media.

Figure 3-1 illustrates the relationships between each of the hardware and software elements that comprise a PCMCIA solution, and identifies the typical supplier of each element. The definition and need for each element is described in the following sections.

The PC Card

A wide variety of hardware applications can be implemented using PC Cards. Many PC Cards consist of memory devices used to emulate floppy or hard drives. These virtual drives provide very fast access and provide a data transfer medium much less susceptible to harsh environmental conditions when compared to magnetic media (such as diskettes and magnetic tape). If these devices are to be used as replaceable media, the system must be able to recognize when a card is inserted or removed and provide the ability to access the card as if it were a floppy disk.

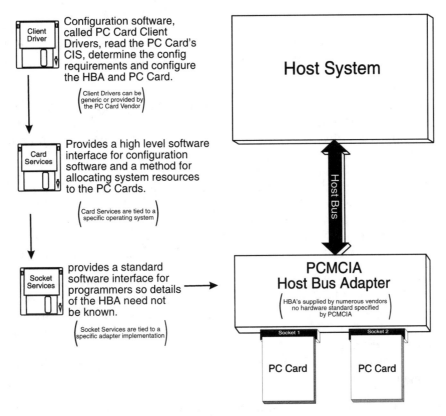

Figure 3-1. Relationship of PCMCIA Software and Hardware

PCMCIA also supports I/O devices such as modems, IDE (ATA) hard drives and LAN controllers. New support has also been added for multifunction devices.

Regardless of the type of PC Card implemented (memory, I/O, or multifunction), PCMCIA systems are designed to permit their automatic detection and configuration. The PCMCIA automatic configuration capability is in some ways similar to that employed by the Micro Channel and EISA system designs, but eliminates the user intervention required with these systems and permits insertion and configuration while power is applied to the system.

In Micro Channel and EISA designs, the manufacturer of an adapter board must supply a configuration file that describes the possible configuration options for the board. The system manufacturer also supplies a configuration file describing the resources used by the basic system, along with a variety of configuration options. A configuration utility program must be run by the user to merge all the configuration information together (system and installed boards). The configuration software then determines an overall conflict-free configuration that satisfies the requirements of the system and all expansion boards.

PC Cards incorporate configuration option information in non-volatile memory within the card itself, rather than requiring a companion diskette that contains the configuration option information. This configuration data is kept in an area within the card known as the (CIS). The CIS is mapped into the PC Card's attribute memory space. Refer to figure 3-2. PC Card enabler software installs each time the system is powered up. This software checks for the presence of PC Cards that are installed. If a PC Card is detected, the software reads the contents of its CIS to determine the type of device it is, the system resources that it requires, and the configuration options that are possible. The enabler is then responsible for configuring the PC Card so it can be accessed.

PC cards, unlike the Micro Channel and EISA boards, can be inserted either before or after the system is powered up. As a result, enablers must remain available for PC Cards in the event a card is installed following system power-up. Hardware notifies the software when a new card is installed, so that it can be properly configured into the system. When a card is removed, again hardware detects the card's removal and notifies software that the device is no longer installed.

The PCMCIA configuration software consists of one or more PC Card enablers that recognize, enable, and configure the PC Card. This software sometimes comes with a particular PC Card (typically as part of a device driver) that the card manufacturer provides when the PC Card is purchased. This type of PC Card enabler is usually responsible for installing only the PC Card for which it was designed. Other PC Card enablers, sometimes called generic or super-enablers, are typically supplied by the system manufacturer.

Generic enablers evaluate the configuration requirements of a card by scanning and evaluating (parsing) the CIS. If the generic enabler recognizes the card type, it will then attempt to configure the card itself or dynamically load the appropriate enabler from a library residing on disk. Ideally, a single PC Card super-enabler would be used to detect and configure all PC Cards. For a variety of reasons (to be discussed later), a single generic or super-enabler is not always possible today. In short, PCMCIA configuration software may consist of one or more PC Card enablers designed to identify and configure PC Cards.

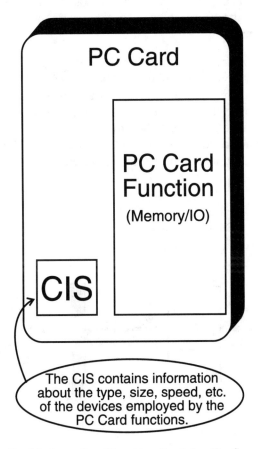

Figure 3-2. The Card Information Structure Contains Configuration Options for the PC Card

Interoperability: PCMCIA Sockets and The PCMCIA Host Bus Adapter

PCMCIA sockets can be designed into a wide variety of PC bus architectures as well as non-PC designs, permitting interoperability of PC Cards. This connection between a given host bus and a PCMCIA socket is provided through a

PCMCIA host bus adapter (HBA). The adapter acts as a bridge, passing host bus transactions to PC Cards installed in PCMCIA sockets. Refer to figure 3-3. Host bus adapters must be programmed by the system in order to gain access to PC Cards. The manner in which the host bus adapter is programmed is determined by the requirements of the particular PC Card installed in the sockets it controls.

Each PCMCIA socket has its own dedicated signal interface provided by the HBA. That is, signals are not bussed between sockets as in most expansion bus architectures. This of course means that the host bus adapter must have a separate interface to each socket along with a single interface to the host system. Access to each socket therefore is controlled through separate sets of socket interface circuitry, each of which must be initialized in order to gain access to a PC Card installed in a given socket.

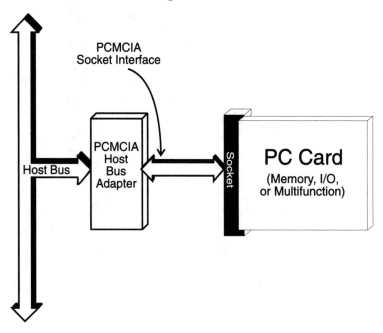

Figure 3-3. PCMCIA Sockets Can Be Incorporated in a Wide Variety of Systems.

Initializing the Host Bus Adapter: Socket Services

Since host bus adapters (HBAs) must have a dual personality — an interface to both the PCMCIA sockets and to the host system — the details of implementing an HBA has been left to the hardware developer and is not included within the PCMCIA specification. This means that a wide variety of HBA designs can (and do) exist for a given type of host interface.

Several chip manufacturers provide PCMCIA host bus adapter chips that system manufacturers can incorporate into their designs. For example, manufacturers of ISA to PCMCIA host bus adapters include: Cirrus Logic, DataBook, Intel, Texas Instruments, Vadem, VLSI Technology, and others. Each of these designs to some extent implement different registers and initialization algorithms. Differences between some HBAs are slight while differences between others are major.

Software must initialize the HBA so that it can pass host expansion transactions to the PC card when it detects an address that resides within the range of addresses used by the PC Card. Since a variety of different HBAs can be used, programmers would have to write their software to interface to each type of host bus adapter in order to ensure proper operation in all system platforms. However, the PC Card specification provides a common software interface called socket services which hides the details of the hardware interface from the programmer. Socket services provides a low-level software interface that gives programmers access to a common set of functions that will permit initialization of any HBA. In IBM PC terminology, these functions can be thought of as merely extensions to the BIOS routines.

Several software vendors have developed socket services for each of the major PCMCIA host adapters. These vendors include: American Megatrends, Award Software, Phoenix Technology, SystemSoft, Ventura Micro Inc., and others. Today most system designers license socket services from a software vendor, making it easier to implement PCMCIA solutions.

Configuring the Card: Card Services & Enablers

PC Cards require configuration software (enablers) that detect their presence, determine their configuration requirements and program them for operation within the system. This is true whether a card is installed when system power is applied or installed after the system is powered up and fully operational.

Configuration software for early PC Cards, built before the introduction of socket services, had to program the host bus adapter to permit access to the card's memory address space. This required that the programmer of the configuration software know the details of the hardware interface and the protocol required to access and program the host bus adapter. Furthermore, these programmers had to poll status registers on the host bus adapter to detect when cards were inserted and removed, or when other status changes occurred at the socket (i.e. low battery detection, write protect switch position, or ready/busy indications). Since different host bus adapters have different hardware interfaces, programmers were required to provide a separate version of their software for each host bus adapter type. The introduction of socket services removed the burden of having to write card enablers to interface directly to the hardware.

In addition, programmers must determine the system resources required by their PC Card and allocate them to the card. The resources that it assigns to its PC Card must not be already allocated to another device in the system. In the past, the programmer had to somehow determine what system resources were available to be allocated, or make an educated guess, hoping that the resources it was about to allocate were not already in use. These issues and others placed a heavy burden on the programmer to ensure that their cards worked in a given system. Fortunately, PCMCIA introduced another software layer called card services that lifts these burdens from the programmer.

Thanks to card services, the job of writing PC Card enablers is a much simpler task today, and far more reliable than was possible with early revisions of the specification. Card services provides a software layer consisting of high-level functions that programmers can call to gain access to a card, determine its configuration requirements, and request the system resources it requires.

One of the primary functions that card services fulfills for enablers is system resource allocation. Card services maintains a data base of system resources that are available for assignment to PC Cards. Once the enabler determines the configuration requirements of the card by reading the card's CIS, it requests that these resources be allocated to its card. If the resource is available, card services returns "success" to the enabler and the resource is then assigned. If the resource has already been used, then card services returns "failure" and another configuration option must be read from the CIS and tried. This process continues until one of the card's configuration options satisfies the request or until all options are exhausted, in which case the card cannot be configured.

Card services also notifies enablers of card insertion and removal and other status change events. This eliminates the need for enablers to continually poll to determine if some status change has occurred.

Accessing PC Cards After Configuration

Once a PC Card has been detected and configured, it behaves like any other device that exists on the expansion (PCMCIA host) bus. This allows applications to access PC Cards directly through the normal methods used in a given operating environment. This access can be done without using the PCMCIA software interface (i.e. card and socket services). Figure 3-4 illustrates the basic software flow during configuration and status reporting, versus run-time access (accesses made to a PC Card by application software once it has been configured). Each of the software components shown in figure 3-4 are discussed in detail in later chapters and the relationships between them are further defined.

The Metaformat

PCMCIA has defined a comprehensive software structure called the metaformat that defines the software support that can be provided with the card. The metaformat is a four layer software model that encompasses the CIS discussed in the previous example. Refer to table 3-1. The only software layer required by all cards is the CIS (layer one), which contains the information necessary to configure the card within the system.

The other layers are intended for memory cards that are used as virtual disk drives. PC Card memory is accessed as a logical disk drive via the operating system's file management system and in conjunction with device drivers that have knowledge of how the PC Card's memory arrays are organized. The additional layers provide information that can be used by file management software, utilities and other software requiring knowledge of a card's memory array characteristics.

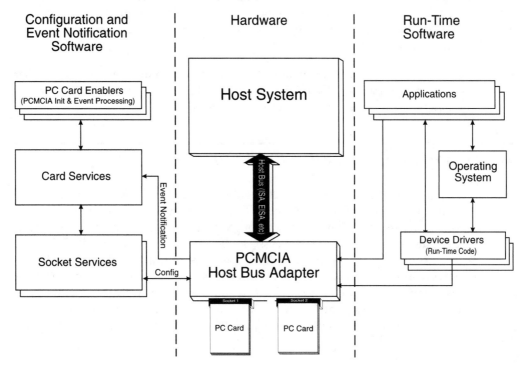

Figure 3-4. Configuration and Status Reporting Software Flow Versus Run Time Software Flow

Few PC Cards today contain information for metaformat layers two through four. In many instances the enablers for memory cards or flash file systems contain information regarding the organization of common devices. The chapter entitled, "The Card Information Structure (CIS)", contains detailed examples of the CIS (layer one of the metaformat) used by typical cards. Refer to Appendix E for a list and description of the tuples defined for layers two through four.

Chapter 3: Tying the Pieces Together

Table 3-1. PCMCIA Card Metaformat

Metaformat Layers	Description
Layer 1 — Compatibility Layer	The compatibility layer includes information necessary for a card to be recognized and configured. This portion of the card standard is commonly referred to as the Card Information Structure (CIS). All 2.0 compliant PC Cards must contain a CIS. The CIS information must be accessible from attribute memory starting at location zero.
Layer 2 — Data Recording Format Layer	This information specifies how data is recorded in the PC Card's memory arrays, and specifies what error checking capabilities are used, if any. Two basic types of data recording are specified: disk-like recording (blocks of data) or memory-like (sequential byte addressable data).
Layer 3 — Data Organization Layer	Defines the logical organization of data within a partition in a memory card. Data within a partition may be organized to support an OS file system, a flash file system, a vendor-specific organization, or an application specific organization.
Layer 4 — System Specific Layer	Specifies application specific information pertaining to a given operating environment. Items currently defined include DOS environment capabilities including: • An interchange format to ensure that PC Cards formatted with a DOS file system can be interchanged with systems implementing all versions of DOS. • Execute in Place (XIP) to support direct execution of application programs from the card. • Ability to configure older cards formatted without a CIS.

Part Two

Socket and Host Bus Adapter Design

Chapter 4

The Previous Chapter

The previous chapter introduced the major concepts of PCMCIA and explained the relationships between the various hardware and software elements employed in a typical PC Card environment.

This Chapter

This chapter focuses on the various physical packages defined by PCMCIA for PC Cards and the related environmental specifications. The chapter also describes the standard socket and low-voltage socket types.

The Next Chapter

The next chapter introduces and defines the memory-only socket interface, including definition of each pin. It also explains and illustrates memory transactions performed to/from PC Card memory functions.

Card Types and Dimensions

Three basic types of physical dimensions are described in the specification for PC Cards. In addition, extensions to type I and type II cards are defined. The card types are:

- Type I
- Type II
- Type III
- Type I extended
- Type II extended

Card Types I, II, and III

Refer to figure 4-1. Type I, II, and III cards all have the same planar or outline dimensions (54.00mm x 85.60mm). Card thickness is also the same within the interconnect area of each card. Only the substrate area of the cards is different. The thickness of each card type in the substrate area is:

- Type I cards = 3.3 mm
- Type II cards = 5.0 mm
- Type III cards = 10.5 mm

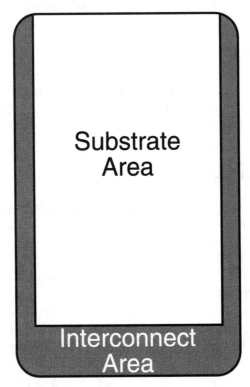

Figure 4-1. The Interconnect Area is the Same Thickness for all PC Cards.

Memory cards typically have a write-protect switch. Some memory cards containing volatile RAM devices also include a battery to prevent loss of data when the card is removed from the socket. The PCMCIA specification defines recommended locations for both the battery and write protect switch as shown in figure 4-2.

Chapter 4: The Physical Specifications

Figure 4-2. Type I Card with Battery and Write Protect Switch

Refer to figure 4-3. Type II cards are most commonly used for I/O devices. The type II package is popular with I/O cards since many of them require more physical space than memory devices due to the state of miniaturization for many of the devices required for I/O designs. These I/O cards typically have an external connector at the end of the card. Previous versions of the PCMCIA standards did not specify the design or location of the external I/O connector. The PC Card standard however, has defined the physical characteristics (i.e. location, pin definition, electrical and mechanical specs) for what the specification calls "open system" LAN and Modem I/O connections. The open system connectors are defined in the PC Card Standard within the PCMCIA Extensions volume. The PC Card standard does not require that manufacturers implement the open system connectors, but these connectors have the advantage of a uniform interface, promoting availability of these connectors from multiple sources.

Note that the card's thickness does not permit some connectors, such as the RJ-11 and RJ-45, to be built into a type II card. As a result, pigtail extension cables are typically used for larger connectors. Other connectors allow phone jack connections without the pigtail cable, such as the Megahertz, XJack implementation.

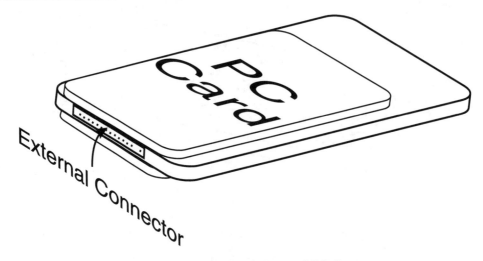

Figure 4-3. Type II Card with External I/O Connector

PCMCIA includes a design to accommodate thicker PC Card devices (such as hard drives). The outline of type III devices is shown in figure 4-4. Most systems that have two type II socket stacked on top of one another can accept a type III card. The type III card plugs into the lower socket, but the body of the type III PC Card requires the space of both sockets.

Figure 4-4. Type III Card Outline

Chapter 4: The Physical Specifications

Extended Card Types I and II

To accommodate large external connectors and to permit designers to encase their electrical and magnetic isolation devices within the shielded PC Card enclosure, PCMCIA defined extended card types I and II. Figure 4-5 shows the outline of the type I and II extended cards. Since the main body of the card is the same as the non-extended designs, these cards will fit into a typical card socket. The extension must be 10mm beyond the standard card length of 85.6mm (i.e. 95.6mm) before the height of the extension can be increased.

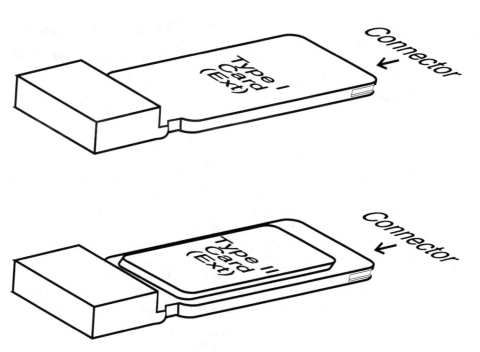

Figure 4-5. Type I and II Extended Cards

The Card and Socket Connectors

Card and Socket Keying

As shown in figure 4-6 PCMCIA cards and sockets are keyed to prevent the card from being inserted upside down. Keying is accomplished at the edges of the PC Card and the socket connector.

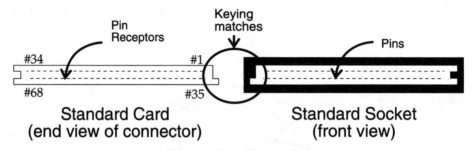

Figure 4-6. Card and Socket Keying-Standard Interface

PCMCIA release 2.0 and 2.1 cards can be designed as dual-voltage cards. These cards always power up at +5 Vcc but can switch to +3.3 Vcc for low power operation. A new generation of low-voltage cards is now possible using the new low-voltage specification. These newer low-voltage cards need not implement the dual-voltage solution described above. Instead, they can be designed for +3.3 Vcc operation only. This means that these cards will not function correctly in systems based on the 2.0 or 2.1 specification, which always apply +5 Vcc to the socket when a PC Card is first installed. Keying is employed on the newer low-voltage cards, preventing them from being inserted into standard dual-voltage sockets as shown in figure 4-7.

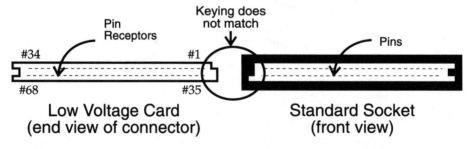

Figure 4-7. Low-Voltage Cards Cannot Be Inserted into Standard Sockets

Chapter 4: The Physical Specifications

To accommodate low voltage cards, a new low voltage socket has been designed. This socket, which might be better named the "universal socket," accepts 5 volt only cards, dual voltage cards, and 3.3vdc cards. This is possible since systems employing the low voltage socket have the ability to apply initial voltages of either +3.3 Vcc or +5.0 Vcc depending on the PC Card's requirements. Two newly defined Voltage Sense (VS) signals determine the initial voltage to be applied to the socket when a PC Card is installed. The Voltage Sense pins are set by the PC Card to indicate the initial voltage that they require.

Low voltage socket keying is shown in figure 4-8.

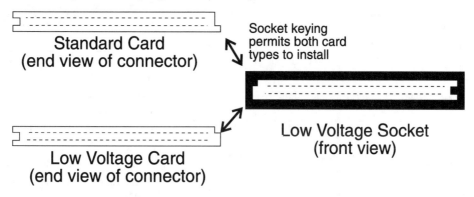

Figure 4-8. Keying Used with Low Voltage Socket

The two voltage sense pins (VS1# and VS2#) provide a means for the host system to detect the voltage level that a given PC Card must initially power up at. Refer to table 4-1. PCMCIA release 2.0 or 2.1 (2.x) compliant systems require that PC Cards always operate at 5 volts when power is first applied, and can later switch to 3.3 volts if configuration software detects that the card supports 3.3 volt operation. These PC Cards are termed dual-voltage cards. The standard PCMCIA socket designed for release 2.x systems have no voltage sense capability since all cards initially power to 5 Vcc.

PCMCIA also supports PC Cards that operate only at 3.3 volts, without initially having to power-up at 5 volts. The specification also supports cards that operate at a future non-specified low voltage, referred to as X.X volts. To accomplish 3.3 and X.X volt only operation, PCMCIA has defined a new socket that can supply the initial voltage required by new low voltage PC Cards. This socket is keyed to accept the newer low-voltage cards, 5 volt-only cards and dual-voltage cards. This is possible since the voltage sense pins determine the initial voltage that should be applied to the socket.

Table 4-1 shows the possible combinations of PC Cards that can be installed into a low-voltage socket. The first column specifies the initial voltage that the PC Card required when power is initially applied to the socket. The second column specifies the keying implemented by the card (i.e. whether the card is keyed to fit into a standard socket or a low voltage socket). Columns three and four specify the state of the voltage sense pins, and column five indicates the initial power that will be applied by the HBA. Note that X.X voltage designates a low level Vcc to be defined in the future.

Table 4-1. Interpretation of Voltage Sense Signals

Initial Power Required	Keying	VS1#	VS2#	Vcc at power up and CIS read
5 volts	standard*	1	1	5 volts applied if available, else no Vcc applied.
3.3 volts	low-voltage	0	1	3.3 volts applied if available, else no Vcc applied
3.3/5 volts	standard*			3.3 volts applied if available, else no Vcc applied.
X.X volts	low-voltage	1	0	X.X volts applied if available, else no Vcc applied.
X.X/3.3 volts	low-voltage	0	0	X.X volts applied if available, else 3.3 volts applied if available, else no Vcc applied.
X.X/3.3/5 volts	standard*			X.X volts applied if available, else 3.3 volts applied if available, else no Vcc applied.

* Standard keying refers to PC Cards keyed to fit into a 2.x compliant socket. These cards also fit into the low voltage sockets.

Pin Length

The PCMCIA Host Bus Adapter connector has three different pin lengths:

- Power pins (Ground & Vcc) — .098" (2.5 mm)
- General interface pins (address, data and control) — .084" (2.1 mm)
- Card detect pins — .059" (1.5 mm)

Chapter 4: The Physical Specifications

When a card is inserted into the host adapter's PCMCIA socket, the power pins make contact first, following by the general interface pins and then the card detect pins. Whether power will be applied to the power pins when a card is inserted depends on the system design. Many implementations apply power to the pins only after the shorter card detect pins make contact, indicating that the card is fully inserted into the HBA socket.

Environmental Characteristics

PCMCIA specifies a very thorough set of environmental tests and operating conditions under which PCMCIA cards and sockets should operate. Refer to the PCMCIA Card Standard for detailed information.

The PC Card standard specifies the following electrical and mechanical specifications for the socket connector and for PC Cards. The following tables list the primary specifications. For a complete list of mechanical and electrical specification and more information regarding the testing criteria and methods see the PC Card Standard's Physical Specification.

Connector Environmental Standards

Table 4-2 is a partial list of specifications defined by the PC Card Standard for connector reliability. All tests and measurements are specified to be made at the following ranges unless otherwise specified:

- temperature — 15ºC to 35ºC
- air pressure — 86 to 106 kPa
- relative humidity — 25% to 85%

Table 4-2. Selected Connector Reliability Specifications

Parameter	Standard/Specification	Testing Criteria
Operating Environment	Operating temp -20º to +60ºC Relative humidity, 95%	
Storage Environment	Storage temp -40º to +70ºC Relative humidity, 95%	
Number of insertions and ejections	10,000	Office Environment (see EIA-364-B Class 1.1)

Table 4-2. Selected Connector Reliability Specifications

Parameter	Standard/Specification	Testing Criteria
Number of insertions and ejections	5,000	Harsh Environment (see EIA-364-B Class 1.1)
Total insertion force	39.2 N maximum	Insert at 25mm/minute
Total pulling force	6.67N min. / 39.2 N max.	Extract at 25mm/minute
Single pin pulling force	Pin shall remain in insulator when .098 N of pulling force is applied.	Pull at 25mm/minute
Single pin holding force	Pin shall remain in insulator when 9.8 N of pushing force is applied.	Push at 25mm/minute
Single socket holding force	Socket shall not be dislodged or damaged when 4.9 N force is applied.	Push socket on axis at 25mm/minute.
Vibration and Frequency	No mechanical damage & no current interruption > 100ns.	MIL-STD-202F Test @ 147m/s^2,10 - 2000Hz
Shock	No mechanical damage & no current interruption > 100ns.	MIL-STD-202F Test @ 409m/s^2 acceleration
Contact Resistance (low level)	40mΩ max (initial value) 20mΩ max change (after test)	MILSTD-1344A Open voltage 20mV, Test current 1mA
Withstanding voltage	No shorting or damage when 500Vrms AC is applied for 1 minute, current leakage of 1mA max.	MIL-STD-202F
Insulation resistance	1000MΩ min (initial value) 100MΩ min (after test)	MIL-STD-202F Apply 500vdc
Current capacity	0.5 A per contact	Based on 30ºC rise above ambient temperature
Insulation Material	UL 94 V-0	UL Standard 94
Ground Return Inductance	18.0 nH max @ 1MHz	ANSI/EIA-364-69

PC Card Environmental Standards

Table 4-3 lists selected environmental specifications for the PC Card. All tests and measurements are specified to be made at the following ranges unless otherwise indicated:

Chapter 4: The Physical Specifications

- temperature — 15ºC to 35ºC
- air pressure — 86 to 106 kPa
- relative humidity — 25% to 85%

Table 4-3. Selected PC Card Environmental Specifications

Parameter	Standard/Specification	Testing Criteria
Operating Environment	Operating temp 0º to +55ºC Max. relative humidity, 95%	96 hours minimum
Storage Environment	Storage temp -20º to +65ºC Max relative humidity, 95%	96 hours minimum
Thermal Shock	Data to be retained by all non-volatile memory after test	MIL-STD-202F Method 107G Test 1 @ -20ºC for 30 min. Test 2 @ 25ºC for <05 min. Test 3 @ 65ºC for 30 min. Test 4 @ 25ºC for <05 min. Repeat all 4 test for 100 cycles
Moisture Resistance	PC Card must function as specified after test and must retain data stored in non-volatile memory prior to test.	MIL-STD-202F Method 106E Test 1 @ 20 to 65ºC for 2.5 hrs. Test 2 @ 65ºC for 3 hrs. Test 3 @ 65 to 25ºC for 2.5 hrs. Test 4 @ 25 to-10ºC for 2.5 hrs. Test 5 @ -10ºC for 3 hrs Test 6 @ -10 to 25ºC for 2.5 hrs Repeat all 6 tests for 10 cycles
Electrostatic Discharge	PC Card must retain data stored in non-volatile memory prior to test.	ISO 7816-1 See Mechanical Specification
X-ray Exposure	PC Card must function as specified after test and must retain data stored in non-volatile memory prior to test.	ISO 7816-1 Wavelength 254 nm Intensity 15000 $\mu W/cm^2$ Exposure time 20 min
EMI	PC Card must function as specified after test and must retain data stored in non-volatile memory prior to test.	ISO 7816-1 Uniform magnetic field of 1000 Oersted Exposure time=10 seconds 100 Oersted Exposure time-Exposure time=10 seconds for rotating media cards.

Table 4-3. Selected PC Card Environmental Specifications (continued)

Parameter	Standard/Specification	Testing Criteria
Card Inverse Insertion	No electrical contact between card and connector except Vcc and ground pins.	See Mechanical Specification
Vibration and High Frequency	PC Card must function as specified after test and must retain data stored in non-volatile memory prior to test.	MIL-STD-202F Method 204D Test B: 147 m/s^2 peak, 10 to 2,000 Hz, 12 cycles per axis, 36 cycles for 3 axes (12hrs). Battery installed, no Vcc.
Shock	PC Card must function as specified after test and must retain data stored in non-volatile memory prior to test.	MIL-STD-202F Method 213B Test Condition A: 490 m/s^2 Standard holding time 11 ms Semi-sine wave
Bend Test	PC Card must function as specified after test and must retain data stored in non-volatile memory prior to test. Dimensions must conform to use requirements after test.	See Mechanical Specification.
Drop Test	PC Card must function as specified after test and must retain data stored in non-volatile memory prior to test. Dimensions must conform to use requirements after test.	See Mechanical Specification.
PC Card Warpage	PC Card must function as specified after test and must retain data stored in non-volatile memory prior to test. Dimensions must conform to use requirements after test.	See Mechanical Specification.

Chapter 5

The Previous Chapter

The previous chapter focused on the various physical packages defined by PCMCIA for PC Cards and the related environmental specifications. The chapter also described the standard and low-voltage socket connector types.

This Chapter

This chapter details the memory-only electrical interface between the PC Card and socket. Each pin is defined and its relationship to the PC Card and the HBA is discussed. The memory-only interface is the interface initially seen by 16-bit PC Cards when they are first inserted into a socket. This permits the memory-mapped CIS to be accessed to determine the PC Card type and interface requirements. If the card is designed for an interface type other than memory-only, then the HBA and PC Card are configured to communicate via one of the other interfaces defined by the PC Card Standard (discussed in the following chapters). Also discusses the timing of socket accesses to PC Cards of differing speeds, including transfers with attribute memory and common memory.

The Next Chapter

The next chapter discusses the electrical interface called the memory or I/O PC Card and Socket interface. This interface is used by standard I/O-based PC Cards.

Overview

The original PCMCIA standard (release 1.0) defined the socket interface for memory cards only. Later releases added additional socket interfaces. The PC Card Standard defines the following socket interfaces:

- Memory only
- Memory or I/O
- ATA (AT attachment for IDE drives)
- DMA (Direct Memory Access)
- AIMS (Auto-Indexing Mass Storage)
- CardBus (32-bit PC Card interface)

Each of these interfaces employs the PCMCIA 68 pins connector. However pin definition changes with each interface type. Most HBAs can be configured to support a variety of socket interfaces. This chapter discusses the memory-only interface. Subsequent chapters discuss the other socket interfaces included in the bulleted list above.

This chapter discusses the PCMCIA memory interface, detailing the electrical interface used PC Cards that employ only a memory function. However, all 16-bit PC Cards must initially operate as memory-only devices. This is necessary since the HBA has no way of knowing whether a PC Card installed required a specific interface other than memory. Therefore, HBAs always present a memory-only interface when a PC Card is initially installed, and all 16-bit PC Cards must operate as memory-only devices when they are inserted into a PC Card socket. A card's client driver is then responsible for reading from the PC Card's CIS (accessible via the memory-only interface) to determine the card type and the socket interface that it requires. The HBA and PC Card can then be dynamically reconfigured under software control to use the specified socket interface. Note however that not all HBAs are designed to support all socket interface types.

The Memory Interface

Two types of memory address space exist within a PC Card: common memory and attribute memory. *Common memory* is the working address space used to map the memory arrays that typically store data and executable files. *Attribute memory* is used for configuration information. The attribute memory address space contains the CIS (Card Information Structure) and configuration registers. Figure 5-1 illustrates the signals that comprise the memory interface which provide access to both common and attribute memory. The signals defined for the memory interface are grouped functionally and described in the following sections.

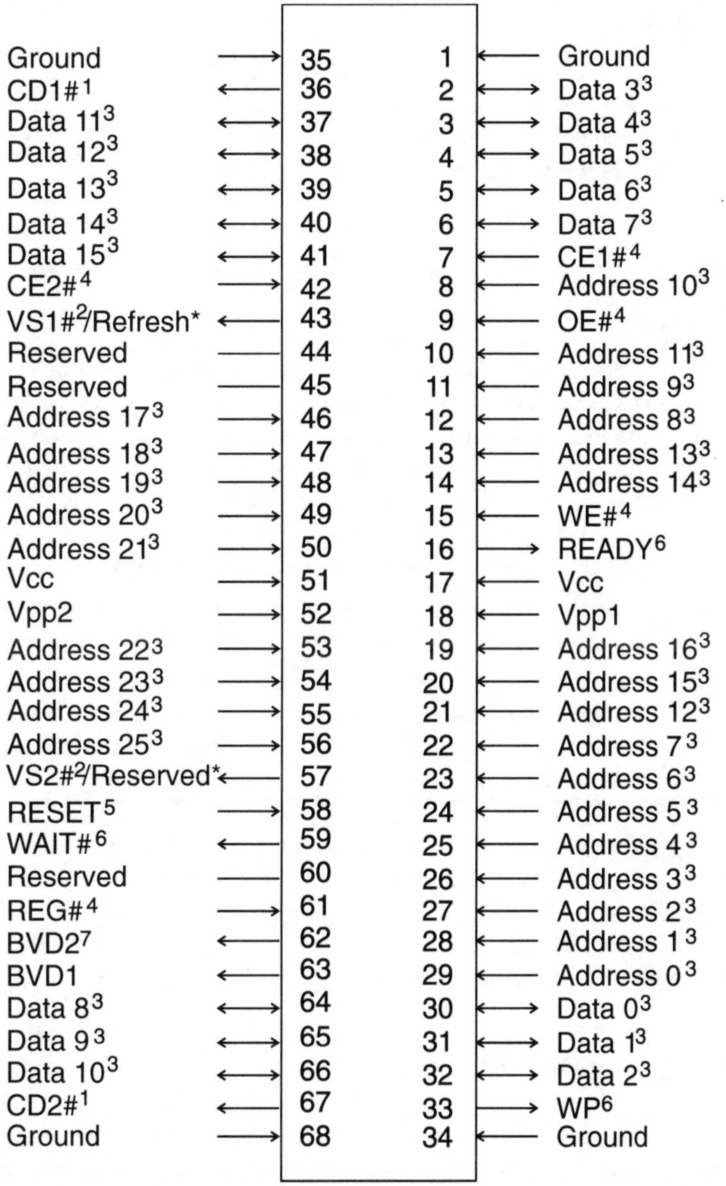

Ground	→ 35	1 ←	Ground
CD1#[1]	← 36	2 ↔	Data 3[3]
Data 11[3]	↔ 37	3 ↔	Data 4[3]
Data 12[3]	↔ 38	4 ↔	Data 5[3]
Data 13[3]	↔ 39	5 ↔	Data 6[3]
Data 14[3]	↔ 40	6 ↔	Data 7[3]
Data 15[3]	↔ 41	7 ←	CE1#[4]
CE2#[4]	→ 42	8 ←	Address 10[3]
VS1#[2]/Refresh*	← 43	9 ←	OE#[4]
Reserved	— 44	10 ←	Address 11[3]
Reserved	— 45	11 ←	Address 9[3]
Address 17[3]	→ 46	12 ←	Address 8[3]
Address 18[3]	→ 47	13 ←	Address 13[3]
Address 19[3]	→ 48	14 ←	Address 14[3]
Address 20[3]	→ 49	15 ←	WE#[4]
Address 21[3]	→ 50	16 →	READY[6]
Vcc	→ 51	17 ←	Vcc
Vpp2	→ 52	18 ←	Vpp1
Address 22[3]	→ 53	19 ←	Address 16[3]
Address 23[3]	→ 54	20 ←	Address 15[3]
Address 24[3]	→ 55	21 ←	Address 12[3]
Address 25[3]	→ 56	22 ←	Address 7[3]
VS2#[2]/Reserved*	← 57	23 ←	Address 6[3]
RESET[5]	→ 58	24 ←	Address 5[3]
WAIT#[6]	← 59	25 ←	Address 4[3]
Reserved	— 60	26 ←	Address 3[3]
REG#[4]	→ 61	27 ←	Address 2[3]
BVD2[7]	← 62	28 ←	Address 1[3]
BVD1	← 63	29 ←	Address 0[3]
Data 8[3]	↔ 64	30 ↔	Data 0[3]
Data 9[3]	↔ 65	31 ↔	Data 1[3]
Data 10[3]	↔ 66	32 ↔	Data 2[3]
CD2#[1]	← 67	33 →	WP[6]
Ground	→ 68	34 ←	Ground

1. Pulled-up to Vcc by HBA (R≥10KΩ).
2. Pulled-up to Vcc by HBA (R=10KΩ-100KΩ).
3. Pulled-down by PC Card (R≥100KΩ).
4. Pulled-up to Vcc by PC Card (R≥10KΩ).
5. Pulled-up to Vcc by PC Card (R≥100KΩ).
6. Pulled-up to Vcc by HBA (R≥10KΩ).
7. Pulled-up to Vcc by HBA.

Figure 5-1. PCMCIA Memory Socket Interface to Host Bus Adapter

Card Power

PC Card memory sockets provide the standard logic supply voltage (Vcc) and programming voltages (Vpp) typically used by EEPROM and Flash devices. Table 5-1 lists the power pins defined by the memory socket.

Table 5-1. Card Voltage Pins

Signal	Function
Vcc & Ground	Card Voltage. Two Vcc pins and four ground pins are used with each socket. Vcc will always be 5 volts when the card is first accessed if the socket is based on the 2.x standard. In these system, if the PC Card supports dual operating voltages (5 volts and 3.3 volts) the operating voltage will be reduced to 3.3vdc during card initialization. The PC Card standard specifies that each Vcc pin supply a maximum of 500mA (1A total per socket). The actual amount of current that can be supplied by the HBA is design specific.
	Systems that support low voltage sockets determine the initial Vcc that is applied to the socket by sampling VS1# and VS2#.
Vpp1 & Vpp2	Programming Voltage. These pins are used for special programming voltages that may be required by programmable memory devices. The card's CIS must specify the required programming voltage. Each Vpp pin must be able to supply 30mA of current.

Two types of sockets are defined by PCMCIA: the standard 2.x compliant socket and a new low voltage (universal) socket. The initial Vcc voltage that a socket can apply to a PC Card depends on the socket type and the HBA design. Figure 5-2 illustrates the voltage switching that PCMCIA HBAs implement if they support the VS1# and VS2# signals.

Release 2.x Socket

The card power pins are listed in table 5-1. For systems that are 2.x compliant, 5 volts is always applied to the Vcc pin when a PC Card is first installed into a socket. Vcc can later be switched to 3.3 volts if the PC Card has dual voltage capability. Support for 3.3vdc operations is detected by a PC Card's client driver when the CIS is interrogated. It should be apparent that any card inserted into a 2.x compliant socket must be able to operate at 5 volts.

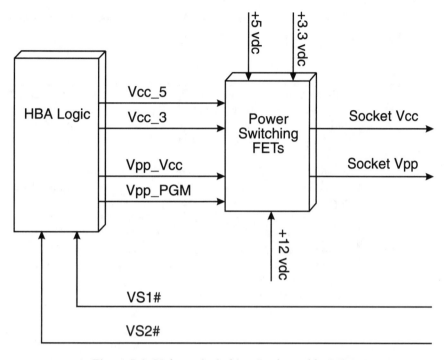

Figure 5-2. Voltage Switching Performed by HBA

Low-Voltage Socket

In systems that implement low-voltage sockets, the initial Vcc applied to the PC Card can be either X.X, 3.3 or 5 volts. The initial voltage is determined by the state of voltage sense pins that have been defined for the low voltage socket. Refer to the chapter entitled "PC Card and Socket Physical Design" for details on the low voltage socket.

Voltage Sense Pins (not used in 2.x systems)

Two Voltage Sense pins (VS1# and VS2#) provide a means for the host system to detect the voltage level that a given PC Card must initially power up at. Refer to table 5-2. PCMCIA release 2.0 or 2.1 (2.x) compliant systems always apply 5 volts when power is first applied, and can later switch to 3.3 volts if configuration software detects that the card supports 3.3 volt operation (via the CIS). These PC Cards are termed dual-voltage cards. The standard

PCMCIA socket designed for release 2.x systems has no voltage sense capability since all cards initially power to 5 Vcc.

Table 5-2. Definition of Voltage Sense Pins

VS1#/Refresh	**Voltage Sense 1 or Refresh**. The values of VS1# and VS2# determine the initial Vcc voltage that is applied to the socket when a PC Card is installed. Both VS pins are pulled to 5 volts by the host system. When a low voltage card is installed, it pulls one or both of the VS pins low to indicate the initial Vcc it requires.
	When a standard 2.x compliant PC Card is inserted into a low-voltage socket, both VS1# and VS2# will remain asserted (because 2.x cards do not implement the VS pins). A 2.x compliant socket defines the VS1# pin as the refresh signal, originally intended to be used with pseudo-static RAM. Its functionality has not been defined and is not used.
VS2#/Reserved	**Voltage Sense 2 or Reserved**. This pin is defined as VS2# for low-voltage sockets and cards and is pulled to 5 volts by the host system. See the description for VS1# above.
	This pin is reserved in a 2.x compliant socket.

PCMCIA also supports PC Cards that operate only at 3.3 volts (i.e. they do not initially power-up at 5 volts). The PC Card standard also supports cards that operate at a future non-specified low voltage, referred to as X.X volts. To accomplish 3.3 and X.X volt only operation, PCMCIA defines a PC Card socket that can supply the initial voltage required by 3.3vdc only PC Cards. This socket is keyed to accept the newer low-voltage cards, as well as, 5 volt-only cards and dual-voltage cards. This is possible because the HBA samples the voltage sense pins to determine the initial voltage required by the PC Card.

Keying on the low-voltage cards prevent them from being inserted into standard 5 volt sockets, thus avoiding the circuit damage that could result if a 3.3vdc card was installed in a 2.x compliant system, which always supplies 5vdc initially to the socket. In summary two types of sockets are specified by PCMCIA.

- Standard Socket — keyed to accept cards that can power up at 5 volts. These sockets accept 5 volt-only cards and cards that can be switched to 3.3 volt operation.

- Low Voltage Sockets — keyed to accept either 3.3 volt, X.X volt or 5 volt cards. Cards designed for 3.3 volt-only operation are keyed to fit only into

Chapter 5: The Memory-Only Socket Interface

this socket, thus preventing possible damage. Note that systems implementing the low-power socket monitor the voltage sense lines; therefore, they can accept PC Cards operating at any of the specified voltages.

Table 5-3 shows the possible combinations of PC Cards that can be installed into a low voltage socket and the resulting Vcc that will be initially applied to the card based on the state of VS1# and VS2#. The X.X voltage designates a Vcc level to be defined in the future.

Table 5-3. Interpretation of Voltage Sense Signals by a Low Voltage Socket

Initial Power Required	Keying	VS1#	VS2#	Socket Vcc at power up
5 volts	standard[1]	1	1	5 volts applied if available, else no Vcc applied.
3.3 volts	low-voltage	0	1	3.3 volts applied if available, else no Vcc applied
3.3/5 volts	standard[1]	PD[2]	1	3.3 volts applied if available, else no Vcc applied.
X.X volts	low-voltage	1	0	X.X volts applied if available, else no Vcc applied.
X.X/3.3 volts	low-voltage	0	0	X.X volts applied if available, else 3.3 volts applied if available, else no Vcc applied.
X.X/3.3/5 volts	standard[1]	PD[2]	0	X.X volts applied if available, else 3.3 volts applied if available, else no Vcc applied.

1. Standard keying refers to PC Cards keyed to fit into a 2.x compliant socket. These cards also fit into the low voltage sockets.
2. PD indicates that the card connects VS1# to ground via a 1KΩ ±10% pull-down resistor.

The Power-Up Sequence

When the HBA recognizes that a PC Card has been inserted into a socket (has detected CD1# and CD2# asserted) it must ensure that the card is powered and the interface signals are enabled in the correct sequence. The PC Card standard specifies the timing and power sequences required. Figure 5-3 illustrates the power-up sequence and the primary timing parameters. Note that RESET is asserted no sooner than 1ms after Vcc has stabilized. Once RESET is deasserted a PC Card has 20ms to perform its initialization before the system begins accessing the card. If the card needs longer than 20ms before being accessed, it must deassert READY until it is ready to be accessed.

Note that during intial power-up the PC Card is not permitted to draw more than 70mA at 3.3vdc or 100mA at 5.0vdc. This limit must be maintained even if the PC Card requires additional current during normal operation.

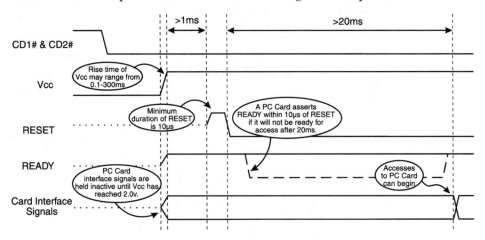

Figure 5-3. The Socket Power-up Sequence

Vpp1 and Vpp2

Vpp1 and Vpp1 (Programming or Peripheral voltages) provide the programming voltage needed by devices such as EEPROM (Electrically-Erasable Programmable ROM) or Flash ROM during write operations. The PC Card standard permits separate voltages to be applied via the Vpp1 and Vpp2 pins; however, this ability may not be supported by given HBA implementations.

When the socket is first powered, Vpp1 and Vpp2 are connected to Vcc. After the CIS is read, an alternative Vpp can be applied to the socket under software control. Twelve volts is recommended as a an alternative Vpp voltage that can be supplied by the HBAs; however, other voltages may also be applied depending on the card's requirements specified in the CIS and the capabilities of the HBA.

Chapter 5: The Memory-Only Socket Interface

Address Signals

Refer to table 5-4. The card address signals consist of the address bus proper (A25:A0) and the card enable signals (CE1# and CE2#). When a transaction to a PC Card begins, the address lines along with CE1# and CE2# are asserted. When both CE1# and CE2# are deasserted, the card is in standby mode (waiting to be accessed). PCMCIA supports 16-bit PC Cards in both 8-bit hosts (e.g. Intel 8088-based systems) and 16-bit host (e.g. ISA expansion buses). The card enable signals addressing modes compatible with both 8- and 16-bit host systems.

Table 5-4. PCMCIA Address Lines—Memory Interface

Signal	Function
A25:A0	**Address Lines 0-25**. Twenty-six address lines permit a total address space of 64 MB for PCMCIA cards. This 64 MB address space is valid for both common memory and attribute memory.
CE1#	**Card Enable 1**. The CE1# signal is an active low signal that specifies access to address locations which are transferred over the lower data path (D7:D0). During accesses by 16-bit hosts, CE1# specifies even location access only. During accesses by 8-bit hosts CE1# specifies access to either an even or odd location, with A0 determining whether an even or odd location is being addressed.
CE2#	**Card Enable 2**. The CE2# signal is an active low signal that specifies access to an odd address location during access by 16-bit hosts. When CE2# is asserted, valid data is always transferred over the upper data path (D15:D8). During access by an 8-bit host, CE2# is always deasserted. When CE1# is deasserted and CE2# is asserted, an odd byte is being accessed by a 16-bit host, and when both CE1# and CE2# are asserted, two bytes are accessed from the card by a 16-bit host.

Table 5-5 identifies the combination of A0, CE1# and CE2# used to access even and odd address locations from PC Cards and shows which data path is used. This addressing scheme permits access to PC Cards by both 8-bit and 16-bit host systems. For example, note that there are two ways to access an odd byte from a PC Card, depending on whether the host system is an 8-bit system (uses only D7:D0) or a 16-bit system (uses D15:D8 and D7:D0).

PCMCIA System Architecture

Table 5-5. Addressing Even and Odd Bytes

Addressing Mode	CE1#	CE2#	A0*	D15:D8	D7:D0
No access (standby mode)	1	1	X	High-Z	High-Z
8/16-bit Mode (even byte)	0	1	0	High-Z	Even Byte
8-bit Mode (odd byte)	0	1	1	High-Z	Odd Byte
16-bit Mode (odd byte only)	1	0	X	Odd Byte	High-Z
16-bit Mode (even & odd byte)	0	0	X	Odd Byte	Even Byte

* "X" indicates a don't care condition.

When a PC Card is accessed in 16-bit mode (by 16-bit hosts), CE1# indicates access to an even address location, while CE2# indicates access to an odd address location (Refer to figure 5-4). Even locations are transferred over data path D7:D0, and odd locations over path D15:D8.

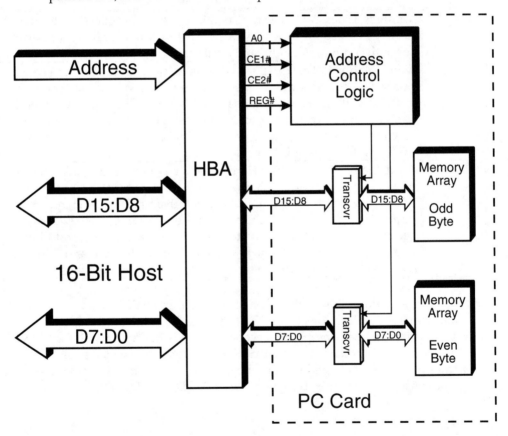

Figure 5-4. Addressing Mode Used by Memory Card with 16-Bit Host

Chapter 5: The Memory-Only Socket Interface

When a PC Card is accessed in 8-bit mode (by an 8-bit host), both even and odd locations must be transferred to or from the PC Card over path D7:D0 (Refer to figure 5-5). In this case, CE2#, CE1# and A0 control data bus steering within the PC Card, ensuring that both even and odd locations are transferred over data path D7:D0.

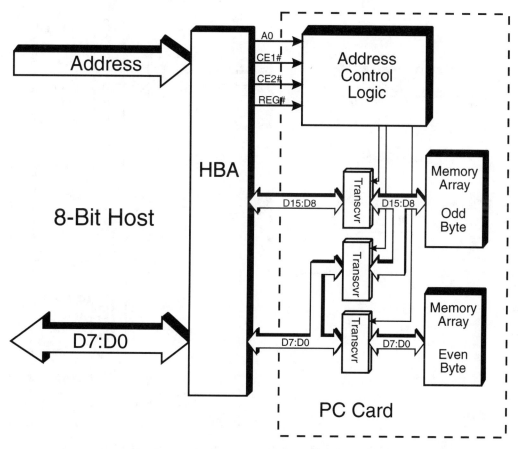

Figure 5-5. Addressing Mode Used by Memory Card with 8-Bit Host

Note that attribute memory devices (i.e. the CIS) only contain valid data at even address locations (Refer to figure 5-6). This simplifies the design of attribute memory when accessed by 8-bit hosts (expansion buses). That is, no data bus steering logic need be implemented, since even address locations are only accessed over D7:D0.

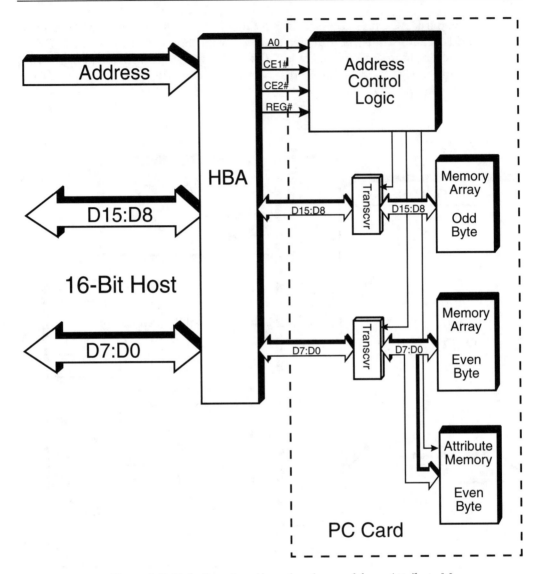

Figure 5-6. Only Even Locations Are Accessed from Attribute Memory over the Lower Data Path

Chapter 5: The Memory-Only Socket Interface

Data Lines

The data lines consist of two 8-bit paths; the lower path, data lines D7:D0 and the upper path, data lines D15: D8 (See Table 5-6.) The data path(s) carrying valid data during a data transfer are defined by the host data bus size and whether an even byte, odd byte or word is being transferred. Note that PCMCIA supports PC memory cards containing only 16-bit devices.

Table 5-6. Data Bus

Signal	Function
D7:D0	**Data lines 7:0** (Lower data path). Transfers data to and from even locations when the host system has a 16-bit data path; transfers data to and from both even and odd locations when host system has a single 8-bit data path.
D15:D8	**Data lines 15:8** (Upper data path). Transfers data to and from odd locations when the host system has a 16-bit data path; not used when the host system has a single 8-bit data path.

PC Memory Card Transaction Definition

Four types of transactions can be performed when accessing a PC Card memory locations:

- Common Memory Read
- Common Memory Write
- Attribute Memory Read
- Attribute Memory Write

The Output Enable signal (OE#), Write Enable or Program signal (WE#) and Register (REG#) signals define the transaction type. Table 5-7 defines each type of PC Card memory command. Table 5-8 shows the possible command signal combinations for common and attribute memory.

Table 5-7. PC Card Command Lines for Memory Interface

Signal	Function
OE#	**Output Enable**. This signal is active low and is asserted during memory read transfers from PCMCIA cards.
WE#	**Write Enable/Program**. This signal is active low and is asserted during memory write transfers to PCMCIA cards. When the PC memory device requires a special programming voltage to perform a write operation, this signal is defined as the "program" command signal.
REG#	**Register Select**. This signal when asserted specifies access to attribute memory.

Table 5-8. PCMCIA Memory Transaction Types

Transaction Type	OE#	WE#	REG#
Common Memory Read	0	1	1
Common Memory Write	1	0	1
Attribute Memory Read	0	1	0
Attribute Memory Write	1	0	0

PC Memory Card Status Signals

PCMCIA supports status reporting for a number of card conditions or events including:

- Card Detection (CD1# and CD2#)
- Ready/busy (READY)
- Write-Protect (WP)
- Low Battery Detection (BVD1 and BVD2)

As described in table 5-9, the memory interface has dedicated signals used for reporting status back to the HBA. Additional information on each of the status conditions is provided in the following section.

Table 5-9. Card and Socket Status Signals

Signal	Function
CD1#	**Card Detect 1**. This signal is asserted while a PC Card is installed in a socket, indicating that one end of the card is making electrical contact within the socket. This pin should be pulled up to 5 volts by the host system.
CD2#	**Card Detect 2**. This signal is asserted while a PC Card is installed in a socket, indicating that the opposite end of the card is making electrical contact within the socket. This pin should be pulled to 5 volts by the host system.
READY	**READY**. Used by the card to inform the system that the card is ready to be accessed. When READY is deasserted the card is processing a command or performing initialization and no access should be attempted to the card until READY is asserted again.
WP	**Write-Protect**. This signal reports the status of the card's write protect switch (if present). If no write protect switch is used the WP pin should be pulled up to Vcc (read only) or pulled low (writeable) based on its read/write capabilities.
BVD1	**Battery Voltage Detect 1**. In conjunction with BVD2, indicates the status of the PC Card's battery, if present.
BVD2	**Battery Voltage Detect 2**. In conjunction with BVD1, indicates the status of the PC Card's battery. JEDEC compliant cards use only BVD1 to report battery status. The host system should pull BVD2 to Vcc on the card to maintain compatibility with JEDEC cards. Otherwise, a JEDEC compliant system will detect a low battery condition which none exists.

* Note that systems based on Release 2.0 or 2.1 of the PC Card Standard do not include the voltage sense capability. These systems always supply 5vdc to a PC Card when it is initially inserted into a socket.

Card Detection

The card detection signals, CD1# and CD2# provide a method of notifying the host system when a PC Card has either been inserted or removed. The host system generates an interrupt when a change in the card detection signals occurs. Host software must take the appropriate action to either configure the PC Card that has been inserted, or to deallocate system resources that were previously assigned to a PC Card that has been removed.

Table 5-10 defines how the card detect signals should be interpreted.

Table 5-10. Interpretation of the Card Detect Signals

CD2#	CD1#	CD Status
1	1	No card inserted
1	0	Card partially inserted
0	1	Card partially inserted
0	0	Card fully inserted

Ready Status

READY is a status signal that indicates when the card is ready to be accessed. When this signal is asserted low, the card is busy and should not be accessed. When the signal is asserted high, the card is ready for access.

The busy condition typically occurs during system initialization if the PC Card requires more than 20 ms to initialize after the reset signal is deasserted. When reset is deasserted, software can normally access a PC Card after a 20ms delay; however, if the initialization is not yet completed by the PC Card, then the busy signal is asserted to prevent premature access to the card. Upon completion of initialization, the READY signal transitions to the ready state.

Busy should also be indicated during normal operation if the PC Card is processing a command or performing some lengthy operation, during which the card cannot be accessed.

Changes in the READY status should generate a system interrupt to notify software that a given PC Card is busy and should not be accessed, or that the PC Card was previously busy and is now ready for access. Software should hook the status interrupt to gain notification of READY status changes. If the interrupt is not hooked by software, then it should periodically poll the READY status.

Write-Protect Status

Some memory cards have write-protect capability. Normally a manual switch is incorporated on the end of the card that selects whether the memory is to be write-protected or not, as reflected by the card's WP signal. When a change in the write-protect status occurs the WP signal is asserted. The HBA senses WP asserted and may (depending on the software defined interrupt mask bit) initiate a status change interrupt to notify software of the change.

Chapter 5: The Memory-Only Socket Interface

The PC Card designer can define which address ranges it wishes to allow the user to write protect and which ranges are always writable. This definition is included in the Card's CIS. Configuration software reads the CIS to determine which ranges of the PC Card's address space can be write protected and programs the HBA so that it will block writes to the specified address ranges when the WP pin is asserted. The state of the WP pin has no effect on writes to address ranges that the CIS defines as always writable.

Low Battery Detection

Two signals (BVD1 and BVD2) report status of PC Card batteries. Batteries are typically implemented on PC Cards that contain volatile memory devices, such as SRAM cards. The PC Card should pull-up both BVD1 and BVD2 to Vcc, indicating a fully operational battery. To indicate a low battery warning or a dead battery the PC Card deasserts these signals as shown in table 5-11.

The JEIDA memory card specification supports low battery detection using only the BVD1 signal. When a JEIDA compliant card is inserted in a socket, it will not pull BVD2 to Vcc, allowing BVD2 to float. If the HBA interprets the BVD2 signal as a logic low, then a PCMCIA compliant system would report a low battery warning when in fact no such condition exists. To alleviate this potential problem, systems designed to support JEIDA memory cards should pull-up BVD2 to Vcc in the HBA.

Table 5-11. Interpretation of Battery Voltage Detection Signals

BVD2	BVD1	Battery Status
1	1	Battery in good condition
1	0	Battery cannot maintain data integrity
0	1	Battery replacement warning — data integrity maintained
0	0	Battery cannot maintain data integrity

Bus Cycle Control

Cards use the WAIT# signal to extend normal access timing to the card. That is, a data transfer between the host bus and a PC Card can be stretched out by the PC Card when it asserts the WAIT# signal.

Normally, when accessing a PC Card, the speed of the transaction is defined by the device speed specified within the card's CIS. Configuration software reads the PC Card's speed and configures the HBA to run transactions to the PC Card based on the programmed value. When the host system accesses the PC Card, the HBA initiates a card transaction and accesses the PC Card at its specified speed.

A PC Card that asserts the WAIT# signal can extend the transfer, if it is unable to complete the transfer within the normal timing. The maximum value that wait can extend the cycle timing can be specified within the CIS in the configuration entry tuple (tuple code 1Bh). The maximum WAIT# duration allowed by the specification is 12µs.

Card Reset

The RESET signal forces the PC Card to reset internal devices and clear its configuration registers. (Note that many memory-only PC Cards do not implement configuration registers.) Reset is typically derived from the system's master reset signal, but can also be asserted under software control via an HBA register or the RESET bit in card's configuration register, if implemented.

The host system holds RESET in a high-impedance state during PC Card power-up. This occurs during system power-up if the card is installed when the host system is turned on, or when the card is installed with power already applied to the system. RESET must remain in high impedance for at least 1 ms after Vcc becomes valid. When RESET is asserted it should remain active for 10µs as specified by the PCMCIA standard.

Chapter 5: The Memory-Only Socket Interface

PC Card Memory Transfers

The PC Card standard specifies standard cycle timing for accessing attribute memory and common memory devices residing within PC cards. These cycle times indicate that a PC card can be accessed at intervals equal to the speed rating specified by the card's CIS. Cycle time includes the setup, command and recovery time required to access a PC Card.

This section focuses on the relationships and functions of the signals used to control access to PC cards, and does not attempt to define all timing parameters and minimum and maximum values. This is the province of the PCMCIA specification.

Table 5-12 lists the specified cycle times for attribute and common memory. Note that attribute memory timing is 300ns, while cycle time for common memory devices range from 100ns to 250ns. A special 600ns cycle time is included for 3.3vdc memory cards requiring slower cycle time.

Table 5-12. Standard Cycle Times for PC Card Memory Devices

Memory Type / Speed	600ns	300ns	250ns	200ns	150ns	100ns
Attribute Memory		X				
Common Memory (5V)			X	X	X	X
Common Memory (3.3V)	X		X	X	X	X

Attribute Memory Read Transfers

The first access made to a PC card is a memory read from the Card Information Structure (CIS), which is mapped into *attribute* memory address space. Address zero is the first location read from, followed by the next even location. Only even locations are accessible within attribute memory space, making it easier to accommodate 8-bit host accesses. This means that only the lower data path (D7:D0) contains valid data when reading from and writing to attribute memory locations. Table 5-13 highlights the only supported addressing mode for attribute memory accesses.

Table 5-13. Addressing Mode Supported by Attribute Transfers

Addressing Mode	CE1#	CE2#	A0	D15:D8	D7:D0
No access (standby mode)	1	1	X	High-Z	High-Z
8/16-bit Mode (even byte)	0	1	0	High-Z	Even Byte
8-bit Mode (odd byte)	0	1	1	High-Z	Odd Byte
16-bit Mode (odd byte only)	1	0	X	Odd Byte	High-Z
16-bit Mode (even & odd byte)	0	0	X	Odd Byte	Even Byte

Since attribute memory contains the CIS, it must be read to determine the card's access timing requirements. However, the speed of the memory device containing the CIS must be known prior to reading it. For this reason, a default access time of 300ns is used for reading attribute memory within all PC cards.

Figure 5-7 shows the typical relationships between signals asserted during attribute memory reads (refer to the PCMCIA standard for minimum and maximum timing values). The HBA starts an access to a given socket when it recognizes an address residing within the PC card. The HBA outputs the target address to the socket at the beginning of the read transfer, along with the REG# signal. The card enable signal, CE1#, is asserted while CE2# remains deasserted, consistent with even byte-only accesses that are permitted to attribute memory. Once the setup time has been satisfied, the read command, OE# (output enable), is asserted, indicating that this is a read from attribute memory. The memory card then returns valid data to the HBA. The HBA keeps the address asserted to the socket to satisfy the recovery (hold) time of the memory device. The PC memory card is now ready for another data transfer.

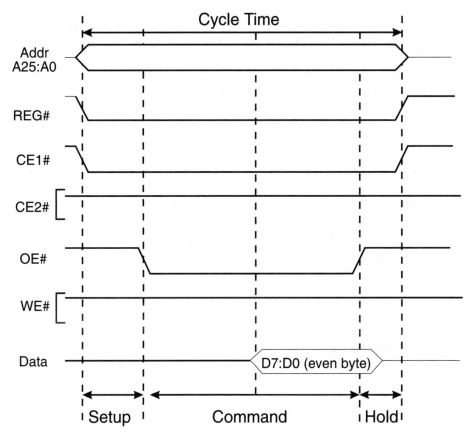

Figure 5-7. Attribute Memory Read Transfer

Attribute Memory Write Transfers

Attribute memory write transfer timing defaults to 250ns cycle timing (consistent with the timing parameters defined for 250ns common memory writes). The only difference between attribute memory write transfers and common memory write transfers is that the REG# signal is asserted during attribute memory writes to distinguish them from common memory writes. Note that the CIS may specify attribute memory write timing, in which case write transfer timing will be determined by the CIS timing entry and not the 250ns default mentioned earlier.

Common Memory Read/Write Transfers

PC Memory cards may be installed in 8-bit host systems or 16-bit host systems. Memory cards respond to two separate address modes, permitting access by either 8-bit or 16-bit host bus systems. The following sections describe accesses by each type of host.

Common Memory Read or Write Transfer (16-Bit Hosts)

The addressing mode used by 16-bit hosts is shaded in table 5-14. Note that 16-bit address mode permits even byte only transfers (over D7:D0), odd byte-only transfers (over D15:D8) and word transfers (over D15:D0). Address lines A25:A1 determine the target word location, while the state of CE1#, CE2# and A0 determines the specific byte or bytes requested within the target word.

Table 5-14. Addressing Mode Supported by PC Memory Card When Connected to 16-Bit Host Systems.

Addressing Mode	CE1 #	CE2 #	A0	D15:D8	D7:D0
No access (standby mode)	1	1	X	High-Z	High-Z
8/16-bit Mode (even byte)	0	1	0	High-Z	Even Byte
8-bit Mode (odd byte)	0	1	1	High-Z	Odd Byte
16-bit Mode (odd byte only)	1	0	X	Odd Byte	High-Z
16-bit Mode (even & odd byte)	0	0	X	Odd Byte	Even Byte

Figure 5-8 illustrates a two byte read from a 16-bit host. Note that REG# is deasserted, indicating an access to common memory. This access results when the host system requests a word from the PC card. The PC card, recognizing that both CE1# and CE2# are asserted, returns an even and an odd byte to the host system. Other combinations of CE1#, CE2# and A0 permit single byte access.

Chapter 5: The Memory-Only Socket Interface

Figure 5-9 shows an example memory write with a 16-bit host system. In this example, an odd byte only is being written.

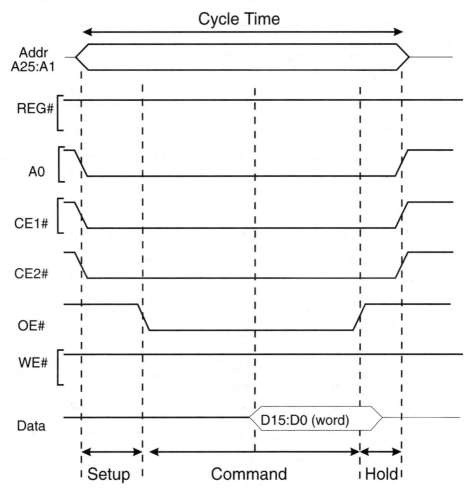

Figure 5-8. Common Memory Read Cycle — Word Transfer

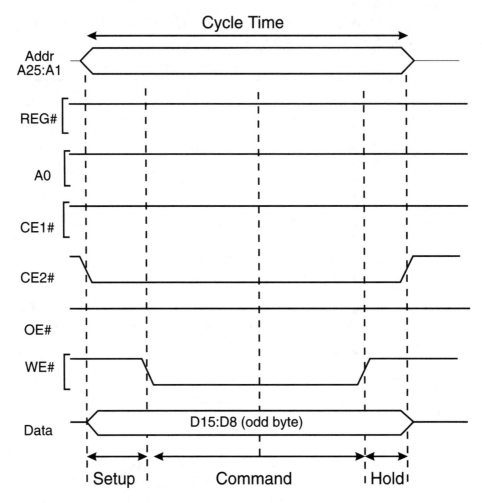

Figure 5-9. Common Memory Write Cycle

Common Memory Read or Write Transfer (8-Bit Hosts)

PC cards must be able to respond to reads and writes from 8-bit hosts that have a single data path (D7:D0). The 8-bit addressing mode permits both even and odd byte accesses over the lower data path, consistent with the needs of the 8-bit expansion bus. As indicated in table 5-15, when the 8-bit addressing mode is used CE2# remains deasserted during all transfers, while CE1# remains asserted. Address A0 specifies whether the access is to the even or odd byte. Note that transfer timing is not affected by the addressing mode used.

Chapter 5: The Memory-Only Socket Interface

Table 5-15. Addressing Mode Supported by PC Memory Card When Connected to 8-Bit Host Systems.

Addressing Mode	CE1#	CE2#	A0	D15:D8	D7:D0
No access (standby mode)	1	1	X	High-Z	High-Z
8/16-bit Mode (even byte)	0	1	0	High-Z	Even Byte
8-bit Mode (odd byte)	0	1	1	High-Z	Odd Byte
16-bit Mode (odd byte only)	1	0	X	Odd Byte	High-Z
16-bit Mode (even & odd byte)	0	0	X	Odd Byte	Even Byte

Common Memory Read/Write Timing with Wait

The WAIT# signal, under PC card control, extends standard cycle time. The maximum duration of WAIT# is 12μs. When WAIT# is asserted by the PC card, command time is extended by the duration of the WAIT# signal. In the event that WAIT# does not extend beyond the standard command time, standard timing will be met. In this instance, timing is not impacted by the assertion of WAIT#.

Figure 5-10 illustrates a memory read transfer with WAIT# asserted. This example illustrates a memory read using 8-bit addressing mode. Note that CE2# is deasserted and CE1# is asserted, while A0 (a logic "1") indicates access to an odd location. Since CE2# is deasserted, the odd location's contents must be transferred via data path D7:D0. The PC card also asserts WAIT#, telling the HBA to extend the cycle time. The cycle completes when WAIT# is deasserted. Refer to the PCMCIA specification for detailed timing information.

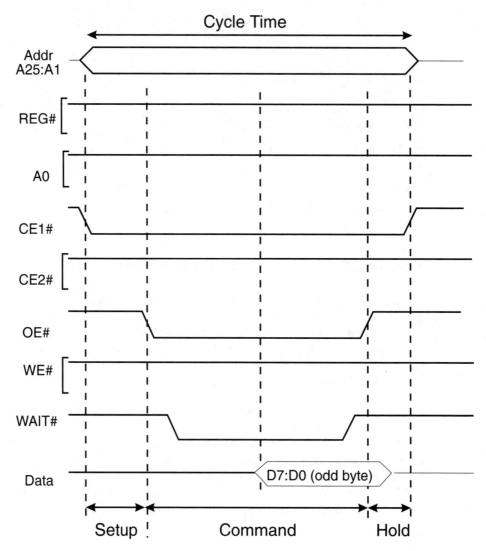

Figure 5-10. Common Memory Read Cycle With Wait Asserted

Chapter 6

The Previous Chapter

The previous chapter detailed the memory-only socket interface. Each pin was defined and its relationship to the PC Card and the HBA was discussed. The memory-only interface is the interface initially seen by 16-bit PC Cards when they are first inserted into a socket. This permits the memory-mapped CIS to be accessed to determine the PC Card type and interface requirements. If the card is designed for an interface type other than memory-only, then the HBA and PC Card are configured to communicate via one of the other interface defined by the PC Card Standard.

This Chapter

This chapter details the memory or I/O socket interface. The memory-only interface is converted into a memory or I/O interface by software after it detects that an I/O PC Card has been installed into the socket interface. Pins that are added or redefined by the memory or I/O interface are discussed along with their relationship to the I/O card function. Some of the memory-only pins are replaced with I/O specific pins when the interface is redefined for I/O. This chapter describes how the functions associated with the replaced memory-only pins are handled.

The Next Chapter

The next chapter defines the electrical interface that permits I/O Cards to use PC compatible DMA transfers. The DMA interface provides a way for standardized I/O cards that use DMA, to take advantage of existing software that is designed to use DMA data transfers.

PCMCIA System Architecture

Overview

The memory-only socket and the Memory or I/O socket have identical pin definitions when a PC Card is initially powered up. That is, when an I/O device is installed in a memory or I/O socket, the pin definition is initially defined as a memory-only configuration, allowing access to the Card Information Structure (CIS), which is mapped in attribute memory address space. Software then reads the CIS, determines the card requires an I/O interface and programs the Host Bus Adapter (HBA) and the I/O card to reconfigure the socket interface to the I/O pin definition.

The memory or I/O interface permits operation of either memory cards, I/O cards or multifunction cards containing combinations of both memory and I/O devices. When a socket contains a memory card, it is defined as a memory-only socket. When an I/O device is installed in the socket, some of the signal definitions change making the socket compatible with both memory and I/O cards.

Since the memory signals are covered in the previous section, this discussion focuses only on the signals that differ from the memory socket implementation.

The I/O Socket Interface

The following discussion describes the dynamic changes made to a memory or I/O socket when a PC Card containing I/O devices is installed. Note that the memory or I/O socket is configured as a memory socket when a PC Card is initially installed, allowing the Card Information Structure (CIS) to be read from attribute memory address space. If configuration software detects that the PC Card contains I/O devices, it then programs the PCMCIA HBA to reconfigure the socket for I/O device support.

The signals added to the socket when an I/O device is installed in a memory or I/O socket are listed in table 6-1. Some of these new signals replace pins that are reserved in the memory-only socket (those signals shown in the gray boxes in figure 6-1), while others replace selected status pins used in the memory-only interface (signals shown in the black boxes).

Chapter 6: The Memory or I/O Interface

Table 6-1. Pins Added/Removed When Converting from Memory-Only to Memory or I/O Interface

Memory Pin	I/O Replacement	Description
Reserved	INPACK#	**Input Port Acknowledge**. This signal is asserted during I/O read transfers from a PC Card when it recognizes the address. The signal enables the socket's data path transceiver so that the addressed PC Card can deliver valid data to the system. This signal is necessary if addresses within an I/O address window overlap with other devices. (Refer to the chapter entitled "The HBA" for a description of I/O address windows.)
Reserved	IORD#	**I/O Read Command**. This signal is asserted during I/O read transfers from PCMCIA cards.
Reserved	IOWR#	**I/O Write Command**. This signal is asserted during I/O write transfers to PC Cards.
READY	IREQ#	**Interrupt Request**. This signal is asserted to inform the system that the PC Card has an interrupt that needs servicing.
WP	IOIS16#	**I/O size is 16-bits**. This signal is asserted during I/O read transfers from PC Cards, if the device size is 16 bits.
BVD2	SPKR#	**Digital Audio Waveform**. Used to send audio information to the system speaker.
BVD1	STSCHG#	**I/O Status Change**. Used to report a card status change.

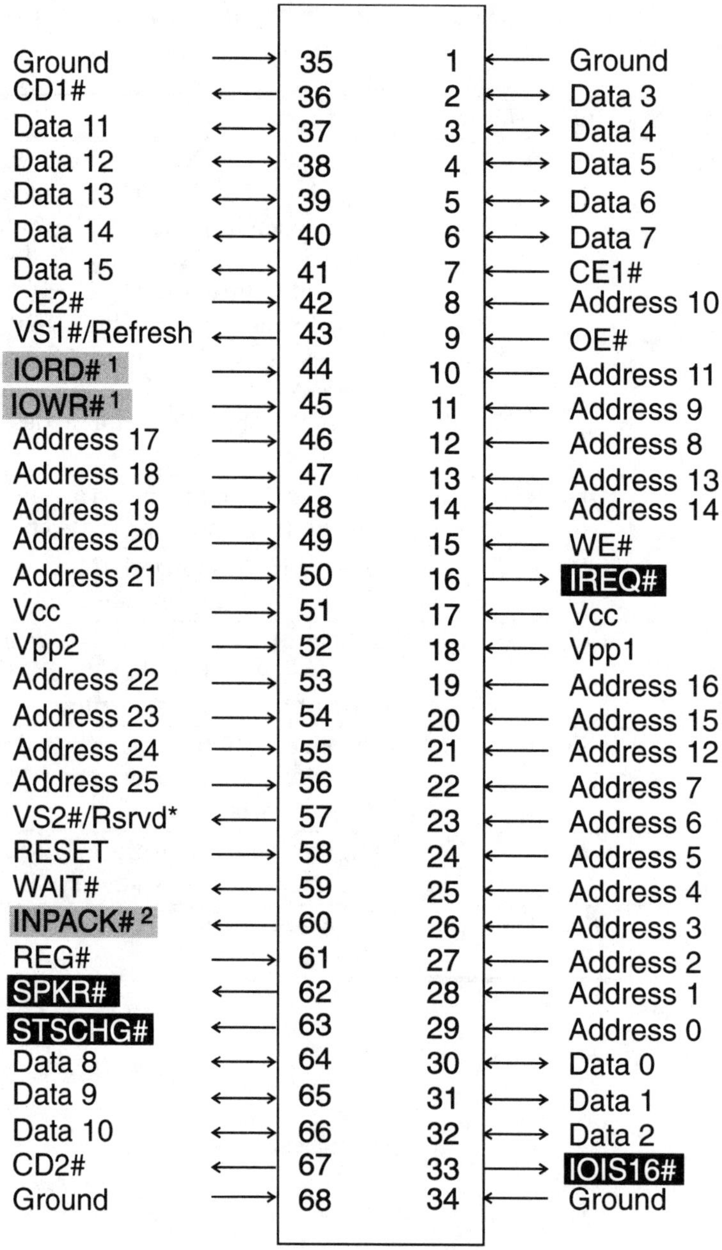

Ground	35	1	Ground
CD1#	36	2	Data 3
Data 11	37	3	Data 4
Data 12	38	4	Data 5
Data 13	39	5	Data 6
Data 14	40	6	Data 7
Data 15	41	7	CE1#
CE2#	42	8	Address 10
VS1#/Refresh	43	9	OE#
IORD# 1	44	10	Address 11
IOWR# 1	45	11	Address 9
Address 17	46	12	Address 8
Address 18	47	13	Address 13
Address 19	48	14	Address 14
Address 20	49	15	WE#
Address 21	50	16	IREQ#
Vcc	51	17	Vcc
Vpp2	52	18	Vpp1
Address 22	53	19	Address 16
Address 23	54	20	Address 15
Address 24	55	21	Address 12
Address 25	56	22	Address 7
VS2#/Rsrvd*	57	23	Address 6
RESET	58	24	Address 5
WAIT#	59	25	Address 4
INPACK# 2	60	26	Address 3
REG#	61	27	Address 2
SPKR#	62	28	Address 1
STSCHG#	63	29	Address 0
Data 8	64	30	Data 0
Data 9	65	31	Data 1
Data 10	66	32	Data 2
CD2#	67	33	IOIS16#
Ground	68	34	Ground

1. Pulled-up to Vcc by PC Card (R≥10KΩ).   2. Pulled-up to Vcc by HBA (R≥10KΩ).

Figure 6-1. PCMCIA Memory or I/O Socket

Chapter 6: The Memory or I/O Interface

PC Memory or I/O Card Transaction Definition

Six types of transactions can be performed when accessing a PC Card containing I/O devices:

- I/O Read
- I/O Write
- Common Memory Read
- Common Memory Write
- Attribute Memory Read
- Attribute Memory Write

Note that multifunction devices containing both common memory and I/O devices support all the transaction commands.

The Output Enable signal (OE#), Write Enable or Program signal (WE#), I/O Read (IORD#), I/O Write (IOWR#), and Register (REG#) signals define the transaction type. Table 6-2 lists each of the PC Card transaction definition signals and indicates the command signal combinations for common memory, attribute memory and I/O accesses. Note that REG# specifies access to either attribute memory address locations or I/O address locations. The memory and I/O command lines determine which address space is being accessed.

Table 6-2. PCMCIA Transaction Definition

Transaction Type	IORD#	IOWR#	OE#	WE#	REG#
I/O Read	0	1	1	1	0
I/O Write	1	0	1	1	0
Attribute Memory Read	1	1	0	1	0
Attribute Memory Write	1	1	1	0	0
Common Memory Read	1	1	0	1	1
Common Memory Write	1	1	1	0	1

I/O registers incorporated into PC Cards can be either 8-bits or 16-bits wide. I/O cards that contain 16-bit registers assert the IOIS16# signal when a 16-bit register is addressed. The HBA can determine the size of the register being accessed by monitoring the IOIS16# signal and match the bus size to the device size. For example, if a 16-bit access is being made to an 8-bit register, the host system (either the HBA or expansion bus controller) will divide the 16-bit access into two 8-bit accesses required by the I/O device.

The IOIS16# Pin

This pin is asserted by an I/O card when it recognizes that the location being accessed is contained within a 16-bit I/O device. When IOIS16# is asserted the HBA will perform a 16-bit transfer if possible. If the HBA is performed a 16-bit transfer but the IOIS16# pin is deasserted, then the HBA will perform two 8-bit transfers to/from target register.

The IREQ# Pin

The interrupt request pin can be driven either as a level or pulse triggered signal. The interrupt trigger used is a function of the interrupt triggering mechanism used by the host expansion bus. When an interrupt is asserted by the PC Card it is routed (steered) by the HBA to the target interrupt request line on the expansion bus. For details regarding the implementation of the IREQ# trigger selection and interrupt steering refer to the chapter entitled, "The Host Bus Adapter."

The INPACK# Pin

The INPACK# pin is asserted by PC Card I/O functions during reads from registers within the card. This pin is used by the HBA to enable data buffers between the PC Card socket and the expansion bus. If an I/O transfer is sent to a PC Card that does not access an internal register, then the data buffers remain disabled leaving the expansion bus electrically isolated from the PC Card socket interface. This is done in case the I/O access that does not belong to the PC Card is for another device somewhere within the system. Keeping the PC Card isolated from the bus eliminats possible bus loading or data bus contention problems.

The STSCHG# Pin

Many PC Cards that incorporate only an I/O function do not implement memory-mapped devices, require no battery backup, implement no write-protect switch, nor do they have a READY state. Therefore, the status signals (READY, WP, BVD1, and BVD2) which are not defined for the memory or I/O interface are not needed. However, some PC Card's may require one or more of these status signals (e.g. multifunction PC Cards containing both memory and I/O functions).

Since status signals (READY, WP, BVD1, and BVD2) used to report status information are not defined for the memory or I/O interface, PCMCIA defines an alternative method for reporting these status changes in lieu of the status pins. A configuration register (called the Pin Replacement Register) located within the attribute memory address space is used by PC Cards that must report status for one or more of the status pins that have been removed from the memory or I/O interface.

To notify the HBA that a status change has occurred, the Status Change (STSCHG#) signal is asserted. When the HBA detects the STSCHG# signal asserted it generates a status change interrupt just as if one of the status pins had been asserted on the memory-only interface. Software must then read the pin replacement register contained within the PC Card's attribute memory address space to determine the source of the status change interrupt.

The SPKR# Pin

The speaker pin is used by I/O-based PC Cards to deliver audio information back to the host system's speaker. The signal is implemented as a binary audio signal with a single amplitude, and is simply ORed with other signals that drive the host speaker. If the I/O card does not require a speaker, the SPKR# pin will be driven high by the PC Card.

PC Card functions using the SPKR# pin must also implement an enable/disable bit (called audio enable) in their Configuration and Status register.

I/O Transfers

Cycle times for I/O devices consist of a single timing standard. The default I/O cycle time requires a minimum of 255ns to complete. A device requiring additional cycle time must assert the WAIT# signal to extend the cycle.

Like PC memory cards, PC I/O cards must also respond to 8-bit and 16-bit host addressing modes. These addressing modes are the same as those discussed for memory cards, and are not repeated here.

Unlike PC memory cards, however, I/O devices within PC cards can be designed with either 8-bit or 16-bit registers, or a combination of both. When access is made to an I/O location within the PC card, the HBA may not know whether the I/O transfer is to or from an 8-bit or 16-bit device. In such cases, the HBA samples the IOIS16# signal to determine the size of I/O device accessed. When the host system accesses a PC card's I/O address space, several situations can result that require action:

- Single byte access by the host system to/from 8-bit register
- Word access by the host system to/from 8-bit register
- Odd byte access by the host system to/from 16-bit register
- Word access by the host system to/from 16-bit register

Single Byte Access to/from 8-Bit I/O Devices

Single byte accesses by the host system must be handled so that the data is transferred over the correct data path. Accesses to and from even locations present no problems since both 8-bit and 16-bit hosts expect even address location transfers to occur over the lower data path (D7:D0). Similarly, accesses to and from odd locations present no problems for 8-bit hosts since they expect both even and odd bytes to be transferred over the lower data path. However, 16-bit host systems expect odd location transfers to occur over the upper data path (D15:D8). Since 8-bit I/O devices transfer both even and odd locations over the lower data path, either the host bus system or the PCMCIA HBA must steer the data to the correct path when accessing odd locations.

When an I/O transfer begins, the HBA does not know whether the access is to an 8-bit or 16-bit device, but defaults to the 8-bit addressing mode. This means CE1# is asserted and CE2# is deasserted, while A0 determines whether an even or odd byte location is to be accessed.

Figure 6-2 illustrates a standard I/O read transfer from an odd location. The location being accessed is from an 8-bit I/O register, indicated by IOIS16# being deasserted. Note also that the cycle time is the standard 255ns.

Data from the odd address location is transferred over the lower data path from the 8-bit I/O register. With most PC-based bus architectures, such as ISA, the host system's bus implements device size lines that control data bus steering when accessing odd locations from 8-bit devices. The HBA notifies the host bus controller of the register size being accessed and the bus controller steers the contents of the odd location to the upper data path. If the host bus does not include a steering mechanism, then the HBA must perform the steering and supply data to the data path expected by the host bus requester.

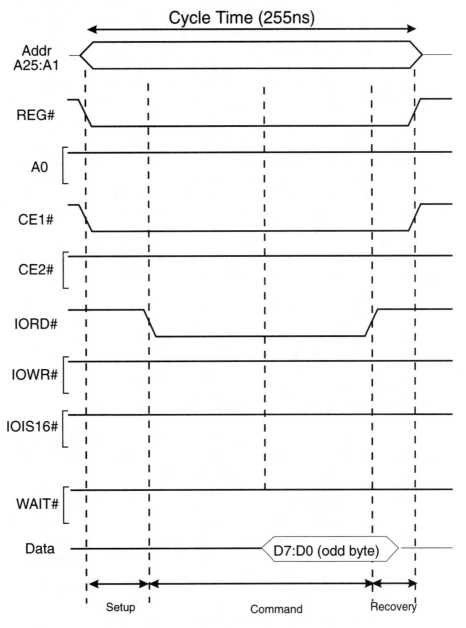

Figure 6-2. Default PC Card I/O Read Cycle.

Word Access to/from 8-Bit I/O Devices

When the host system performs a 16-bit data transfer with 8-bit registers on the PC card, the host's request to transfer an entire word (two bytes) requires two accesses to the PC card. The host system is responsible for converting the word access into two separate byte accesses to the PC card. Depending on the host bus architecture, either the host bus control logic or the PCMCIA HBA must automatically initiate the additional 8-bit access.

Systems based on most PC bus architectures (such as ISA, EISA, and the Micro Channel) employ signal lines and logic designed to manage accesses to and from devices of different sizes. In these instances, the HBA can utilize the host system's resources to run an additional cycle to the 8-bit PC card. When the HBA samples the PC card's IOIS16# line deasserted, it can use the host bus size lines to inform the host that the access is to an 8-bit device. The HBA completes the first byte transfer (even byte) and waits for the second transfer (odd byte) to be initiated by the host. The host, knowing that the odd byte is from an 8-bit device and that the data will be returned on the lower data path (D7:D0), steers the content of the lower data path to the upper path (D15:D8).

Some host systems may not employ device size translation logic for HBAs to use. In these instances, the HBA must run the additional transfer to the PC card and return the entire word requested by the host system in what appears to be a single cycle to the host.

Byte Accesses to/from 16-Bit Register

When the host transfers a single byte (whether with an even or odd location), the transfer can complete in a single cycle when a 16-bit I/O device is accessed. As in the examples discussed earlier, the HBA, not knowing whether the device is 8-bit or 16-bit, starts the transfer by using 8-bit addressing mode. Since even location accesses are identical for both 8-bit and 16-bit addressing mode, no adjustment need be made by the HBA or the PC card and the transfer completes normally regardless of the state of the IOIS16# signal. Transfers to and from odd byte locations when accessing 16-bit devices either require:

- adjustment of the address mode to ensure that data is transferred to and from the PC card over the correct data path, or
- data steering the between upper and lower data paths if 8-bit mode addressing is used.

Chapter 6: The Memory or I/O Interface

Word Accesses to/from 16-Bit I/O Registers

Word transfers to and from 16-bit I/O registers can complete in a single cycle. Refer to figure 6-3. Typically, when an I/O transfer begins the address mode defaults to 8-bit addressing mode, in expectation that an 8-bit register may be accessed. However, when the IOIS16# signal is asserted by the 16-bit target device, the HBA can also assert CE2#, causing the PC card to respond to the word transfer.

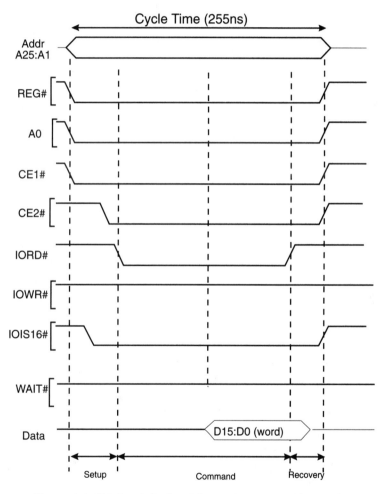

Figure 6-3. I/O Read Cycle without WAIT#- Word Transfer

Chapter 7

The Previous Chapter

The previous chapter detailed the memory or I/O interface between the PC Card and socket. Configuration software reconfigures the memory-only interface into a memory or I/O interface after it detects that an I/O PC Card has been installed into the socket interface. Pins that are added or redefined by the memory or I/O interface are discussed along with their relationship to the I/O card function. Some of the memory-only pins are replaced with I/O specific pins when the interface is redefined for I/O. The previous chapter described how the functions associated with the replaced memory-only pins are handled.

This Chapter

This chapter defines the DMA compliant electrical interface, permitting I/O Cards to use PC compatible DMA transfers. The DMA interface allows I/O devices that use DMA to take advantage of existing compatible software when performing data transfers.

The Next Chapter

The next chapter discusses the PC Card ATA interface. A PC Card ATA interface provides a PC compatible hardware and programming interface that simplifies the job of implemented hard drive solutions in the PCMCIA environment. This chapter defines the various ways that a PC Card ATA can be mapped in the system along with the electrical interfaces that are used. Differences between the PC compatible ATA implementation versus the PC Card ATA interface are also discussed.

PCMCIA System Architecture

Background

Release 2.x systems do not support DMA transfers. As a result, standard PC hardware and software solutions that use DMA will not work with 2.x compliant systems. This makes the job of implementing devices such as floppy drives and Sound Blaster in the PC Card environment extremely difficult. These devices use the IBM PC compatible DMA subsystem to transfer data between themselves and main system memory. Standard software supporting these type devices are designed to program the DMA subsystem in order to transfer data to/from these devices.

Previous implementations of PC Cards that use DMA required definition of additional hardware and software that extends beyond the Release 2.x specification. Some HBA manufacturers included DMA support and some system vendors implemented solutions using these HBAs. These solutions however, did not enjoy industry-wide support because the PCMCIA Standard did not define a standard implementation.

Review of PC Compatible DMA Transfers

PC compatible DMA employs a DMA controller (DMAC) that is programmed to orchestrate a transfer between an I/O device and main system memory. Once programmed, the DMAC handles a block transfer and its termination. The DMAC used in ISA compatible PCs performs a "fly-by" transfer; that is, it is able to transfer data between memory and an I/O device (read and write) in a single DMA cycle without latching the data internally, a job that would normally require two separate bus cycles (a read followed by a write) by the processor.

Upon completion of the overall data transfer, the I/O device interrupts the microprocessor to indicate completion. In response, the microprocessor temporarily suspends its current task and performs an I/O read from the I/O device to check the completion status of the transfer. If the I/O device indicates no errors were encountered, the microprocessor may continue processing.

A DMA Example

This example describes a DMA transfer between the floppy drive controller and system memory. The example defines the signal involved in the transfer and describes the sequence of events that occur to initiate, perform, and terminate a DMA transfer.

Four distinct steps must occur to initiate and complete a DMA transfer:

- Set-up the DMA channel for the transfer.
- Command the I/O device to initiate the block data transfer.
- Grant the system buses to the DMA controller so it can run the bus cycle.
- Notify the microprocessor that the transfer is complete.

Each DMA Channel within the DMA controller has its own set of I/O registers that the programmer uses to set up the data transfer. The set of I/O registers associated with each DMA Channel allows the programmer to specify:

- The Transfer Count (number of bytes to be transferred).
- The start memory address (start address in memory where data will be read from or written to).
- The direction of transfer with reference to (type of transfer).

After the DMA Channel has been set up by the programmer, the I/O device must be programmed to initiate the overall block data transfer. As an example, the programmer would issue the proper series of I/O write commands to a floppy disk controller to initiate a disk read operation.

Having set up the respective DMA channel and issued the proper commands to the I/O device (in this case, the floppy disk controller and DMA channel two), the microprocessor can then go on to another task. The entire data transfer and its termination will be handled by the I/O device and its respective DMA Channel.

Each I/O device designed to use the DMA transfers employs three dedicated DMA signals defined by the ISA bus:

- **DREQ** (DMA Request) — output by the I/O device to request a DMAC transfer be performed.

- **DACK#** (DMA acknowledge) — input to the I/O device notifying it that the transfer has started.
- **TC** (Terminal Count) — input to the I/O device notifying it that the block transfer has been completed.

When performing a floppy disk transfer, the programmer may only perform data transfers in multiples of the sector size. When running MS-DOS, a sector on a floppy disk contains 512 bytes of information. This would be the smallest data transfer possible when transferring information between a disk drive and memory.

Refer to figure 7-1 for a block diagram of the components involved.

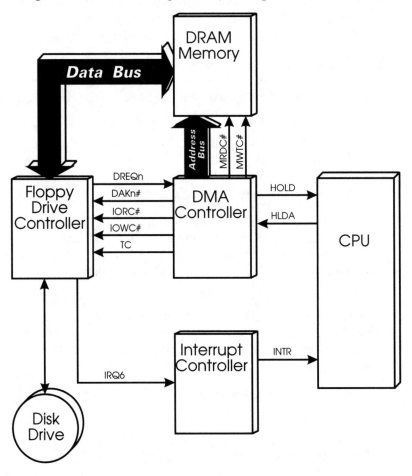

Figure 7-1. Example DMA Transfer Mechanism

1. The programmer issues a series of I/O writes to DMA channel two's registers to set up the start memory address, transfer count and the direction of the transfer with reference to memory. In the disk read example, assume that the start memory address is 1000h, the transfer count is 512 bytes (one sector) and that this is a write transfer (with reference to memory).

2. The floppy controller must be programmed with the disk read command, the cylinder number, the head (or surface) number, the start sector number and the number of sectors to be read. In this example, we will assume a one sector (512 bytes) read from cylinder three, head one, sector five.

3. Upon receiving the parameters and the disk read command, the disk controller initiates a seek operation to position the read/write head mechanism over cylinder three. It must then wait for the disk to spin until the start of sector five is detected under the read head on surface one. As the disk is a mechanical device, this will take some time.

4. In the example of a read operation from a floppy disk controller, some time will elapse before the disk controller has read the first byte from disk.

5. When the first byte has been transferred from the disk to the disk controller, the floppy disk controller must then request that its associated DMA Channel transfer the data. The floppy disk controller asserts DMA request line two (DREQ2) that goes to the DMAC.

6. The DMAC responds by asserting HOLD to seize the buses (address, data, and control buses) from the microprocessor. The HOLD line goes directly to the microprocessor's hold request input.

7. When the microprocessor completes the current bus cycle, it will tri-state all of its bus output drivers, thereby floating the buses. The microprocessor also asserts HLDA to tell the requesting device (the DMAC in this case) that it is now the bus master.

8. The DMAC then responds to DREQ2 from the disk controller by activating DMA Acknowledge (DACK2#) and the I/O read command line (IORC#). These two lines go to the disk controller.

9. The disk controller drops DREQ2 and begins the access to the data register to place data onto the data bus.

10. The DMAC activates the Memory Write Command line (MWTC#) and places the address from channel two's start address register onto the address bus.

11. The data on the data bus is written into memory at the address currently on the address bus.

12. The DMAC then increments channel two's memory address register by one to point to the address in the RAM where it will store the next byte it receives from the disk controller.

13. The DMAC also decrements the byte transfer count. If the transfer count is not exhausted, the data transfer is not complete and the DMAC must wait for another DMA Request (DREQ2) from the floppy drive controller, indicating that it has another byte to transfer. The DMAC also deasserts HOLD to give control of the buses back to the processor and awaits the next DREQ2 assertion from the floppy disk controller. The microprocessor reattaches itself to the buses (exits the tri-state condition) and deasserts the Hold Acknowledge line (HLDA) to tell the DMAC it has resumed control of the buses. The microprocessor is now bus master again. (step 6).

14. When the transfer count is exhausted, the data transfer is complete. The DMAC will once again deassert the hold request line (HOLD) to tell the microprocessor that it no longer needs the buses.

15. The DMAC also generates EOP (End-of-Process). This supplies the signal TC (Terminal Count reached) to the disk controller. The disk controller will then generate a device-specific interrupt request to the 8259 Interrupt Controller which in turn generates INTR (Interrupt Request) to the microprocessor to inform it that the transfer operation is complete.

The DMA controller supports a variety of transfer modes. This example describes a transfer in which the DMAC surrenders control of the buses after each transfer, called Single Transfer Mode. This transfer mode keeps the processor and other bus masters (e.g. the refresh logic) from be starved for control of the system bus. Other transfer modes are supported by the DMAC including Block Transfer Mode and Demand Transfer Mode.

DMA Channels Supported by ISA

The DMAC used in ISA machines is the Intel 8237, providing four separate DMA channels. Two 8237s are used in a master/slave configuration, providing a total of seven DMA channels. Each DMA channel employs its respective DREQn and DACKn# signals (where n= 0, 1, 2, 3, 5, 6, 7), corresponding to the DMA channel number. Each DMA channel is used by a separate I/O device to handle block data transfers with memory.

ISA compatible machines support both 8- and 16-bit DMA channels, specifying the width of the data path used during the transfer. DMA channels 0-3 are 8-bit only DMA channels and DMA channels 5-7 are 16-bit only DMA channels. An I/O device wishing to use DMA transfers must select one of the DMA channels corresponding to the width of transfer it supports.

Chapter 7: The DMA Interface

For more detailed information regarding DMA refer to the MindShare book entitled, *"ISA System Architecture,"* published by Addison-Wesley.

The DMA Socket Interface

The DMA interface defines three DMA signals (DREQ#, DACK, and TC) required by an I/O device in order for it to use the DMA transfer mechanism. Figure 7-2 illustrates the memory or I/O interface signals that can be reassigned to the respective DMA related signals.

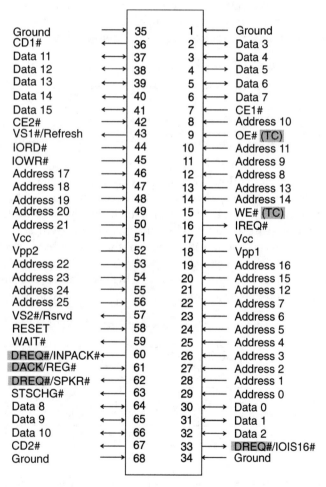

Ground	→	35	1	← Ground
CD1#	←	36	2	↔ Data 3
Data 11	↔	37	3	↔ Data 4
Data 12	↔	38	4	↔ Data 5
Data 13	↔	39	5	↔ Data 6
Data 14	↔	40	6	↔ Data 7
Data 15	↔	41	7	← CE1#
CE2#	→	42	8	← Address 10
VS1#/Refresh	←	43	9	← OE# (TC)
IORD#	→	44	10	← Address 11
IOWR#	→	45	11	← Address 9
Address 17	→	46	12	← Address 8
Address 18	→	47	13	← Address 13
Address 19	→	48	14	← Address 14
Address 20	→	49	15	← WE# (TC)
Address 21	→	50	16	→ IREQ#
Vcc	→	51	17	← Vcc
Vpp2	→	52	18	← Vpp1
Address 22	→	53	19	← Address 16
Address 23	→	54	20	← Address 15
Address 24	→	55	21	← Address 12
Address 25	→	56	22	← Address 7
VS2#/Rsrvd	←	57	23	← Address 6
RESET	→	58	24	← Address 5
WAIT#	←	59	25	← Address 4
DREQ#/INPACK#	←	60	26	← Address 3
DACK/REG#	→	61	27	← Address 2
DREQ#/SPKR#	←	62	28	← Address 1
STSCHG#	←	63	29	← Address 0
Data 8	↔	64	30	↔ Data 0
Data 9	↔	65	31	↔ Data 1
Data 10	↔	66	32	↔ Data 2
CD2#	←	67	33	→ DREQ#/IOIS16#
Ground	→	68	34	← Ground

Figure 7-2. DMA Signal Interface

The DREQ# Pin

DREQ# can be assigned to any one of three memory or I/O interface pins, thereby replacing the standard I/O signals as follows:

- Pin 33 (replaces IOIS16#)
- Pin 60 (replaces INPACK#)
- Pin 62 (replaces SPKR#)

The pin assigned to fulfill the DREQ# signaling function is specified by the PC Card's CIS. This DREQ# pin assignment information is contained within the miscellaneous features field of the Configuration Table Entry tuple (tuple code 1Bh). The miscellaneous features field definition is illustrated in table 7-1.

Table 7-1. Definition of the Miscellaneous Features Field that Defines DMA support

7	6	5	4	3	2	1	0
EXT	RFU (0)	Pwr Dn	Read Only	Audio	Max Twin Cards		
EXT	RFU (0)	RFU (0)	DMA width	DMA Request Signal		RFU (0)	RFU (0)

The first byte within the miscellaneous features field was defined for 2.x compliant systems and contains no definition for DMA. The newer PC Card Standard defines an extension that includes the DMA related information. Bit 7 of the first miscellaneous features extension byte is set to indicate that the second byte is present. Bits 2 and 3 of the second byte specifies which interface pin the PC Card uses for DREQ#. A PC Card that uses DMA forfeits the functionality of the signal replaced by DREQ#. The binary values in bits 2 and 3 are interpreted as shown below:

Table 7-2. Interpretation of DMA Request Assignment Bits

Bit 3	Bit 2	Definition
0	0	DMA not supported
0	1	DREQ# uses SPKR#
1	0	DREQ# uses IOIS16#
1	1	DREQ# uses INPACK#

Note that the data width of the DMA transfer is also specified by bit 4 of the second miscellaneous features byte. A value of "0" indicates an 8-bit DMA data transfer is supported and a value of "1" indicates support for 16-bit DMA transfers. Configuration software is responsible for checking the DMA data width and selecting the corresponding DMA channel that supports the data width indicated by the PC Card.

The DACK/REG# Pin

The DACK is shared with the REG# pin to differentiate normal I/O transfers from DMA transfers. When an I/O register access begins the HBA asserts either IORD# or IOWR#, signaling the start of the transfer. It further specifies the type of I/O access using the DACK/REG# pin. The access is treated as a normal I/O transfer when REG# asserted (in which case the PC Card decodes the address to select the target register) and when DACK is asserted the transfer is recognized as acknowledgment of a DMA transfer (in which case the DMA data register is selected directly and the address is ignored).

The TC Pin

When TC is asserted by the DMA controller, it is indicating that the block transfer has completed. Note that only one TC pin is defined by the ISA expansion bus, therefore the DMA controller also asserts the respective DACKn# signal to identify the I/O device that TC is intended for. The PC Card upon recognizing TC belongs to it, asserts its IREQ# pin, thereby signaling the system that its DMA transfer has ended.

TC is assigned to pin 9 (replacing OE#) to specify completion of a DMA write transfer and pin 15 (replacing WE#) to specify completion of a DMA read transfer.

DMA with PC Card

Figure 7-3 illustrates a PC Card using DMA transfers. Notice that the HBA must invert the DREQ# and DACK signals to/from the ISA bus, since it defines these signal active in the opposite logic state. DMA transfers complete just as they do to/from any I/O device supporting the DMA transfer mechanism. Additionally the HBA must implement DMA channel steering logic so that the PC Card's DREQ# and DACK signals connect to the selected ISA DREQn and DACKn# signals.

DMA transfer width may be either 8-bit or 16-bit as specified in the miscellaneous features field of the Configuration Table Entry tuple (table 7-1). The HBA determines the DMA transfer size (8- or 16-bit) via the SA0 and SBHE# signals on the ISA bus and in turn asserts either CE1# (8-bit transfer) or CE1# and CE2# (16-bit transfer). Refer to the chapter entitled, The "Host Bus Adapter" for additional information regarding the DMA implementation.

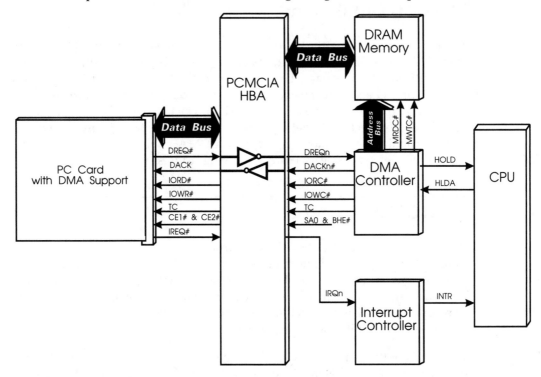

Figure 7-3. Block Diagram of PC Card implementing DMA Transfers

DMA Transfer Timing (PC Compatible)

DMA Bus Cycle

In the PC environment, DMA transactions are performed by an Intel compatible 8237 DMA controller (DMAC). The DMAC transactions consist of four states, each with a duration of one DMA clock period. When the DMAC has

Chapter 7: The DMA Interface

gained ownership of the system buses, it uses its own clock when executing bus cycles. This clock is referred to as the DMA clock and is 1/2 the expansion bus clock frequency. Depending on the PC and the selected processor speed, this will yield a DMA clock of either 3MHz (6MHz AT), 4MHz (8MHz ISA-compatible machine), or 4.165MHz (8.33MHz ISA-compatible machine).

Table 7-3 lists the clock period for the three possible processor speed settings:

Table 7-3. Typical DMA Clock Speeds in the PC Environment

Speed Setting	DMA Clock Frequency	DMA Clock Period
6MHz	3MHz	333.3ns
8MHz	4MHz	250ns
8.33MHz	4.165MHz	240ns

Prior to receiving a DMA Request, the DMAC is in the idle state, Si. When a DRQ is sensed, the DMAC enters a state where it asserts HOLD (Hold Request) to the microprocessor and awaits the HLDA (Hold Acknowledge). This state is called So. The DMAC remains in the So state until HLDA is sensed active.

The DMAC can then proceed with the DMA transfer. S1, S2, S3 and S4 are the states used to execute a transfer (of a byte or word) between the requesting I/O device and system memory. In addition, when accessing a device that is slow to respond, a DMA transfer cycle can be stretched by deasserting the DMAC's READY input until the device is ready to complete the transfer. This will cause the DMAC to insert wait states, Sw, in the bus cycle until READY goes active again.

The following actions take place during states S1-S4. See figure 7-4 for the actual timing of a single transfer:

State	Actions Taken
S1	During single transfer mode, S1 is used to output the middle byte of the memory address, A8:A15 during each transfer. The middle byte of the memory address is output onto data bus pins D0:D7. The DMAC also pulses its Address Strobe (ADSTB) output during S1 and on the falling edge of ADSTB the new middle byte of the address to be latched into the external DMA address latch. Address lines A8:A15 receive the middle portion of the address during S2.
	During Block and Demand transfers, the middle byte of the memory address only changes once every 256th transfer. For this reason, when in these modes the DMAC only enters the S1 state every 256th transfer to update the middle byte of the address.
S2	During S2, the lower byte (A0:A7) of the memory address is output directly onto the address bus, A0:A7. The DMAC's AEN output is set active causing the external DMA address latch to output the middle portion of the address and to act as an enable for the DMA Page Register addressing. In addition, DACKn# is asserted to tell the I/O device that the transfer is in progress. When DACK# is asserted, the HBA starts the PC Card data register access.
S3	S3 will only occur in a bus cycle if Compressed Timing hasn't been selected for this DMA channel. See text below for a discussion of Compressed Timing. During S3, the MRDC# or the IORC# line is set active. If the DMA channel is programmed for extended writes, the MWTC# or IOWC# line is also set active during S3.
S4	If the DMA channel was not programmed for extended write, the MWTC# or IOWC# is set active at the start of S4. If extended write had been selected, the write command line was already set active at the start of S3. The actual read/write takes place at the trailing edge of S4 when both the Read and Write command lines are de-asserted by the DMAC. This completes the transfer of a byte or word between memory and the requesting I/O device.

When Compressed Timing is selected, S3 is eliminated from the DMA transfer cycle. The only real purpose of S3 is to allow the Read command line to be asserted for twice the duration it is when Compressed Timing is active. Not all memory and I/O devices will tolerate this abbreviated Read command line, so it must be used cautiously.

When Extended Write is selected, it causes the Write command line to be set active during S3 rather than S4, effectively doubling the duration of the Write command line's active period.

It should be obvious that Extended Write and Compressed Timing are mutually exclusive because S3 is essential for Extended Write and is eliminated when Compressed Timing is selected.

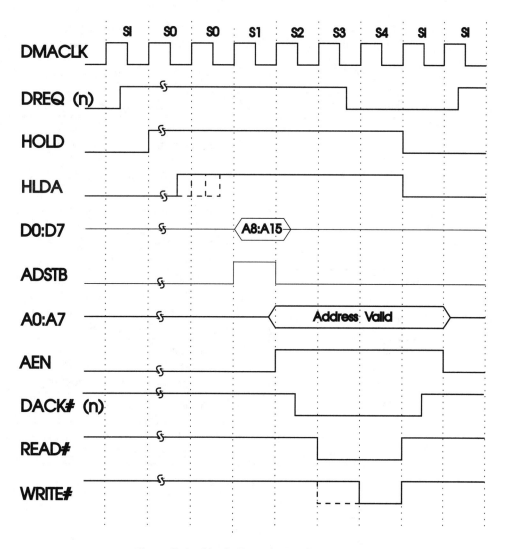

Figure 7-4. Single Transfer Mode Timing

PCMCIA System Architecture

The HBA must satisfy the timing requirements of the DMA controller implemented in the host system. Note that the duration of the PC Card access is during the assertion of the DACK# from the ISA bus (DMA clocks S2, S3 and S4).

Changes to Socket Services

Several socket service functions have been modified to support DMA. These functions are listed in table 7-4 and the DMA change is described.

Table 7-4. Socket Service Functions Modified to Support DMA

Socket Service Function	Code	Description of Change
GetSocket	8Dh	Provides status information regarding the current setting of the specified HBA socket interface. Includes two bits that specify whether the DREQ# signal is currently assigned to the socket (00b=DREQ# not assigned to socket), and if so, which socket interface pin is used to signal DREQ#. (01b=SPKR#; 10b=IOIS16; 11b=INPACK)
InquireSocket	8Ch	Defines attribute bits indicating whether the socket supports DMA transfers. If supported, also defines a bit-map of DMA channels supported.
SetSocket	8Eh	Changes the current settings of the HBA socket interface. Includes the same definition used by Get socket
GetStatus	8Fh	Provide status regarding the HBA socket interface and PC Card configuration. This information incorporates the changes made to GetSocket.

Chapter 7: The DMA Interface

Changes to Card Services

Several of the card services have also been modified to support DMA. The services affected are listed in table 7-5 along with a description of the changes made. The services shown in shaded boxes were added with the PC Card 95 release.

Table 7-5. Modifications Made to Card Services to Support DMA

Service Name	Code	Description of Change
AdjustResouceInfo	35h	Obtains status of or makes changes to the system resource table managed by card services. If DMA is supported, DMA channel resources will be included in the resources table, and the ability to modify DMA resource information within the table will be defined for this service.
GetConfigurationInfo	04h	Provides the current configuration of the PC Card and socket. This service includes DMA configuration information.
ModifyConfiguration	27h	Modifies the current configuration of the socket configuration. Adds support for enabling or disabling the DMA channel.
RequestConfiguration	30h	Requests that card services perform the configuration that has been specified. This service adds the ability to enable or disable the DMA routing, if a Request-DMA service was called for this PC Card.
RequestDMA	3Ah	Requests that a DMA channel be assigned to the PC Card being configured.
ReleaseDMA	3Bh	Releases a DMA channel previously assigned to a PC Card with the RequestDMA service.

Chapter 8

The Previous Chapter

The previous chapter defined the DMA compliant electrical interface, permitting I/O Cards to use PC compatible DMA transfers. The DMA interface allows PC Cards using DMA to take advantage of existing compatible software when performing data transfers.

This Chapter

This chapter discusses the PC Card ATA interface. A PC Card ATA interface provides a PC compatible hardware and programming interface that simplifies the job of implemented hard drive solutions in the PCMCIA environment. This chapter defines the various ways that a PC Card ATA can be mapped in the system along with the electrical interfaces that are used. Differences between the PC compatible ATA implementation versus the PC Card ATA interface are also discussed.

The Next Chapter

The next chapter focuses on the optional Auto-Indexing Mass Storage (AIMS) interface. The chapter describes the programming interface and the transfer mechanism used by AIMS cards.

The ATA Interface

IDE Disk drives use the ATA (AT Attachment) interface common in many ISA-compatible PCs. The ATA interface is a 40 pin interface that connects IDE drives to an ATA host bus adapter (HBA) interface (refer to figure 8-1). The interface includes register select signals, three address lines, 16 data lines and control signals. Functions performed by the ATA host adapter include address decode and data buffering.

Devices implemented as ATA drives in the PCMCIA environment include actual small form-factor disk drives (i.e. 1.8 inch disks) and Flash cards that use the ATA interface and emulate a disk drive. The ATA interface is attractive because the software interface used by ATA devices is standardized and quite common. Standard BIOS routines are built into virtually every PC to support the ATA interface, eliminating the need for specialized device driver code to access the ATA card.

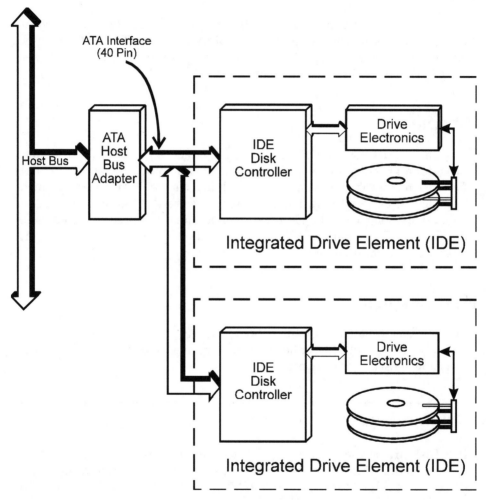

Figure 8-1. Typical ATA Interface to IDE Drive

The ATA Interface

PCMCIA does not require that the HBA include the ATA host adapter functionality. In the PCMCIA environment, the ATA host adapter functions (address decode and data buffering) are incorporated into the ATA PC Card proper as shown in figure 8-2. As a result, PC Card ATA devices can interface via the standard I/O socket interface.

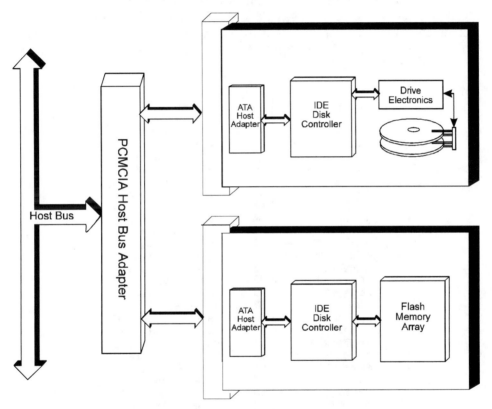

Figure 8-2. PC Card ATA Disk and Memory Devices

The PCMCIA specification includes an interface definition, which lists the minimum signals required to communicate with an ATA PC Card. However, virtually all PCMCIA host bus adapters support the standard memory or I/O interface, which contains all the signals required to support the ATA interface. Figure 8-3 illustrates the minimal interface required to support ATA Cards. Notice that all of the signals defined are included in the standard memory or I/O socket interface.

It should be noted that some PCMCIA host bus adapters provide an ATA interface (defines the standard 40 pin interface required by IDE drives) at the PC Card socket. This interface is not specified nor supported by PCMCIA. These designs integrate the ATA host bus adapter into the PCMCIA HBA. This interface permits system manufacturers to connect a 40 pin standard small form factor IDE drive via the PC Card socket. One advantage of the small form factor ATA drive interface is that it can provide performance advantages over the standard I/O interface that requires the ATA host bus adapter be integrated into the PC Card itself. This performance gain results from the elimination of address setup time (required by standard PC Cards) when transferring data to and from the ATA drive. See the chapter entitled, "An Example Adapter - CL-PD6722."

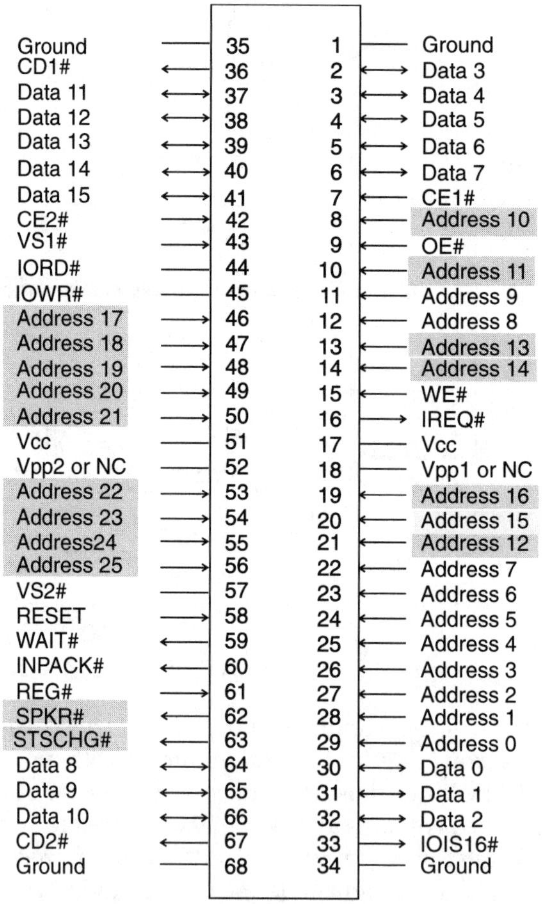

Ground	35	1	Ground
CD1#	36	2	Data 3
Data 11	37	3	Data 4
Data 12	38	4	Data 5
Data 13	39	5	Data 6
Data 14	40	6	Data 7
Data 15	41	7	CE1#
CE2#	42	8	Address 10
VS1#	43	9	OE#
IORD#	44	10	Address 11
IOWR#	45	11	Address 9
Address 17	46	12	Address 8
Address 18	47	13	Address 13
Address 19	48	14	Address 14
Address 20	49	15	WE#
Address 21	50	16	IREQ#
Vcc	51	17	Vcc
Vpp2 or NC	52	18	Vpp1 or NC
Address 22	53	19	Address 16
Address 23	54	20	Address 15
Address24	55	21	Address 12
Address 25	56	22	Address 7
VS2#	57	23	Address 6
RESET	58	24	Address 5
WAIT#	59	25	Address 4
INPACK#	60	26	Address 3
REG#	61	27	Address 2
SPKR#	62	28	Address 1
STSCHG#	63	29	Address 0
Data 8	64	30	Data 0
Data 9	65	31	Data 1
Data 10	66	32	Data 2
CD2#	67	33	IOIS16#
Ground	68	34	Ground

Figure 8-3. Minimum Signals Required for ATA Socket Interface

Differences Between Standard ATA and PCMCIA ATA

Note that the ATA interface consists of signals and functionality not completely supported by the PCMCIA ATA interface. Note for example, that the normal ATA interface supports daisy chaining another drive via a ribbon cable connector. Since PC Card ATA drives have the ATA adapter integrated into the PC Card, the daisy chain approach is not supported with the PCMCIA solution. Table 8-1 lists the ATA signals not defined by PCMCIA's ATA interface and identifies the functionality that may be impacted or lost.

Table 8-1. Signals Defined by ATA But Not Used By PCMCIA

ATA Signals Not Supported	Related Functionality
PDIAG (Passed Diagnostics)	Asserted by drive 1 to inform drive 0 that it has completed diagnostics. This pin allows drive 0 to report diagnostic status for drive 1. The diagnostic command must be run for each socket containing an ATA PC Card.
DASP (Drive Active/Second Drive Present)	This is a multiplexed signal indicating that a drive is active. During initialization, this signal is asserted by drive 1, indicating its presence. This functionality is provided by PCMCIA using the Socket and Copy Registers.
CSEL (Cable Select)	Used by the ATA host adapter to select drive 0 or drive 1. PCMCIA Drives use the Socket and Copy Registers to differentiate between drive 0 and 1. Each are accessed at a separate socket based on the copy number.
DMARQ and -DMACK (DMA Request and DMA Acknowledge)	These signals permit ATA drives to use DMA transfers when transferring data to and from the 16-bit data register. This capability is not supported by PCMCIA.

ATA System Resource Requirements

ATA devices contain two register blocks called the command register block and control register block. Each of these register blocks must be assessible by the system. PC Card ATA devices support either I/O or memory-mapping these registers using one of four addressing modes listed in table 8-2.

Standard mapping in the ISA environment includes the assignment of two separate I/O address ranges to map ATA drive registers into. If these ranges are not available, another range of I/O addresses can be used. If neither of the standard I/O address ranges are available, then a contiguous block of 16 I/O locations is acquired for mapping the command and control block registers into.

Alternatively, the registers can be mapped into memory locations. When memory-mapping is chosen, a contiguous 2KB block of memory locations are used. The command and control registers are mapped into the first 16 bytes of the 2KB memory block, while the last 1KB of the block is used as a high speed buffer to transfer data to and from the PC card. The address modes listed in table 8-2 (except for the memory-mapped option) are mandatory for compliance with the PCMCIA ATA specification.

Table 8-2. ATA Addressing Options Supported by PCMCIA

Address Mode	Command Block	Control Block
I/O - Primary ATA drive address	1F0h - 1F7h	3F6h - 3F7h
I/O - Secondary ATA drive address	170h - 177h	376h - 377h
I/O - Any 16-byte contiguous range	XXX0h - XXXFh	
Memory - Any aligned 2KB address range	Card must respond to locations XXX0h - XXXFh and X400h - X7FFh within the 2KB range	

In addition to mapping the registers, an interrupt request line must also be supported for I/O addressing. Normally IRQ 14 is used by ATA drives. When configured for memory-mapped registers, the socket interface does not define an interrupt line, therefore software polling must be used.

Supporting Two Drives

It is possible for two ATA drives to be simultaneously installed into PCMCIA sockets of the same HBA. When accessing these drives, some method must be used to individually select these drives as either drive 0 or drive 1. This is accomplished in a standard ATA environment via the daisy-chained cable with the cable-select signal or by jumpers (switches) on the drive. In the PCMCIA environment, a configuration register, called the Socket and Copy Register, can be used to identify two ATA PC cards mapped to the same address space. The copy number programmed into the Socket and Copy Registers is used by the HBA to differentiate drive 0 from drive 1.

Chapter 9

The Previous Chapter

The previous chapter discussed the PC Card ATA interface. A PC Card ATA interface provides a PC compatible hardware and programming interface that simplifies the job of implemented hard drive solutions in the PCMCIA environment. The chapter defined the various ways that a PC Card ATA can be mapped in the system along with the electrical interfaces that can be used. Differences between the PC compatible ATA implementation versus the PC Card ATA interface were also discussed.

This Chapter

This chapter focuses on the optional Auto-Indexing Mass Storage (AIMS) interface. The transfer mechanism is described, along with the registers that must be programmed to initiate the transfer.

The Next Chapter

Next, host bus adapter design is discussed, including the functionality that must be implemented, along with the optional features.

The AIMS Interface

The AIMS (Auto-Indexing Mass Storage) interface is designed to support cards that store large data structures to support functions such as imaging and multimedia. This interface creates a standard PC card interface for electronic cameras and other portable equipment requiring large amounts of data storage.

The interface uses a block transfer mechanism. Memory accesses occur through the card's registers. The specification describes the signal interface and the register set required by an AIMS card. The registers can be mapped into either memory or I/O address space. See figure 9-1 for the AIMS interface pin definition.

Note that the AIMS interface specifies only an 8-bit data bus and seven address lines. The interface can be mapped into the host system's memory or I/O address space. The actual interface provided by the HBA will be a memory-only interface or the memory or I/O interface; however, the AIMS card only uses the pins illustrated in figure 9-1.

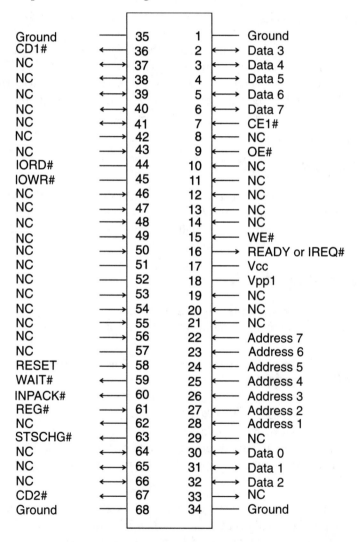

Figure 9-1. AIMS Socket Interface Signals

Chapter 9: The AIMS Interface

The AIMS Register Set

The memory array incorporated into an AIMS PC Card is accessed via a register set that includes:

- Address register (32-bit) — specifies the target memory address within the AIMS card that is being accessed.
- Data register (8-bits) — contains read or write data.
- Command register (8-bits) — contains the commands written by the AIMS device driver that specifies the operation to be performed.
- Mode register (8-bits) — provides status information regarding the card functions and controls the operation of the interrupts.
- Block count register (16-bits) — specifies the number of blocks to be erased when the erase command is issued to the command register.

Since AIMS cards can also support the memory or I/O interface, two additional registers are required:

- Configuration Option Register
- Pin Replacement Register

These registers are located in attribute memory address space at the location specified by the Configuration tuple within the CIS.

The Block Transfer

Transfers to or from an AIMS PC Card is controlled by a specific device driver that is aware of the AIMS transfer mechanism. This driver must program the AIMS card to perform the desired block transfer. The AIMS design is based on the expectation that flash memory will be employed as the memory array, and therefore, the block size is related to the flash block size for reading, writing, and erasing memory locations.

The following list describes the block transfer process initiated by the AIMS device driver:

1. Transfers are initiated by loading the address register with the starting block address to be transferred to or from the AIMS card. This requires four 8-bit writes to load the entire 32-bit address register.

2. Once the start address has been specified, then a command is issued to the command register. (Note that the mode register should be read to ensure the card is READY before writing to the command register.)

3. The AIMS card executes the command by either reading data from its memory array and placing it into the data register, or accepting write data into the data register and writing it to the memory array.

4. If no errors occur during the transfer, the address register auto-increments. The read or write transfer continues with the address being automatically incremented by the AIMS card each time another byte is successfully transferred.

5. The block transfer terminates when the device driver issues either an End of Read (EORD) or an End of Write (EOWR) command to the AIMS card.

6. When the AIMS card has stopped the transfer, sets any error conditions in the mode register and notifies the host system that the transfer has ended (by asserting READY for memory-mapped implementations or by asserting IREQ# for I/O-mapped implementations). The device driver then checks transfer status to determine the results of the transfer.

If a write operation is specified, the device driver would have issued an erase command prior to issuing the write command.

The AIMS Commands

A variety of commands are defined by the AIMS specification. Two basic types of commands are defined: type C and type D. Type C commands have a defined end state (e.g. an "end of write" command), whereas, the type D commands execute the specified command repetitively (e.g. a "write blocks" command). The AIMS commands are listed in table 9-1.

Chapter 9: The AIMS Interface

Table 9-1. Commands Supported by AIMS Cards

Name	Code	Type	Registers Used	Description
Write Blocks	38h	D	Address Command Status Data	Initiates block write operation. Address auto-increments until the write operation terminates when the "end of write" command is issued.
End of Write	4Fh	C	Command Status	Terminates a write block transfer. The AIMS card either generates an IREQ# or asserts READY upon completion of the transfer.
Read Blocks	40h	D	Address Command Status Data	Initiates block read operation. Address auto-increments until the read operation terminates when the "end of read" command is issued.
End of Read	3Fh	C	Command Status	Terminates a read block transfer. The AIMS card either generates an IREQ# or asserts READY upon completion of the transfer.
Erase Blocks	C0h	C	Address Block Count Command Status	Initiates a block erase operation. The operation continues until the specified number of blocks (contained the block count register) have been erased.
Execute Diagnostics	90h	C	Command Status	Initiates PC Card diagnostics. When the diagnostic completes the card reports any error conditions and notifies the system via READY or IREQ#.
Enter Diagnostic Mode	88h	C	Command Status	Places the card into the diagnostic mode. Note that the effects of accessing the AIMS registers is vendor specific when in diagnostic mode.
Return Internal Error Code	9Ah	C	Command Status Data	Provides access to error codes by reading the data register.
Write Verify Blocks (optional)	3Ch	D	Address Command Status Data	Initiates a write block transfer, like the write block command, except the card verifies the data just written prior to incrementing the address and accepting the next write data.

Accessing the AIMS Registers

The AIMS registers are identified by the PC Card address (A7:A1) and by indicating either a read or write transfer. These registers are mapped in either the host system's memory address space or I/O address space.

- When memory-mapped the registers are accessed with REG#=1 and the OE# and WE# commands are used to specify either read or write.

- When I/O-mapped the registers are accessed with REG#=0 and the IORD# and IOWR# command lines specify either a read or write operation.

Table 9-2 lists the registers and the address locations used to access each AIMS register. Note that the address offset applies to both memory- and I/O-mappings.

Table 9-2. AIMS Registers

Register Name	Read/Write	Address Offset
Address Register 0	Read/Write	00h
Address Register 1	Read/Write	02h
Address Register 2	Read/Write	04h
Address Register 3	Read/Write	06h
Block Count Register (low byte)	Write	08h
Block Count Register (high byte)	Write	0Ah
Command Register	Write	0Ch
Mode Register	Read/Write	0Eh
Data Register	Read/Write	10h
Vendor Unique Register	undefined	12h
Vendor Unique Register	undefined	14h
Vendor Unique Register	undefined	16h
Reserved	undefined	18h-1Eh

Chapter 10

The Previous Chapter

This chapter focuses on the optional Auto-Indexing Mass Storage (AIMS) interface. The transfer mechanism is described, along with the registers that must be programmed to initiate the transfer.

This Chapter

This chapter discusses the role of the PCMCIA Host Bus Adapter. Individual Host Bus Adapter functions are discussed. A functional block diagram of an HBA adapter is provided along with detailed explanations of each function.

The Next Chapter

The next chapter discusses the CIS and its role in the PC Card configuration process. The basic structure of the CIS configuration table required by I/O cards is described, along with the method used by configuration software to interpret the configuration table entries.

Introduction

As illustrated in figure 10-1, the PCMCIA Host Bus Adapter (HBA) resides physically between the PCMCIA host bus (usually an expansion bus such as ISA, EISA, Micro Channel or PCI) and the PCMCIA sockets. Since PCMCIA is host bus independent, this chapter focuses on the specific HBA requirements without detailing the exact nature of the expansion bus interface. Refer to the following MindShare books for information on other expansion buses: *ISA System Architecture; EISA System Architecture;* and *PCI System Architecture,* all published by Addison-Wesley.

Figure 10-1 also illustrates the software flow to and from the HBA. Two distinct software paths are illustrated:

- configuration and event notification path (PCMCIA specific)
- run-time path (normal program flow and execution)

Note that client drivers are shown in both software paths. These client drivers typically contain both PCMCIA specific code and standard run-time code (i.e. during execution of application program). The PCMCIA code within a client driver interacts directly with card services. The client driver is responsible for configuring the PC Card and programming the HBA so it can bridge the appropriate transactions from the host expansion bus to the PCMCIA sockets and cards. The client drivers are also responsible for processing PC Card status change events.

As illustrated in figure 10-1, client drivers do not access the HBA directly, but rather call card services, which in turn call socket services which access the HBA directly. Socket services provide a standard calling interface for card services to use. In this way, card services can call socket services functions to request that specific HBA functions be programmed as specified by the client driver.

Once the PC Cards have been configured, the PCMCIA-specific software has done its initial job and becomes dormant in memory. Application programs can now access the PC Card just as they do any other device that resides on the host's expansion bus. During PC Card configuration, the HBA is programmed to recognize addresses that reside on the PC Card. When the HBA recognizes an address belonging to a PC Card, it bridges the expansion bus cycle to the PC Card's socket.

PCMCIA software only runs again if the client driver needs to reprogram the HBA or if a PC Card status change event occurs. When the HBA detects a card event change it generates an interrupt that "wakes up" card services which calls socket services to determine the source and type of the status change event. Card services then calls the client driver, notifying it of the event. The client driver then processes the event as required.

Chapter 10: The PC Card Host Bus Adapter

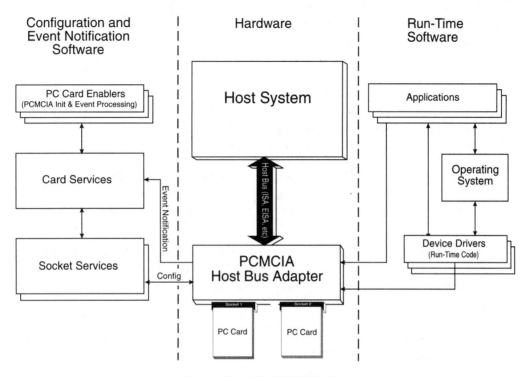

Figure 10-1. The PCMCIA Environment

In summary, the HBA is initially accessed by PCMCIA software that programs it to recognize accesses made to the PC Card. Once programmed, the HBA recognizes target addresses within the PC Card and passes the bus transaction to the card socket. The HBA also monitors status change events and generates an interrupt to inform card services of these events.

Host Bus Adapter Functions

The host bus adapter (HBA) provides the interface between the host bus and the PC Card sockets. This interface must be able to translate host bus accesses to PC Card socket accesses. Specific functions that must be supported by the HBA, include:

- Power switching
- Card detection
- Address translation

- Socket data buffering and control
- Socket data transfer timing and control
- Host bus transfer control
- PC Card interrupt steering
- DMA channel steering
- Socket status reporting
- Status change interrupt generation and steering
- Power Conservation (Power Management)

Note that a given HBA may support other interfaces including ATA (AT Attachment), AIMS (Auto-Indexing Mass Storage) and other custom interfaces. This chapter focuses on the memory and I/O interfaces and their related functions.

Figure 10-2 illustrates the primary functions associated with an HBA designed with two socket interfaces. HBAs are typically designed using an HBA chip supplied by one of several vendors. The functions in figure 10-2 incorporated into a specific chip can vary from vendor to vendor.

The Socket Interface

Since the PCMCIA socket interfaces are not bussed together, but rather are specified as independent socket interfaces, separate signal lines are required for each socket. This means that 68 pins must be included for each socket supported by an HBA. As a result, typical HBA implementations contain either one or two socket interfaces due to the number of pins required for the socket interface. (Some HBA designs may share some of the interface pins between sockets, reducing the total number of pins required for each socket.)

Maximum Number of HBAs

Some system implementations may require that four or more sockets be implemented. This means that more than one physical HBA chip is likely to be implemented (based on typical chip designs — two sockets/chip). Similarly, an additional HBA may be added in systems that have expansion slots. The theoretical maximum number of HBAs that a single system can support depends on the socket services software interface. With the Intel x86 binding (software function calling protocol) the maximum number is 256 adapters.

Other factors may also limit the number of HBAs that can be supported, such as the amount of space available in ROM or main DRAM.

Maximum Number of Socket Per HBA

The maximum number of sockets per HBA may also be determined by the socket services interface. The maximum number of sockets possible with the Intel x86 binding is 16 per adapter, governed by field width of the socket selection parameter within the Inquire, Get, and SetWindow functions.

Data Buffers / Transceivers

Each socket must be isolated from the expansion bus so that PC Cards can be inserted and removed when system power is applied. These buffers (usually transceivers) prevent transients from being introduced on the expansion bus signal lines when a PC Card is inserted or removed from the socket. Some HBA chips integrate the isolation buffers while others chips require external buffers.

Card Detection

The Card Detect pins (CD1# and CD2#) provide a way for the adapter to detect the presence of PC Cards when they are inserted into a PCMCIA socket. When power is applied to the system, the HBA can check the Card Detect pins to determine if power should be applied to the socket. The CD pins also provide notification that a PC Card has been either inserted or removed from a socket.

The HBA ties the CD1# and CD2# pins to Vcc through a 10K (or larger) pull-up resistor. Since these pins are tied to ground inside of each PC Card, when the card is fully inserted both pins will be pulled low, indicating that a card is installed in the socket.

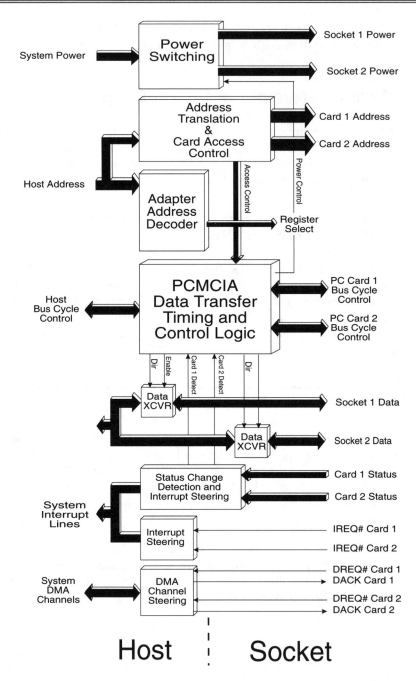

Figure 10-2. Host Bus Adapter Functional Block with Two Sockets

Chapter 10: The PC Card Host Bus Adapter

The HBA should be designed to generate a "socket status change" interrupt when a change is detected at the CD1# and CD2# pins. This interrupt, sometimes called the HBA, or management interrupt, notifies system software that some card event has taken place. Note that a status change interrupt can be caused by a number of card events (in addition to card insertion and removal). See the section entitled, "Card Event Notification" later in this chapter for information on other events that generate a status change interrupt, and for the steps taken by software when such an interrupt occurs. Ultimately, if card insertion or removal is detected, software will either configure the card or release resources that have been previously assigned to the PC Card.

Power Switching

The HBA must have the ability to switch different supply voltages to Vcc, Vpp1 and Vpp2 as required by the PC Card. The HBA must also be able to completely enable or disable Vcc, Vpp1 and Vpp2.

Vcc Power Controls

The initial Vcc that is applied to the PC Card socket depends on the version of specification that it supports. The following sections define the 2.1 HBA mechanism for applying Vcc followed by the new low voltage socket defined by the PC Card standard.

Vcc and 2.1 Compliant HBAs

The PCMCIA 2.x compliant HBA must be able to supply a Vcc of 5vdc and 3.3vdc to support dual-voltage cards. When a card is installed in release 2.x compliant systems, 5vdc is initially supplied to the card. Software then reads the CIS (the DEVICE_OC tuple specifies 3.3vdc support) to determine if the card has dual-voltage capability (operates at 3.3 vdc). If so, software must be able to direct the HBA to switch 3.3vdc to the card's Vcc pins.

In order to change Vcc, configuration software must remove power from the socket, select the new Vcc, and repower the socket. The PC Card will not retain any information from the previous power-up sequence. When Vcc is reapplied the entire initialization and configuration process must occur anew.

Vcc and Low Voltage Sockets

Systems based on the PC Card Standard must monitor the voltage sense pins (VS1# and VS2#) to determine the voltage that should initially be supplied to the Vcc pins (see table 10-1). The initial Vcc voltage applied depends on the voltages that the system and HBA is capable of delivering to the card's Vcc pin. Voltages supported are likely to include 3.3 vdc and 5 vdc. The X.X vdc referred to in table 10-1 is defined by PCMCIA as a low voltage supply to be defined in the future.

Table 10-1. Interpretation of Voltage Sense Lines.

Initial Power Required	Keying	VS1#	VS2#	Vcc at power up and CIS read
5 volts	standard*	1	1	5 volts applied if available, else no Vcc applied.
3.3 volts	low-voltage	0	1	3.3 volts applied if available, else no Vcc applied
3.3/5 volts	standard*			3.3 volts applied if available, else no Vcc applied.
X.X volts	low-voltage	1	0	X.X volts applied if available, else no Vcc applied.
X.X/3.3 volts	low-voltage	0	0	X.X volts applied if available, else 3.3 volts applied if available, else no Vcc applied.
X.X/3.3/5 volts	standard*			X.X volts applied if available, else 3.3 volts applied if available, else no Vcc applied.

* Standard keying refers to PC Cards keyed to fit into a 2.x compliant socket. These cards also fit into the low voltage sockets.

Vpp1 and Vpp2 Control

Socket pins Vpp1 and Vpp2 supply programming voltages for memory devices that require a special programming voltage. These pins can also be used to provide additional voltages for peripheral cards. Initially, these pins supply the same voltage as Vcc until the card's CIS is read to determine what special programming or peripheral voltages are required. PCMCIA recommends that Vpp1 and Vpp2 be tied to Vcc initially and then switched (as required by the card). PCMCIA also recommends that +12 vdc be available as an alternate supply for Vpp1 and Vpp2.

Chapter 10: The PC Card Host Bus Adapter

Some cards require the same supply voltage on Vpp1 and Vpp2, while others may require separate voltages be applied to Vpp1 and Vpp2. Whether the HBA can supply separate supplies to each Vpp pin is design dependent.

Address Translation

Translation of the address from the host bus to the PCMCIA socket may be required due to:

- The form of address used by the host expansion bus may need to be converted to the form expected by PC Cards. The nature of the translation depends on the nature of the host bus address.
- The maximum address space supported by the host system differs from the maximum address space supported by PC Card sockets.
- The PC Card responds to a fixed address range already allocated to another device in the system.

In short, the HBA must, if necessary, translate the host address to the form recognized by PC Cards, and remap the address presented on the host bus to the appropriate address within the PC Card.

Memory Address Mapping

The host address may need to be remapped to a different location within the PCMCIA address space for a variety of reasons including:

- The host and socket address space are not the same size.
- System software may constrain the addresses that a card can be mapped to within system address space.
- PC Card address decoder may not be programmable.

Direct Mapping

System addresses can be mapped directly to the same locations within the PC Card's memory address space. In this case, no re-mapping is required by the HBA. For example, assume that a 10MB flash memory card is installed in a host system whose expansion bus supports 16MB of address space. The 10MB flash memory card could be directly mapped within the system's address space (as shown in figure 10-3). This example also assumes that the flash card's address decoder can be programmed to the range of addresses specified. If the flash card's address decoder can not be programmed, then the range of addresses that it responds to is fixed and the same fixed address range within system memory address space would have to be allocated in order for the PC Card to direct-map the card.

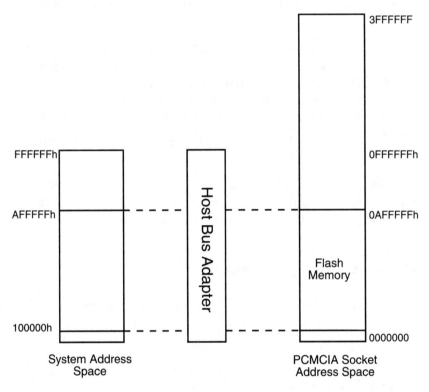

Figure 10-3. PC Card with Memory That Can Be Direct Mapped into the System Address Space.

Remapping the Host Address to PC Cards with Fixed Addresses

The previous example illustrates mapping a flash card with a programmable address decoder directly into the system address space. Next, consider a 10MB flash card whose address decoder is not programmable and whose addresses reside in the PC Card's common memory from address 0 to 10MB. In order to directly map the flash card into system memory address space, it must be mapped within the same system address space (0-10MB). Since much of the first megabyte of memory address space is reserved for other system devices and functions, this creates a problem in PC environments. Mapping the flash card in this space would cause data bus contention if an address within the range assigned to two memory devices was accessed.

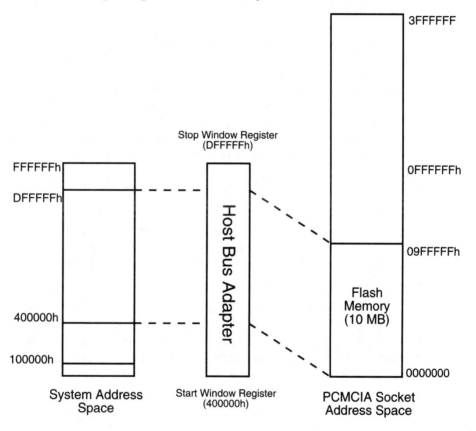

Figure 10-4. Example of Address Translation Logic Remapping the System Address to the Bottom of the Common Memory Address Space.

Successfully mapping the 10MB flash card requires that the address be mapped within system address space to a location that doesn't conflict with standard memory devices installed in the system. For example, consider a system containing system DRAM memory that is mapped up to 4MB. Refer to figure 10-4. The flash card could be mapped within system memory starting at address location 400000h to DFFFFh. Since the flash card resides in common memory from address location 000000h to 9FFFFFh, the system address must be remapped to this address space in order to access the flash card. Consequently, the HBA must provide a means of remapping system addresses to the appropriate address space in the PC Card's address space.

System Address Space Smaller Than Socket Address Space

If the host system is incapable of addressing the entire 64MB of PC Card address space, then the HBA must have the ability to remap system address space such that all PC Card locations are accessible. Assume for example, that a 20MB flash card is installed in a socket whose HBA connects to an ISA host bus. Since the maximum memory address space supported by the ISA bus is 16MB, the system cannot possibly address all the locations within the 20MB flash card in a direct fashion. Therefore, remapping must be employed to permit access to all flash memory address locations.

This concept is shown in figure 10-5. To accomplish this remapping, system address space must be mapped twice: once to access the first 10MB address range and once to access the second 10MB address range. Using this technique, the HBA can be dynamically programmed to redirect, or remap accesses within the system address space (via an offset value) to different regions within the PC Card's memory array, permitting access to the entire 64 MB of address space.

Note that the technique described above is common in 8088-based systems that employ a maximum of 1 MB of memory address space, much of which is not available for mapping PC Cards. The host address space typically used by PC memory cards is within the address range from D0000h to DFFFFh.

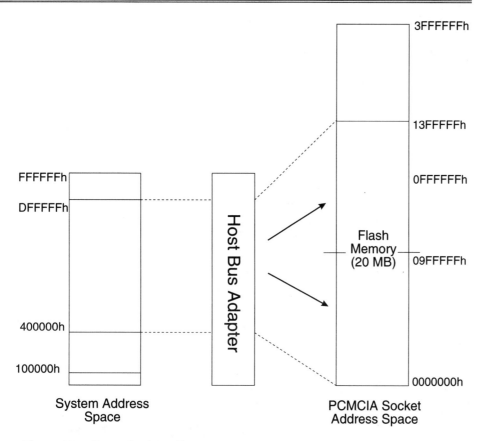

Figure 10-5. Example of Small System Address Range Being Remapped to a Larger PCMCIA Memory Device.

System Address Space Larger Than Socket Address Space

Accesses can also be made to PC Cards from system addresses beyond the 64MB maximum address range supported by the PC Card socket. Once again the system addresses are remapped to locations within the PC Card's address space. Refer to figure 10-6.

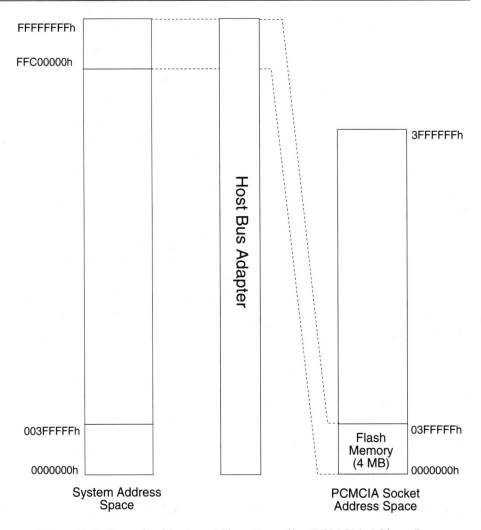

Figure 10-6. Example of System Address Exceeding PCMCIA Address Range.

Memory Address Windows

Address windows are used by HBAs to determine the range of host system memory addresses to which a particular card responds and to remap the system memory address to a location within the PC Card's memory address space. The HBA address windows are typically implemented with programmable window address registers, permitting software to program the range of memory addresses to which the PC Card in a given socket can respond, and what PC Card memory address it should be remapped to. Note that a given PC Card may have several different blocks of addresses that it must respond to, each requiring a separate address window. HBAs typically have several address windows that can be programmed for both memory and I/O devices.

Each address window consists of a:

- Start window address register
- Stop window address register
- Window offset address register (mapping register)

When the host system accesses some device within the system, the HBA must determine if the address on the host bus is within any of the programmed address windows. If so, the host access is to a location within the PC Card installed in a socket, and the HBA initiates a transfer to or from the socket. Otherwise, the host access is ignored. In short, the HBA acts as the PC Card's address decoder by passing only those transactions to the PC Card that are intended for it.

In addition to determining if the host address targets a socket, the HBA also remaps the address if necessary. Remapping is typically accomplished via an offset register. This register is programmed with a value that, when added to the host address, redirects (remaps) it to the desired location within the PC Card's memory address space. Refer to figure 10-7.

When the host address must be mapped to a lower address, the offset value equals the number of address locations that must be subtracted from the host address. Since the HBA always adds the contents of the offset register to the host address, the programmer uses the two's complement of the offset value, resulting in a negative offset (as shown in figure 10-7).

Overlapping Memory Windows

When two PC Cards are installed, each is mapped into it's own socket address space. Normally, each will be accessed within separate host address ranges. This prevents contention between the two devices. If, however, the host has insufficient address space to map both devices into separate ranges, then the address windows of the two sockets may overlap, creating the potential for contention (as shown in figure 10-8).

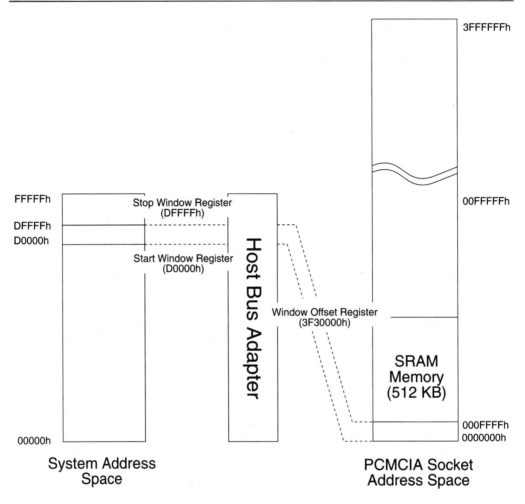

Figure 10-7. Registers Define the Size of the Memory Window and the Size of the Off-set for Remapping the System Address.

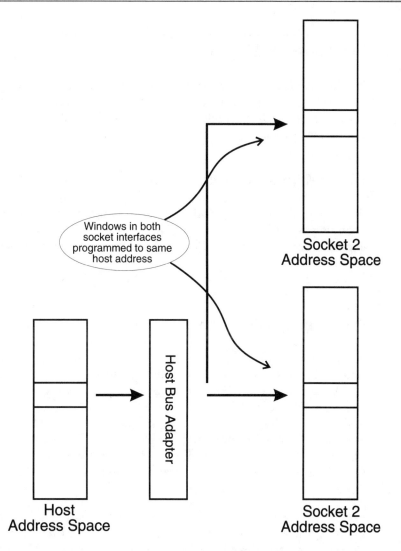

Figure 10-8. Example of Overlapping Memory Windows Causing Contention

When memory windows overlap, only one window can be enabled at a time, thereby preventing contention. This highlights the requirement that memory windows, once programmed, support the ability to be enabled and disabled under software control.

I/O Address Mapping

PC Cards containing I/O registers must be mapped into the system's I/O address space. If the system has only memory address space, then the HBA must map memory addresses into the PC Card's I/O address space. The following discussion assumes that the system has I/O addresses.

Direct Mapped I/O Addresses

Figure 10-9 illustrates PC Card registers being mapped directly to the corresponding system I/O addresses. The HBA in this example, would bridge the expansion bus cycle to the PC Card when an I/O address is detected within the ranges of the addresses used by the PC Card. In this example, two I/O windows must be used to specify the address ranges required by the card.

Overlapping I/O Windows

Sometimes I/O windows must be programmed to overlap with addresses of I/O devices residing elsewhere in the system. Consider the example in figure 10-10. Assume that the HBA has two I/O address windows for a given socket, and that the PC Card requires three I/O address ranges that are spread widely across the system I/O address space. Since only two address registers exist, one must be programmed to encompass two of the three address ranges. This large window may encompass address locations used by another PC Card in a different socket or locations used by some other device residing elsewhere in the host system.

When an I/O read access occurs from a location within the large address window, the HBA responds by starting a data read transfer from the socket. The PC Card decodes the socket address to determine if the address is to one of its registers. If so, the INPACK# (Input Acknowledge Port) signal is asserted by the PC Card and the transfer completes from the PC Card. The INPACK# signal enables the data transceiver so that data from the socket is returned over the host data bus.

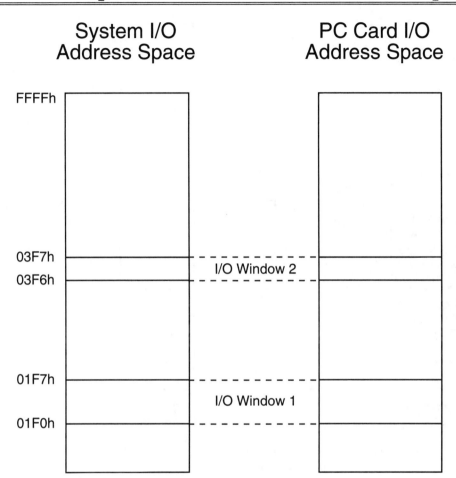

Figure 10-9. PC Card I/O Addresses Mapped Directly to System I/O Addresses

If the address decoded by the PC Card is not recognized, the INPACK# signal is not asserted. Since INPACK# is not asserted, the HBA also ignores the host access and the socket's data bus transceivers remain disabled.

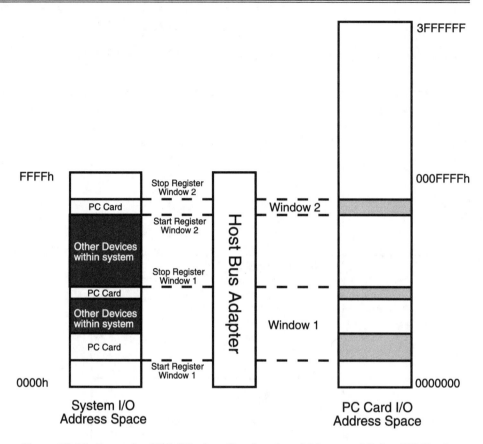

Figure 10-10. Example of I/O Window Overlapping Addresses of Other I/O Devices in the System.

It may be necessary to program I/O address windows that overlap between two sockets (as illustrated in figure 10-10). When I/O windows overlap, PCMCIA permits simultaneous reads from both sockets, relying on the PC Card decode and the INPACK# signal to prevent contention.

Other Information Associated with Address Windows

When the HBA detects that a host address is within the range of an address window, it initiates a data transfer to or from the PC Card. Since PC Cards can contain devices of varying speeds, it is also necessary to program the access time of the device residing within the targeted address window.

Additionally, PC Card device size information must also be associated with I/O address windows. This is necessary since I/O registers within PC Cards can be either 8-bit or 16-bit; therefore, the data path(s) used to transfer data to and from the PC Card can vary. The HBA must be able to detect I/O device size to determine which data path or paths the I/O device uses.

When client drivers read the CIS, they determine PC device speed and size and program this information into the HBA window(s) allocated for the card. In this way, the HBA knows the exact nature of the transfer it must run to the device being accessed. (For more information refer to the section entitled "PC Card Device Size" later in this chapter.)

Socket Transfer Timing and Control

The socket transfer timing and control logic has multiple interfaces: a host bus interface and one or more socket interfaces. When a read or write transfer is detected on the host bus, the address translation logic determines if the address is intended for one of the PC Cards, while the timing and control logic determines whether the access is a read or write to memory or I/O. When an address falls within one of the address windows, the address translation logic notifies the timing and control logic, triggering the appropriate socket access.

Access must be made to the socket to either read or write data based on the type of host cycle being run.

Interface Control

The HBA configures each socket at power up as a memory-only interface. However, once the card's client driver determines its configuration requirements, an alternative socket interface may be required. For example, the client driver must reconfigure the HBA from a memory-only to a memory or I/O interface when it detects an I/O card. Since some signal definitions change when a socket is configured for memory or I/O, the HBA must multiplex selected lines to alternative functions. A given HBA may also support other interface types such as DMA or AIMS, requiring additional socket interface redefinition.

Socket Access Timing

PCMCIA specifies standard cycle timing for common memory, attribute memory and I/O registers. (Refer to the Chapters entitled, "The Memory Interface" and "The Memory or I/O Interface" for details regarding cycle timing for the respective card types.) The timing and control logic accesses memory cards based on the timing specified in the CIS. The cycle timing of a PC Card's memory is specified within its CIS during card initialization. Each bank of memory with different cycle timing must be listed separately within the CIS. Each memory bank can be accessed via a separate address window that specifies the cycle timing required by the target bank. Cycle timing information is loaded into a card's memory or I/O window registers during card configuration. The PC Card standard requires that access timing information be programmed as part of the address window definition for each socket/device.

Stretching Socket Access Timing

PCMCIA also incorporates a WAIT# signal that is used for stretching the access timing. This capability is optional but typically supported for devices that may not always be able to respond to a socket read or write within the programmed timing.

Word or Byte Access

Host systems may have the ability to access single byte locations (from either even or odd locations) or entire words in a single bus cycle. When the HBA detects that an address being accessed by the host system resides in a given socket, it translates the address, if necessary, and starts a socket transfer. The address specifies the start location being accessed within the PC Card, but does not specify whether a single byte is being accessed or an entire word. The HBA must be able to detect the size of the host transaction and assert CE1# and/or CE2#, commanding the PC Card to transfer one or two bytes of data. For example, an ISA system uses SA0 and SBHE# to indicate the number of bytes being transferred. The HBA must translate these signals to the form understood by the PC Card (A0, CE1# and CE2#).

The actual combinations of CE1# and CE2# asserted by the HBA depends on the size of the host bus (as shown in table 10-2).

Table 10-2. Address Sent to Socket

Host Transfer Size	Location(s) Accessed	Socket Signals Asserted		
		A0	CE1#	CE2#
8-Bit	Even Byte	0	0	1
8-Bit	Odd Byte	1	0	1
16-Bit	Even Byte	0	0	1
16-Bit	Odd Byte	1	1	0
16-Bit	Word	0	0	0

PC Card I/O Device Size (IOIS16#)

PC Card memory devices are always implemented as 16-bit devices. However, I/O PC Card can implement either 8-bit registers, 16-bit registers, or both. Device size is read from the card's CIS and programmed into the I/O address window, or alternatively, the IOIS16# signal can be sampled by the HBA to distinguish between accesses to 8-bit or 16-bit registers.

Some host expansion buses include device size lines that are asserted by the addressed target, informing the host system of the size of the device being accessed. The data path over which the data is expected and the bus cycle timing varies depending on the device size reported. For this reason, the size information reported by a PC Card may need to be transferred to the host system so that transfer timing and data path steering can be adjusted by the host system (e.g. the ISA bus controller) A given HBA will be designed to control both the socket access and the host access, ensuring that the transfer appears correctly to both.

Card Interrupt Steering and Handling

During initialization, a system interrupt request line is assigned to each PC Card that uses interrupts. The HBA is programmed to steer the PC Card interrupt (IREQ#) to the system interrupt request line allocated to the card during the configuration process. Figure 10-11 illustrates ISA interrupt steering for a dual socket HBA. The number of ISA interrupts that an HBA supports is implementation specific.

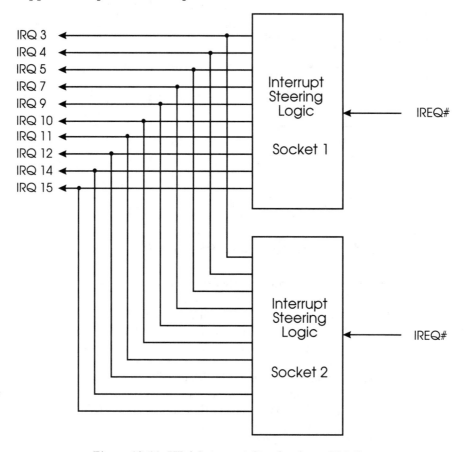

Figure 10-11. HBA Interrupt Steering in an ISA System

The IREQ# signal sent from a PC Card may be signaled by one of the following methods:

- Level mode
- Pulse mode

PC Cards must be designed to support level mode interrupts, whereas, pulse mode interrupts are optional.

Level Mode Interrupts

Normally, a PC Card is programmed for level interrupt mode. When in level mode, the IREQ# pin is pulled up to Vcc on the PC Card and asserted low to signal an interrupt. The interrupt is kept asserted until the interrupt service routine reads the PC Card's status register, thereby resetting the interrupt indication and causing IREQ# to be deasserted.

As illustrated in figure 10-12, when level mode interrupts are used the HBA must invert the IREQ# signal from the PC Card to generate a positive-edge triggered interrupt required by ISA systems. While the IREQ# signal is asserted by the PC Card using level mode, no other device can trigger a positive-edge interrupt (the interrupt line is driven high by the HBA from the time of trigger until the interrupt is serviced). Similarly, when no interrupt is being asserted by the PC Card the HBA continually drives the IRQn line low also preventing other ISA devices from generating a positive-edge trigger. Another device attempting to trigger a positive-edge will be unsuccessful and, more importantly, hardware damage can result.

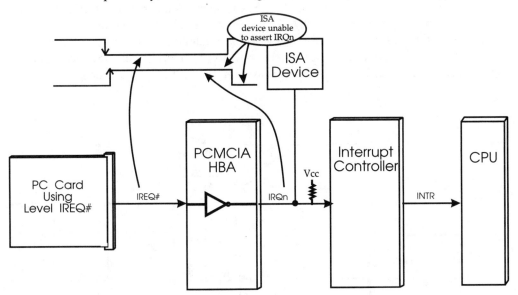

Figure 10-12. ISA Interrupt Sharing Not Permitted with Level Mode IREQ#

Level mode interrupt signaling can be used in ISA systems, where no sharing is supported, or in host environments permitting interrupt sharing via low level interrupt triggering, such as PCI and EISA systems.

Pulse Mode Interrupts

Since the level interrupt mode defeats the capability of interrupt sharing in an ISA system, pulse mode interrupts were implemented to allow sharing. Pulse mode interrupts allow a PC Card to share the same IRQn line with another device. On the trailing-edge of the negative pulse, a positive edge trigger will be recognized by the ISA interrupt controller. Note that the pulse must be equal to or greater than 0.5 microseconds in width. The HBA must use an open collector driver to permit other devices to drive the same IRQn line.

When an interrupt is not being triggered by the PC Card the IRQn line is pulled to Vcc. This permits another ISA device to trigger an interrupt by driving the IRQn line low and then cease driving it, thereby, causing a negative pulse whose trailing edge creates the positive-edge trigger. ISA devices designed to share interrupts also use an open collector driver for their IRQn line.

Only during the negative transition of the pulse are other devices prevented from triggering an interrupt. As a result using pulse mode interrupts to permit interrupt sharing in ISA hosts may still result in conflicts when two simultaneous interrupts are triggered by the devices sharing the interrupt line. Additionally, two interrupt pulses that do not overlap but that occur in close proximity to each other may also cause an interrupt trigger to be missed.

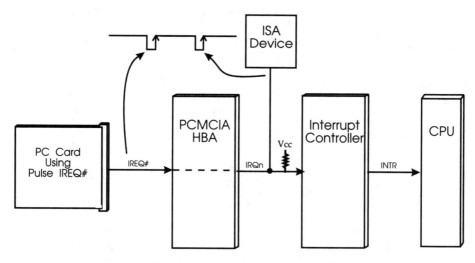

Figure 10-13. Pulse Mode Interrupts Permit Interrupt Sharing in an ISA System.

Card Event Notification (The Status Change Interrupt)

PC Cards can report PCMCIA status events such as low battery warnings, write-protect switch position change, READY indications, and card detection. When the socket signals a status change, the HBA must be able to generate an interrupt, notifying PCMCIA software (card and socket services) that a status change event has taken place. The PCMCIA status change interrupt (sometimes called management interrupt) must be steered to the appropriate system interrupt line under software control. The HBA should also have the ability to mask out specific status change events under software control so that they do not generate an interrupt.

The HBA must also implement status registers indicating which socket(s) experienced a status change event, which status event has occurred and the current state of each status indicator. During the interrupt service routine, socket services will read these status registers within the HBA to determine which socket or sockets have encountered a status change. When socket services has been notified that a status change has occurred at a given socket, it then reads another status register within the HBA to determine the actual event causing the interrupt.

DMA Support

DMA support is an optional feature for a PC Card compliant system. As illustrated in figure 10-14, HBAs supporting DMA transfers must contain logic to:

- select the PC Card's DREQ# signal from one of three pins: SPKR#, IN-PACK#, or IOIS16#.
- deliver the DACK signal from the ISA bus to the PC Card's REG# pin.
- deliver the TC signal from the ISA bus to the PC Card's OE# pin upon completion of a DMA write transfer.
- deliver the TC signal from the ISA bus to the PC Card's WE# pin upon completion of a DMA read transfer.
- steer DREQ# from the PC Card to any of the seven ISA DREQ lines.
- steer any of the seven DACK# signals from the ISA bus to the PC Card's DACK pin.

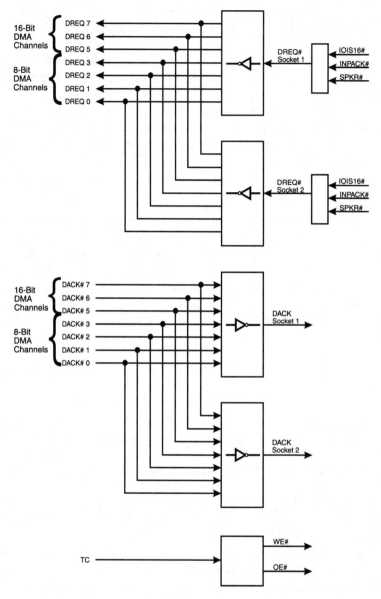

Figure 10-14. HBA Functions Required to Support PC Card DMA

The HBA also determines the width of the DMA transfer by monitoring the Expansion bus and asserting the card enable pins to reflect the transfer size (either 8- or 16-bits). Refer to the Chapter entitled "The DMA Interface" for additional information.

Chapter 10: The PC Card Host Bus Adapter

Power Conservation Modes

Most PCMCIA HBAs support some form of power conservation. For example, when no PC Card activity has occurred within a specified time period, as many functions as possible are powered down to conserve power. Only the logic necessary to detect card insertion and removal and system bus activity must remain active. Depending on the HBA design, it may also support additional power saving modes (where even more of the adapter functionality is powered off).

Card Lock Mechanism

PCMCIA includes optional support for card interlock mechanisms. A PC Card interlock has two major advantages over systems without an interlock.

1. Prevents the user from removing a PC Card while the card is in use. Such implementations may employ motor driven mechanisms used to insert and eject PC Cards. If the user requests that the card be ejected, software can remind the user that an applications currently using the card should be closed before removing the card.

2. Prevents PC Cards from being removed from a system by unauthorized personnel. Security mechanisms may employ a simple mechanical lock that prevents a card from being ejected from the socket. A key may be required to release the lock. These mechanisms may also be motor driven and require that a password be entered before software will start the motor to eject the card.

One major obstacle to the more complex solutions is the additional weight, size, and power required, making them less attractive in the mobile computing environment. The card lock functionality is optional and currently is not in widespread use.

Error Detection and Correction (EDC)

Support exists within socket services to support EDC, thereby providing a method to enhance reliability of HBA designs. The author is unaware of any current HBA solutions that implement error detection and correction generation. Since EDC generators are not typically used, the design and implementation of EDC generators is not covered in this book.

Part Three

PC Card Design

Chapter 11

The Previous Chapter

The previous chapter discussed the role of the PCMCIA Host Bus Adapter. Individual Host Bus Adapter functions are discussed.

This Chapter

This chapter discusses layer one of the metaformat, commonly referred to as the card information structure, or CIS. The chapter details the role of the CIS in the PC Card configuration process. Tuples are also introduced and their format and structure are described. The basic structure of the CIS's configuration table required by I/O cards is also described.

The Next Chapter

Configuration registers are discussed in the next chapter, providing a complete description of each register specified by the PC Card standard. Configuration register implementations for both single and multiple function cards are covered.

Overview

PC Cards include a data structure called the Card Information Structure (CIS) that is stored in non-volatile memory. The CIS provides a method for software to determine what kind of PC Card is installed, along with its speed, size, and the system resources required by the card. Having determined this information, the PCMCIA Host Bus Adapter (HBA) can be programmed to allow access to the PC Card, and the card itself can be configured by writing to its configuration registers. Configuration registers are required by I/O cards but are optional for memory cards. Both the CIS and configuration registers are mapped in the attribute memory space.

PCMCIA System Architecture

As shown in figure 11-1, the CIS is read by PC Card client drivers during card initialization to determine the configuration options supported by the card. The PC Card client accesses the CIS via card and socket services. Once the card type and resource requirements have been read from the CIS, the PC Card client driver programs the HBA and configures the PC Card, again via card and socket services. No further access is typically made to the CIS after the card has been initialized. The memory or I/O device can now be accessed via the host expansion bus, as would any other expansion device. Note that the CIS is only accessed by programs that are PCMCIA aware. Most application programs have no knowledge that they are accessing devices implemented in PC Card packages.

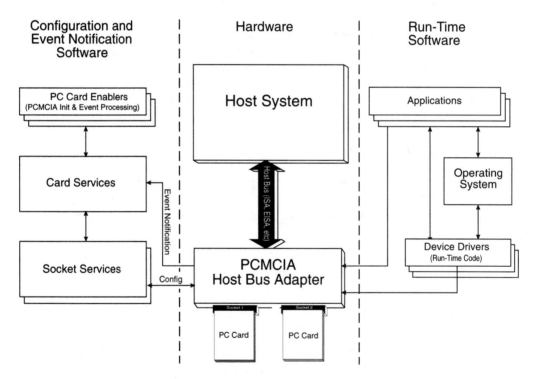

Figure 11-1. PCMCIA Software Flow

The Card Information Structure (CIS)

The CIS is mapped into the attribute memory address space starting at address zero as illustrated in figure 11-2. The CIS consists of a linked list of data blocks, or tuples, that describe the function and characteristics of a PC Card. Configuration software accesses this data to determine the characteristics and configuration requirements of a given PC Card. Tuples are identified by a unique code which in the first byte of each tuple.

Note that CIS data is mapped only to even locations within the attribute address space; thus, information is returned only on the lower data path (D7:D0). This simplifies card designs for accommodating eight-bit host systems that connect only to the lower data path.

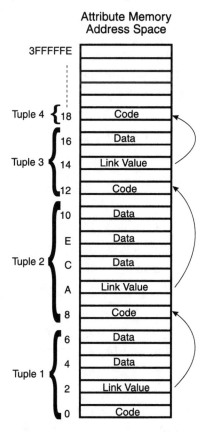

Figure 11-2. Example CIS Layout Consisting of a Linked List of Four Tuples

Tuples

A tuple is defined in Webster's Ninth New Collegiate Dictionary as a "set of elements." A tuple in PCMCIA terminology refers to a defined set of data items that characterize some facet of a PC Card. The PCMCIA standard specifies tuples intended to be used by PC Card designers for providing information about their device. Tuples provide information such as the PC Card's device speed and size. Tuple information is most often used by configuration software to determine the configuration requirements of the card. However, other tuples provide information that can be used by utility programs and applications to ascertain additional capabilities of the card.

Tuple Format

All tuples have a general format defined by PCMCIA (refer to table 11-1). The first one-byte element (entry 0) of every tuple is a tuple *type code* that defines the tuple's function. The second entry (entry 1) of every tuple is a one-byte link value (in hex) that specifies the number of additional bytes remaining in the tuple. The number and definition of these remaining bytes depends on the type of tuple.

Table 11-1. Basic Tuple Format

Byte	Standard Tuple Format	
0	TPL_CODE	Tuple type code (XXh). See table 11-7 for tuple codes.
1	TPL_LINK	Link to next tuple (number of bytes (in hex) remaining in tuple).
n	TPL_DATA	Tuple specific data block (definition, format and length defined by individual tuples).

The CIS consists of a linked list of tuples. Each tuple specifies a link value that identifies the start of the next tuple. Processing software can read the CIS entries and interpret the meaning of the tuples that contain configuration information for the PC Card.

The exact set of tuples incorporated into the CIS depends primarily on the type of card and its capabilities. For example, the Device Information Tuple may contain all the information needed to determine the resources required by a simple SRAM card, while other card types might require numerous tuples to define the configuration of the card.

A Sample Tuple

Consider the information provided by the Device Information tuple shown in table 11-2. This tuple defines a 100ns SRAM card containing 1MB of memory. The first byte within the tuple contains a value of 01h defining this tuple as a device information tuple. The second byte (03h) specifies the number of bytes remaining in the tuple. The device information tuple contains two bytes within the tuple's data area. One that defines the memory card type, speed, size, and whether the write-protect switch affects the range of memory being defined, and one that defines the size of the memory device.

The memory card device type is specified in the tuple as a hexadecimal code value. In this example, the device code is a 6h. As shown in table 11-3, a device code of 6h identifies the card as SRAM. Similarly, the SRAM's cycle time is specified with a speed code of 4h. This indicates a device speed of 100ns as shown in table 11-4. The size of the device can be determined by reading the unit size code and multiplying the unit size by the number of units specified. The unit size code of 5h, specifies memory banks of 512KB (refer to table 11-5) and the number of units field contains a 1h, indicating two memory units are implemented for a total size of 1MB. Finally, the tuple is terminated by FFh. This tuple includes a termination byte because the data within the tuple can vary in length (i.e. more than one memory device can be described by the Device Information tuple). The termination bytes make it easier for parsing software to recognize the end of variable length tuples. Tuples that do not vary in length do not define a termination byte.

Table 11-2. Example Device Information Tuple for an SRAM Card

Byte	Value	Device Information Tuple
0	01h	Tuple Code (01h)
1	03h	Link to next tuple (3h)
2	64h	*Device Type=bits 7:4 (6h); WP=bit 3 (0);Speed=bits 2:0(4h)
3	0Dh	*Device Size= # of units [bits 7:3 (1)] times unit size [bits 2:0 (5h)]
4	FFh	FFh (marks end of device info field)

* Refer to the following tables for an interpretation.

Table 11-3. Device Type Codes

Code	Name	Meaning
0	DTYPE_NULL	No memory device. Generally used to designate a hole in the address space. If used, speed field should be set to 0h.
1	DTYPE_ROM	Masked ROM
2	DTYPE_OTPROM	One-time programmable PROM
3	DTYPE_EPROM	UV EPROM
4	DTYPE_EEPROM	EEPROM
5	DTYPE_FLASH	Flash EPROM
6	DTYPE_SRAM	Static RAM (JEIDA has Nonvolatile RAM)
7	DTYPE_DRAM	Dynamic RAM (JEIDA has Volatile RAM)
8-Ch		Reserved
Dh	DTYPE_FUNCSPEC	Function-specific memory address range. Includes memory-mapped I/O registers, dual-ported memory, communication buffers, etc., which are not intended to be used as general-purpose memory.
Eh	DTYPE_EXTEND	Extended type follows.
Fh		Reserved

Table 11-4. Device Speed Codes

Code	Name	Meaning
0h	DSPEED_NULL	Use when device type = null
1h	DSPEED_250NS	250 nsec
2h	DSPEED_200NS	200 nsec
3h	DSPEED_150NS	150 nsec
4h	DSPEED_100NS	100 nsec
5h-6h		(Reserved)
7h	DSPEED_EXT	Use extended speed byte.

Table 11-5. Unit Size Codes

Code	Units
0	512 bytes
1	2 K
2	8 K
3	32 K
4	128 K
5	512 K
6	2 M
7	Reserved

The Configuration Table

I/O devices require that the CIS contain a configuration table that is not required by memory cards. This table consists of multiple entries each of which describes a set of configuration options that the PC Card needs for normal operation. A comparison can be made between each configuration table entry and each possible switch and jumper setting required when configuring an ISA card. Each configuration table entry reflects the possible resource combinations that the PC Card can be configured for.

The Configuration Entry Tuple

Figure 11-3 illustrates a CIS that contains a configuration table. Directly preceding the configuration table is the configuration tuple that specifies which configuration registers are implemented by the PC Card and where they are mapped within attribute memory address space. The configuration tuple also specifies the index number of the last entry within the configuration table. As illustrated in figure 11-3, the configuration table consists of a series of configuration table entry tuples (CFTABLE_ENTRY). Each entry contains up to seven data structures that describe operational characteristics of the PC Card. These structures include:

1. **A power description byte** — the power parameters specified within this structure may apply to Vcc only, Vcc and Vpp1 and Vpp2 (Vpp1=Vpp2), or separately to Vcc, Vpp1, and Vpp2. The specific power parameters de-

scribed by the structure are also selectable as defined by the parameter selection byte within the power description structure.

2. **Configuration timing information** — this structure defines the maximum length of time that the PC Card will keep READY deasserted and the maximum duration of the WAIT# signal.

3. **I/O address space description** — defines up to sixteen ranges of I/O address space required by the PC Card for this configuration. The structure defines the exact base I/O address and the number of address locations within the range

4. **Interrupt request description** — specifies the system interrupt request line required for this configuration. A single IRQ can be specified or a group of IRQs can be defined, any of which will satisfy the configuration requirements. Also included in the description is information that defines the deliver mode (level or pulse), whether interrupt sharing is supported, and alternative interrupt signal definitions (i.e. NMI, I/O check, bus error, vendor specific interrupt).

5. **Memory address space description** — specifies up to eight ranges of memory address space required for this configuration. Both the Host processor address and the PC Card address can be specified. When both the host and PC Card address are the same, no address translation is required since the host address is directly mapped into the common memory address space. If no host address range is specified, then any range of host address space can be used and mapped by the HBA to the specified range within common memory address space. A base address and range value are specified for each block of addresses needed for this configuration.

6. **Miscellaneous information structure** — contains information regarding support for special features required by this configuration. Two bytes are defined by the PC Card standard. The first byte identifies the PC Card's support for power down (for power management software), whether the SPKR# pin is used, and the number of identical PC Cards that are supported for the max twins cards option (e.g. support for multiple ATA drives). The second byte defines support for DMA, including the DMA transfer size and specifies which pin the PC Card uses for DREQ#.

7. **Subtuple information** — permits definition of additional information relating to this configuration. Subtuples are included as extensions to the configuration table entry tuple and may include information such as the operation system for which the configuration was intended and the physical device being implemented in this configuration.

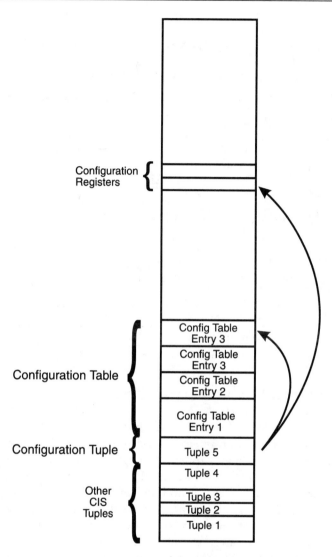

Figure 11-3. The Configuration Table Consists of a Number of Entries, Describing the Configuration Options Supported by the PC Card.

Table 11-6 shows the format of the configuration table entry tuple. The actual structures that are implemented within this tuple are specified by the feature selection byte.

Table 11-6. Format of the Configuration Table Entry Tuple

Byte	Name	Description of Entry
0	TPL_CODE	Configuration Entry tuple code (CISTPL_CFTABLE_ENTRY, 1Bh)
1	TPL_LINK	Link to next tuple (n-1, {2 minimum})
2	TPCE_INDX	Configuration table index byte — this byte contains the index number of the entry, specifies whether the interface byte will follow, and specifies whether this entry is a default entry or not.
..	TPCE_IF	Interface description byte — this field is present only when the interface bit of the Configuration-table index byte is set
..	TPCE_FS	Feature selection byte indicates the optional structures present
..	TPCE_PD	Power description structure
..	TPCE_TD	Configuration timing information structure
..	TPCE_IO	I/O address space description structure
..	TPCE_IR	Interrupt request description structure
..	TPCE_MS	Memory address space description structure
..	TPCE_MI	Miscellaneous information structure
..n	TPCE_ST	Additional information about the configuration in subtuple format

Interpreting the Configuration Table

When parsing software (usually a card services client driver) processes an entry within the configuration table, it must determine if the resources specified are available. (Refer to the chapter entitled, "Client Drivers" for a discussion of resource acquisition.) If all resources that have been requested are available then the configuration is satisfied and no additional configuration table entries need be evaluated. If however, one or more of the resources required to satisfy the configuration are not available, then parsing software must evaluate subsequent entries in an attempt to find alternative system resources that will satisfy the PC Card's configuration requirements.

The first entry within the configuration table is typically specified as a default entry. Default entries indicate that all configuration information specified within the entry should be retained even in the event that the full configuration was not satisfied. For example consider the configuration table illustrated in figure 11-4. The first entry is a default entry that specifies a power structure, a configuration timing structure, an I/O address space structure, an interrupt request structure and a miscellaneous information structure. Assume that parsing software was able to satisfy all configuration information specified by this entry except the interrupt request line. Software then proceeds in the following manner:

1. Since this is a default entry, all resources successfully acquired are retained. This eliminates the need to re-specify all the parameters that apply globally to the card's configuration regardless of which I/O address space and IRQ line is assigned to the card. In this example, since the entire configuration was not satisfied, parsing software proceeds to the next entry, attempting to find alternative resources that the PC Card can use.

2. Assume that entry 2 is not a default entry and contains only an I/O address structure and IRQ structure. Parsing software recognizing a non-default entry knows it must successfully acquire all configuration options specified, and if unable to do so must release the partial configuration by returning the resources previously acquired. Furthermore, since a pair of resources is being requested, the parsing software recognizes that the I/O address space acquired when attempting to satisfy the previous default entry must be released in favor of the new I/O address space and IRQ lines specified by this entry. If both configuration options are acquired successfully, then the configuration is completed. If not, the incomplete configuration is released and parsing software proceeds to the next entry.

3. Assume that entry 3 is not a default entry and contains another set of I/O addresses and another IRQ line. Once again parsing software attempts to acquire both resources, and if not successful must release any resource acquired and proceed to the next entry. As before, if both are acquired the configuration is complete.

4. Entry 4 is the last configuration entry and contains the final I/O address space and IRQ options for configuring the PC Card. If these resources cannot both be acquired, then the parsing software must report to the user that the card cannot be configured.

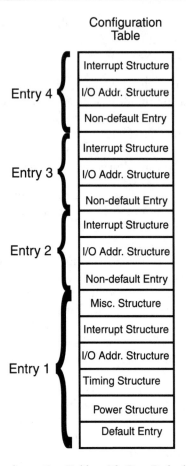

Configuration
Table

Figure 11-4. Example Configuration Table with One Default and Four Non-Default Entries

Once parsing software has obtained the configuration resources from the system it must configure the HBA and PC Card so that they respond to the resources. Parsing software uses the index number of the configuration table entry that specifies the successful configuration when configuring the PC Card. The index number is written into the PC Card's configuration option register, telling the PC Card which set of configuration options were successfully acquired.

Multiple Function PC Cards

Multi-function PC Cards require a separate CIS and configuration register set for each function within the card. As illustrated in figure 11-5, a global CIS is required when implementing a multi-function PC Card. The global CIS contains a long link multi-function tuple (LONGLINK_MFC) that lists the entry points of each function's CIS. The first entry within the target CIS must contain a LINKTARGET tuple to verify the correct start address specified by the LONGLINK_MFC tuple. Note that the configuration registers used by each function are identified by the configuration tuple within each CIS.

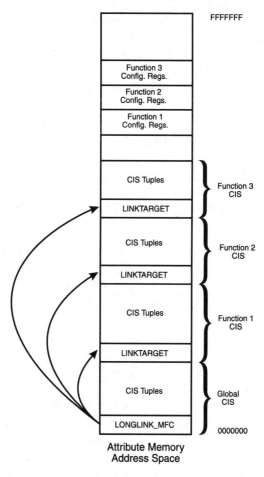

Figure 11-5. Configuration Table Structure Used by a Triple-Function PC Card

PCMCIA System Architecture

Devices Commonly Used for the CIS

Both ROM and FLASH are commonly used to implement the CIS. The clear advantage of FLASH is that the CIS can be easily updated. The CIS is quite small (usually not larger than 1 KB) and in the case of SRAM cards it can be as few as six bytes.

CIS Access Timing

Attribute memory (the CIS and configuration registers) must be accessed by card enabling software to determine the type of card installed and how it should be configured. Attribute memory is accessed by the HBA based on a default 300ns cycle time. This ensures that the CIS can be accessed regardless of the speed of other devices within the card. See the chapter entitled "The Memory-Only Interface" for details regarding attribute memory accesses.

Summary of Layer 1 Tuples

Table 11-7 lists the tuples that are currently defined by the PCMCIA specification for the CIS (layer 1 of the metaformat). Tuples are also defined for layers 2 and 3, but are not discussed here. Refer to the PCMCIA specification for details.

Table 11-7. Tuples defined for Compatibility Layer One (CIS)

Code (h)	CISTPL_NAME	Description and Purpose
00	NULL	Null Control tuple — Used as a place holder. Ignored by tuple processing software.
01	DEVICE	Device Information for Common Memory — Contains information about the card's common memory devices, including speed, type, write protect and size.
02-05	Reserved	Reserved for future versions of the device information tuple or for CardBus implementations.
06	LONGLINK_MFC	Long-Link for Multi-Function Card — Specifies the number of functions within this PC Card (i.e. sets of configuration registers) and defines the location of each function-specific CIS within the card.
07-0F	Reserved	Reserved for future versions or for CardBus tuples.

Chapter 11: The Card Information Structure (CIS)

Table 11-7 Tuples Defined for Compatibility Layer One (Continued)

Code (h)	CISTPL_NAME	Description and Purpose
10	CHECKSUM	Checksum Control — Provides a means for verifying the contents of the CIS in memory. Multiple checksum control tuples can be implemented within a single CIS.
11	LONGLINK_A	Long-Link Control to Attribute Memory — Specifies the continuation of a tuple string to a location in **attribute** memory, beyond the limits of the 1 byte link field. The entry point specified must contain a Link Target tuple.
12	LONGLINK_C	Long-Link Control to Common Memory — Specifies the continuation of a tuple string to a location in **common** memory, beyond the limits of the 1 byte link field. The entry point specified must contain a Link Target tuple.
13	LINKTARGET	Link Target — Verifies the continuation of a valid tuple string. The Link Target tuple is the first tuple at the entry point specified by a Long-Link tuple.
14	NO_LINK	The No Link tuple tells processing software that when the end of the current tuple chain is reached (i.e. the Termination Tuple has been detected) that no more tuples exist in the chain to be processed. (See Termination tuple — code FFh for more information.)
15	VERS_1	Level 1 (also layer 1)Version identifies the PCMCIA compliance level of the CIS (also called the compatibility layer or metaformat layer one). Following the Version information, production information is provided in a series of ASCII strings each ended by zero (Called AS-CIIZ).
16	ALTSTR	Alternate Language String — Includes additional languages for ASCII strings used in the product information tuple (code 15h). Also used for the Level 2 Version / Product Information tuple (code 40h).
17	DEVICE_A	Device Information to Attribute Memory — Contains information about the card's attribute memory devices, including speed, type, write protect and size. (optional)
18	JEDEC_C	Specifies the JEDEC (Joint Electronic Device Engineering Council) manufacturer and programming algorithm required by programmable devices listed in the device information tuple (01h) for common memory. Entries in the JEDEC identifier tuple have a one-to-one correspondence to the entries in the device information tuple.

Table 11-7 Tuples Defined for Compatibility Layer One (Continued)

Code (h)	CISTPL_NAME	Description and Purpose
19	JEDEC_A	Specifies the JEDEC (Joint Electronic Device Engineering Council) manufacturer and programming algorithm required by programmable devices listed in the device information tuple (17h). Entries in the JEDEC identifier tuple have a one-to-one correspondence to the entries in the device information tuple.
1A	CONFIG	Configuration tuple — Specifies the address of the configuration registers in attribute memory space and specifies which configuration registers are implemented in the card. Also identifies the last configuration entry within the configuration table, and provides a method of appending subtuples to the basic configuration tuple. Subtuples define additional information related to the card's configuration. Subtuple codes 80h-BFh are reserved for vendor specific items, while C0h- FEh are reserved for future PCMCIA standard definition. Currently, only the Custom Interface subtuple has been defined.
1B	CFTABLE_ENTRY	Configuration Table Entry — Provides configuration options supported by the card. Each configuration table entry provides additional configuration options. The entire set of configuration entries within the CIS is called the configuration table.
1C	DEVICE_OC	Other Conditions Device Information (common memory) — Specifies the characteristics of devices mapped in the common memory address space, when operating under conditions other than the defaults. For example, if the card is a dual voltage card (operates at both 5 volts and 3.3 volts) the characteristics of the common memory devices may be altered depending on which voltage is applied. There must be a one-to-one correspondence between the information fields listed in the Device Information tuple and the Other Conditions Device Information tuple.

Table 11-7 Tuples Defined for Compatibility Layer One (Continued)

Code (h)	CISTPL_NAME	Description and Purpose
1D	DEVICE_OA	Other Conditions Device Information (attribute memory) — Specifies the characteristics of devices mapped in the attribute memory address space, when operating under conditions other than the defaults. For example, if the card is a dual voltage card (operates at both 5 volts and 3.3 volts) the characteristics of the attribute memory devices may be altered depending on which voltage is applied. There must be a one-to-one correspondence between the information fields listed in the Device Information tuple and the Other Conditions Device Information tuple.
1E	DEVICEGEO	Device Geometry (common memory) — Device geometry provides the erase, read, and write characteristics of programmable devices. This tuple consists of multiple entries for each device identified in the device information tuple.
1F	DEVICEGEO_A	Device Geometry (attribute memory) — Device geometry provides the erase, read, and write characteristics of programmable devices. This tuple consists of multiple entries for each device identified in the device information tuple.
20	MANFID	PCMCIA Manufacturers Identification — Contains the PCMCIA manufacturer identification code and manufacturer card identifier and revision information.
21	FUNCID	Function Identification — Categorizes the card's functional type and specifies whether the card should be initialized during basic system initialization or when the operating system loads. A multi-function device may also be specified, in which case additional Function Identification tuples for each of the card's functions will follow.
Code (h)	CISTPL_NAME	Description and Purpose

Table 11-7 Tuples Defined for Compatibility Layer One (Continued)

Code (h)	CISTPL_NAME	Description and Purpose
22	FUNCE	Function Extension — Provides detailed information about a specific function previously identified by the function identification tuple. This tuple contains additional information useful to application programs or utility programs that are PCMCIA aware. Function extensions, if applicable, follow each Function Identification tuple in the tuple chain. Extensions are useful for defining the capabilities of various types of devices such as modems and network interface cards.
FF	END	Termination tuple — Indicates that this tuple is the last tuple in the string. However, by default parsing software will continue processing tuples at location zero in common memory. This implied jump to common memory occurs unless this tuple string contains either a LONGLINK OR NO_LINK tuple. If a no-link tuple has been encountered, the tuple string ends without further processing. If a valid long-link tuple has been encountered, tuple processing continues at the location specified, contingent on the presence of a LINKTARGET tuple at the target location. If there is neither a long- link nor a no-link tuple within the tuple string, tuple processing should continue at location zero in common memory.

Sample CIS implementations for SRAM, FAX/MODEM, Flash Card and ATA Hard Drive are discussed in later chapters.

Note that the CIS must start at address location zero in attribute address space or at the location specified by the LONGLINK_MFC tuple in multiple function PC Cards.

Chapter 12

The Previous Chapter

The previous chapter discussed the CIS and its role in the PC Card configuration process. Tuples were introduced and their format and structure were described. The basic structure of the CIS's configuration table required by I/O cards was also described.

This Chapter

This chapter discusses the configuration registers and provides a complete description of each register specified by the PC Card standard. Configuration register implementations for both single and multiple function cards are covered.

The Next Chapter

The next chapter describes a sample SRAM card implementation, including a functional block diagram of the SRAM card along with a sample CIS.

Configuration Registers

Each PC Card's I/O function must implement configuration registers. The PC Card standard defines the following configuration registers:

- Configuration Option Register — mandatory for all I/O functions
- Configuration and Status Register — optional
- Pin Replacement Register — optional
- Socket and Copy Register — optional
- Extended Status Register — optional
- I/O Base Address Register(s) — mandatory for multi-function PC Cards
- I/O Limit Register — optional

The format of each register is listed in table 12-1. These configuration registers are mapped into the attribute memory space at the location specified within the CONFIG tuple. Note that each function of a multiple function PC Card will have a dedicated set of configuration registers.

Table 12-1. Format of the Function Configuration Registers

Offset	7	6	5	4	3	2	1	0
0	Configuration Option Register							
	SRESET	LevlREQ	Function Configuration Index					
2	Configuration and Status Register							
	Changed	SigChg	IOIS8	RFU	Audio	PwrDwn	Intr	IntrAck
4	Pin Replacement Register							
	CBVD1	CBVD2	CREADY	CWProt	RBVD1	RBVD2	RREADY	RWProt
6	Socket and Copy Register							
	RFU	Copy Number			Socket Number			
8	Extended Status Register							
	Event3	Event2	Event1	Req Attn	Enable3	Enable2	Enable1	Req Attn Enable
10	I/O Base 0							
12	I/O Base 1							
14	I/O Base 2							
16	I/O Base 3							
18	I/O Limit							

Each of these registers have read/write capability and are mapped at even locations, consistent with the design of attribute memory. The definition of each configuration register is detailed below.

Configuration Option Register

The configuration option register (COR) configures PC Cards that have programmable address decoders. Once a card's client driver successfully parses the CIS and obtains the system resources required by the card, it assigns the resources to the card via the COR.

As discussed earlier in this chapter, the configuration table within the CIS specifies the configuration options that a given card supports. Each entry

Chapter 12: Function Configuration Registers

within the CIS contains a different combination of resources that satisfies a card's resource requirements. When the configuration options described by a particular configuration entry are found to be available, the index number of that configuration entry is written to the COR (refer to table 12-2). The index number programs the card to utilize the resources specified within the associated configuration table entry.

As shown in table 12-2, the COR also specifies whether the card should use level or pulse mode interrupts and provides a means for software to reset the card. Note that some memory cards may implement this register to support software reset as shown in the flash example. (See the chapter entitled, "A FLASH Card Example.")

Table 12-2. Configuration Option Register format and Definition

7	6	5	4	3	2	1	0
SRESET	LevlReq	Configuration Index					

SRESET	**Software Reset**. Setting this bit to one (1) places the card in the reset state. This is equivalent to assertion of the RESET signal except that this bit is not cleared. Returning this bit to zero (0), leaves the card in the same state that follows a hardware reset. This bit is set to zero by power up and hardware reset.
LevlReq	**Level Mode IREQ#**. Level Mode Interrupts are selected when this bit is one (1). Pulse Mode Interrupts are selected when this bit is zero (0).
Conf Index	**Configuration Index.** This field is written with the index number of the entry in the card's Configuration Table that corresponds to the configuration option chosen for the card. When the Configuration Index is 0, the card's I/O is disabled and will not respond to any I/O cycles and will use the memory-only interface.
	Multi-function Card Index definition. The PC Card standard specifically defines the use of each bit within the configuration index.
	Bit 0 — Enables/disables specific function. 1=enabled; 0=disabled
	Bit 1 — Specifies I/O addressing used. 1=I/O addresses specified by the base and limit registers are passed to function; 0=all host I/O address are passed to the function. (This bit is valid only when function is enable via bit 0.)
	Bit 2 — Enables IREQ# routing. 1=This function will deliver interrupts to the PC Card's IREQ# line; 0=interrupts disabled for this function. (This bit is valid only when function is enabled.)
	Bits 3-5 — vendor specific

Card Configuration and Status Register

This register contains a variety of functions used to control the card and report status, as shown in table 12-3. These functions include:

- Status change indication and reporting (bits 6 and 7)
- PCMCIA host expansion bus interface size (bit 5)
- Audio enable (bit 3)
- Power down control for power conservation (bit 2)
- Interrupt pending status (bit 1)

Status Change

Prior to being configured, an I/O card interfaces to the HBA as a memory only device. While in this state, any status change event must be reported directly over the appropriate status change pin. However, when the card is configured, (the COR is written) the card switches to the I/O interface and status change events are now reported via the pin replacement register (PRR) and the card configuration and status register (CSR).

The status changed bit (bit 7) and the signal change bit (bit 6) of the CSR determine whether a status change has occurred when the card is configured for the I/O interface and whether it should be reported over the I/O interface's STSCHG# pin. When a status change event occurs, the appropriate bit is set in the PRR and the status changed bit (Chng) is set in the CSR. When a status change occurs, the card asserts the STSCHG# pin to notify the HBA of the event. The Chng bit remains set until the PRR bit is reset indicating that the status change event has been processed.

The signal change bit (SigChg) is used by the HBA to disable the card from asserting the STSCHG# pin again until the current status change event has been processed. Software must clear this bit when processing a status change interrupt for the card. This permits the next status change event to be reported once the previous event has been processed.

Chapter 12: Function Configuration Registers

Table 12-3. Card Configuration and Status Register and Definition

7	6	5	4	3	2	1	0
Chng	SigChg	IOis8	Resrv (0)	Audio	PwrDn	Intr	IntrAck

Chng	**Status Change Detected**. This bit indicates that one or more of the Pin Replacement Register bits (CBVD1, CBVD2, CRDY, or CWProt) is set to one, normally causing the STSCHG# signal to be asserted. However, if the SigChg bit (see below) is 1 and the card is configured for an I/O interface, the STSCHG# pin is asserted when this bit is set.
SigChg	**Signal Change Enable/Disable**. This bit is set and reset by the host to enable and disable a status-change signal from the status register. When this bit is set and the card is configured for the I/O interface, the Chng bit controls pin 63 (STSCHG#). If no status change signal is desired, this bit should be set to zero and the STSCHG# signal will be held deasserted when the card is configured for I/O.
IOis8	**I/O Cycles Occur Only as 8-bit Transfers**. When the host can provide I/O cycles only using the D7:D0 data path, the PCMCIA software will set this bit to a 1. The card is guaranteed that accesses to 16-bit registers will occur as two byte accesses rather than a single 16-bit access. This information is useful when 16-bit and 8-bit registers overlap.
Resrv	Reserved bits must be 0.
Audio	**Audio Enable**. This bit enables audio information to be sent to the HBA via the speaker pin when configured for an I/O interface.
PwrDn	**Power Down**. This bit is set to one to request that the card enter a power-down state. PCMCIA software must not place the card into a power-down state while the card's READY pin is in the low (Busy) state.
Intr	**Interrupt Request Pending**. This bit represents the internal state of the interrupt request. This value is available whether or not interrupts have been configured. How the Intr bit is cleared is dependent of how the IntrAck bit is configured.
	IntrAck=0 — Intr reflects the function's interrupt request status. If the interrupt is cleared within the function, then Intr is reset by the function.
	IntrAck=1 — Intr remains set even though the interrupt condition has been cleared. It is reset by system software to indicate it is ready to receive another interrupt (implemented to support interrupt sharing).

Table 12-3. Card Configuration and Status Register and Definition(Continued)

7	6	5	4	3	2	1	0
Chng	SigChg	IOis8	Resrv (0)	Audio	PwrDn	Intr	IntrAck

IntrAck	**Interrupt Acknowledge.** This bit determines the response of the Intr bit. The functionality associated with the IntrAck bit permits two or more functions to share the PC Card's IREQ# pin.
	IntrAck=0 — when IntrAck is reset Intr functions as described above to support a single interrupt implementation.
	IntrAck=1 — This causes the Intr bit to remain set even though the interrupt service routine has already serviced the interrupt. Normally, the interrupt service routine clears the interrupt pending bit in a function specific register, causing the Intr also to be cleared. However, to support interrupt sharing the Intr bit is not cleared until PCMCIA specific software is ready to handle the next interrupt request. When cleared by the PCMCIA software, other interrupt requests that are pending can now be asserted over the PC Card's IREQ# pin. (Refer to the chapter entitled, "Multiple Function PC Cards."

Size of Host Expansion Bus

The IOis8 bit reflects the size of the expansion bus that the HBA connects to. When this bit is set, I/O cycles will always occurs as individual 8-bit transfers over the lower data path (D7:D0). When the bit is reset, accesses to 16-bit registers will occur in a single cycle.

Audio Enable

The Audio bit is set to enable audio information to be sent over the I/O interface's SPKR pin. Whether or not the I/O card has audio capability is specified within the miscellaneous information structure within the configuration table entry.

Power Conservation Mode

Some cards support a low power mode that can be used for power conservation. Power management software can set the power down (PwrDn) bit, placing the card in a low power state, if supported. Note that this bit should not be set if the card is in the busy state as indicated by the PRR.

Interrupt Pending

The Intr bit is set by the card when its interrupt request (IREQ#) pin is asserted. If the PC Card implements a single I/O function, the Intr bit remains set until the interrupt service routine is executed, at which time the Intr bit is reset.

Pin Replacement Register

Cards using a memory only interface report status change directly to the HBA via the status change pins. However, when a card uses the I/O interface, the status change pins are replaced by other I/O specific interface signals. As a result, the HBA has no visibility of status change events that may occur on the I/O card. The pin replacement register (PRR) replaces the HBA functions that are normally used to indicate the status of change events for the memory interface.

Refer to table 12-4. The PRR specifies the current state of the status change events (bits 3:0) and whether a change has occurred for a particular event (bits 7:4). The current state of the events (RWP, RREADY, RBVD2, and RBVD1) can be read directly from the lower four bits of the PRR register. When a change occurs for any of these items, its corresponding changed bit is set in the upper group of bits. In this way, processing software can read the upper four bits to determine which event(s) has occurred and therefore, the one needing to be processed. When a given event is processed, the lower portion of the register can be read to check the new state of the event that signaled the change. When the event is processed, software should reset the changed bit, thus permitting another event to be reported.

Table 12-4. Pin Replacement Register

7	6	5	4	3	2	1	0
CBVD1	CBVD2	CRdy	CWP	RBVD1	RBVD2	RREADY	RWP
CBVD1, CBVD2		**Changed BVD1 and BVD2.** These bits are set to one when the corresponding bit (RBVD1 and/or RBVD2) changes from one state to another. These bits may also be cleared by the host.					
CREADY		**Changed READY.** This bit is set to one when the bit RREADY changes state. This bit may also be cleared by the host.					

Table 12-4. Pin Replacement Register (Continued)

CWProt	**Changed Write Protect.** This bit is set to one when the bit RRWProt changes state. This bit may also be cleared by the host.
RBVD1, RBVD2	**Current State of BVD1 and BVD2.** These bits represent the internal state of the Battery Voltage Detect circuits on cards that contain a battery. They correspond to the values that would be on pins 63 and 62, BVD1 and BVD2 respectively. When this bit is set, the corresponding changed bit is also set. When this bit is cleared, the corresponding changed bit is unaffected.
RRdy	**Current State of Ready.** This bit represents the internal state of the READY signal. This bit reflects the state of READY (since the READY pin has been reallocated for use as Interrupt Request on IO Cards). When this bit is set, the corresponding changed bit is also set. When cleared, the corresponding changed bit is unaffected.
RWProt	**Current State of Write-Protect Switch.** This bit represents the current state of the Write-Protect switch. This bit reflects the state of the Write Protect switch when pin 24 is being used for IOIS16#. When this bit is set, the corresponding changed bit is also set. When cleared, the corresponding changed bit is unaffected.

Socket and Copy Register

Refer to table 12-5. This register is used for I/O cards that can coexist with one or more identical cards within the system and respond to the same I/O address ranges. This capability can be used for ATA (IDE) drives that are designated as drive 0 and drive 1. Each responds to the same I/O address space but can be uniquely identified with the socket and copy register. The first card configured will be assigned as copy zero and each card configured thereafter receives the next sequential copy number. The socket number identifies the socket that a given copy occupies.

Table 12-5. Socket and Copy Register

7	6	5	4	3	2	1	0
Reserved (0)		Copy Number			Socket Number		

Reserved	This bit is reserved for future standardization. This bit must be set to zero (0) by software when the register is written.
Copy Number	Cards that can coexist with other cards (twin cards) that are configured identically, should have a copy number identifying this particular copy of the card. (0 to MAX twin cards, MAX = n-1) This field indicates to the card that it is "nth" copy of the card installed in the system that is identically configured. The first card installed receives the value 0. This permits identical cards designed to do so to share a common set of I/O ports while remaining uniquely identifiable and consecutively ordered.
Socket Number	This field indicates to the card that it is located in the nth socket. The first socket is numbered 0. This permits any cards designed to do so to share a common set of I/O ports while remaining uniquely identifiable.

Extended Status Register

This register has been added to the PC Card standard to extend the number of events that can be reported via the STSCHG# pin and to give software the ability to detect and clear the event. The extended status register is organized as an upper nibble (whose bits are set when the corresponding function event occurs) and a lower nibble (that enables and disables setting the "Changed" bit in the CSR). When a status change interrupt occurs PC Card software can read the extended status register to determine if an associated bit has caused an the interrupt.

Table 12-6 illustrates the format of the extended status register. Notice that only the "Requires Attention" and "Requires Attention Enable" bits are defined.

Table 12-6. Format and definition of the Extended Status Register

D7	D6	D5	D4	D3	D2	D1	D0
Event3	Event2	Event1	Req Attn	Enable3	Enable2	Enable1	Req Attn Enable

Field	Description
Event3	Reserved for future expansion/definition, must be reset (0)
Event2	Reserved for future expansion/definition, must be reset (0)
Event1	Reserved for future expansion/definition, must be reset (0)
Req Attn	This bit is latched within one (1) ms of an event occurring on the PC Card, (such as the start of each cycle of the ring frequency to indicate the presence of ringing on the phone line in the case of a modem card). When this bit is set to a one (1), and the *Req Attn Enable* bit is set to a one (1), the *Changed* bit in the Configuration and Status register will also be set to a one (1), and if the *SigChg* bit in the Configuration and Status register has also been set by the host, the STSCHG# pin (63) will be asserted. The host writing a one (1) to this bit will reset it to zero (0). Writing a zero (0) to this bit will not have any effect.
Enable3	Reserved for future expansion/definition, must be reset (0)
Enable2	Reserved for future expansion/definition, must be reset (0)
Enable1	Reserved for future expansion/definition, must be reset (0)
Req Attn Enable	Setting this bit to a one (1) enables the setting of the *Changed* bit in the Configuration and Status register when the *Req Attn* bit is set. When this bit is reset to a zero (0), this feature is disabled. The state of the *Req Attn* bit is not affected by the *Req Attn Enable* bit.

I/O Base Registers

The PC Card standard defines these I/O base registers for use by multiple function cards, but they can also be used by single function cards. These registers define the base I/O address to which the function's I/O registers will be mapped into the host processor's address space. The number of registers used depends on the address space supported by the host processor. Since Intel compatible x86 processors have only 64KB of address space, only the first two registers are needed to specify a base address anywhere within the entire 64KB space.

Chapter 12: Function Configuration Registers

I/O Limit Register

This register relates to the I/O base registers by specifying the maximum range of I/O addresses that can be mapped beginning at the base address. This register is bit mapped such that the most significant bit that is set determines the number of address lines used to decode the address and therefore the maximum block of address space supported. The most significant bit and all bits of lesser significance must be set within the register. This results in the possible number of address lines as listed in table 12-7. Note that the largest block of I/O address space that can be defined is 256 bytes.

This register is optional and need not be implemented for each function if all functions within the PC Card use the same number of I/O registers.

Table 12-7. Address Limit Associated with Function Base Address Register

Bit Position								Maximum
7	6	5	4	3	2	1	0	Number of
# of Address Lines Defined by Bit position								Address
8	7	6	5	4	3	2	1	Locations
0	0	0	0	0	0	0	0	Not defined
0	0	0	0	0	0	0	1	2
0	0	0	0	0	0	1	1	4
0	0	0	0	0	1	1	1	8
0	0	0	0	1	1	1	1	16
0	0	0	1	1	1	1	1	32
0	0	1	1	1	1	1	1	64
0	1	1	1	1	1	1	1	128
1	1	1	1	1	1	1	1	256

Chapter 13

The Previous Chapter

The previous chapter discussed the configuration registers and provided a complete description of each register specified by the PC Card standard. Configuration register implementations for both single and multiple function cards were covered.

This Chapter

This chapter describes a sample SRAM card implementation, including a functional block diagram of the SRAM card along with a sample CIS.

The Next Chapter

The next chapter describes a sample flash card implementation, including a functional block diagram of the card, a sample CIS, and configuration registers implemented by the card.

An SRAM Card Example

Figure 13-1 illustrates the functional blocks associated with an SRAM memory card. Note that this is an example implementation of a 2MB SRAM card. The contents of the CIS are illustrated and discussed in the next section.

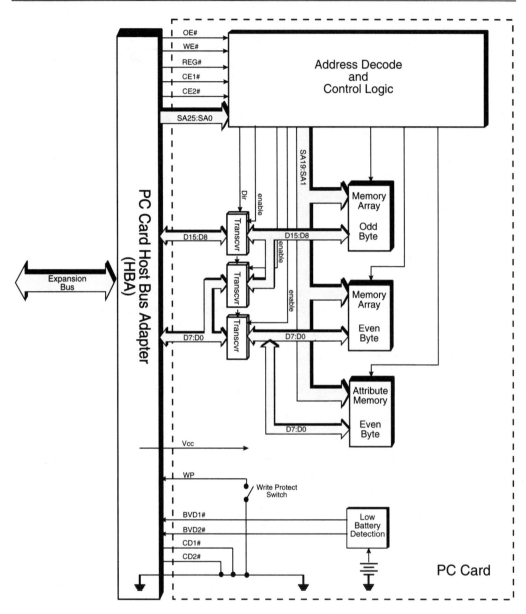

Figure 13-1. Block Diagram of 2MB SRAM PC Card

The SRAM CIS

The following example illustrates the CIS implemented within a typical SRAM card. SRAM PC Card design is relatively simple when compared to I/O cards. As shown in figure 13-2, a typical SRAM CIS may consist of four tuples. The sections following figure 13-2 describe the purpose and contents of each tuple in the SRAM example. Refer to appendix A for a detailed listing and analysis of the tuples contained in this SRAM example.

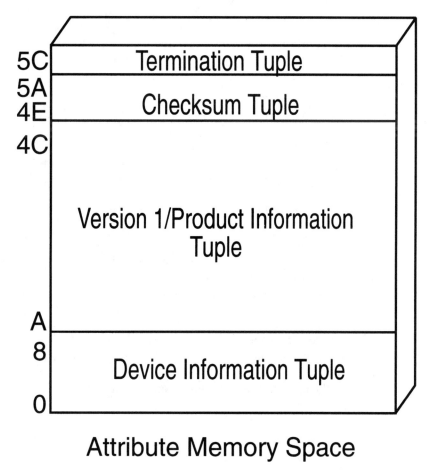

Figure 13-2. Map of Attribute Memory Addresses on Example SRAM Card

Device Information Tuple

As described earlier, the Device Information tuple defines all the information needed to characterize an SRAM memory card. The device information tuple defines the following operational characteristics:

- Device Type (SRAM in this example).
- Device Speed (250ns is this example).
- Write-Protect switch (WPS) definition. Whether the memory defined within the tuple is affected by the write-protect switch (WPS is used).
- Size of the memory array (2MB in this example).

Since no configuration table exists, the memory array described is mapped by default at base address zero within common memory address space.

Level 1 Version / Product Information Tuple

This tuple contains the PCMCIA version of the CIS and ASCII characters describing the product. The data area within the SRAM level 1 version/production information tuple consists specifically of:

- Major version 4 (relates to JEIDA release 4.0).
- Minor version 1 (relates to PCMCIA release 1.0) A major version number of 4 and a minor version number of 1 indicates 2.x compliant CIS.
- ASCII string indicating manufacturer and card description.
- ASCII string indicating model number of card.
- ASCII string indicating serial number card.

The ASCII character strings contained within the product information portion of the tuple are defined by the PC Card manufacturer. The manufacturer and card description information within this tuple are typically read and displayed by PCMCIA configuration software when a card is configured. This notifies the user that the card has been recognized and identified.

Checksum Tuple

The checksum tuple provides a way for processing software to verify that the data read from the CIS is correct. The checksum data block information includes:

- Offset from checksum tuple to the start address of the range to be checked.
- Number of locations to be checksummed from the start address.
- Checksum value.

More than one checksum tuple can be used within a CIS. This example contains a single checksum tuple used to check the CIS from location zero to location 4Ch.

Termination Tuple

The termination tuple consists only of the tuple code FFh. In this example, when processing software encounters the termination tuple, it will continue tuple processing by going to location zero in common memory. Common memory may contain additional tuple information written there by PCMCIA aware software that formats the SRAM memory for use as a virtual drive.

This capability stems from 1.0 compliant cards that did not require that a CIS be implemented. When processing software attempts to read the CIS, a value of FFh will be returned when no CIS is implemented. This is interpreted by software as a termination tuple. Software then reads from location zero in common memory where a link-target tuple will be found. The software then looks for a BIOS Parameter Block (BPB) that characterizes the size of the SRAM to be used as a virtual drive.

Chapter 14

The Previous Chapter

The previous chapter described a simple SRAM card implementation, including a functional block diagram of the SRAM card along with a sample CIS.

This Chapter

This chapter describes a flash card implementation, including a functional block diagram of the card, a sample CIS, and configuration registers implemented by the card.

The Next Chapter

The next chapter describes an example FAX/Modem implementation, including a functional block diagram, a sample CIS, and configuration registers implemented by the card.

An Example Flash Card Implementation

Figure 14-1 illustrates the functions associated with an Intel series II Flash-Card. This example is based on a 10MB flash memory array and includes a CIS contained within the flash control ASIC. This card also incorporates flash memory that implements a ready/busy (RDY/BSY#) pin and takes advantage of the memory socket's READY pin.

PCMCIA System Architecture

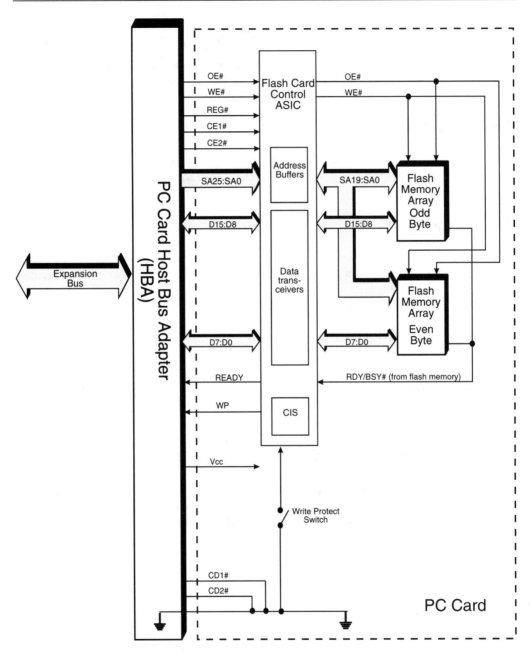

Figure 14-1. 20MB Flash Card Functional Diagram

A Flash Memory CIS Example

Following is an example of a flash memory card's attribute memory address space. As shown in figure 14-2, this flash card implements both a CIS and configuration registers. The sections following figure 14-2 describe the purpose and contents of each tuple used by the flash card in this example. Appendix B contains a detailed listing and explanation of the tuples in this flash memory card example.

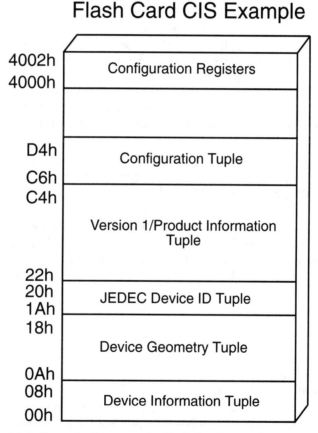

Flash Card CIS Example

4002h 4000h	Configuration Registers
D4h C6h	Configuration Tuple
C4h	Version 1/Product Information Tuple
22h 20h 1Ah	JEDEC Device ID Tuple
18h	Device Geometry Tuple
0Ah 08h 00h	Device Information Tuple

Figure 14-2. Example Contents of a Flash Card's Attribute Address Space

Device Information Tuple

The device information tuple identifies the basic characteristics of the card. The device information tuple determines the following parameters:

- Device Type (flash memory).
- Device Speed (150ns).
- Write-Protect switch (WPS) definition. Whether the memory defined within the tuple is affected by the write-protect switch (WPS used).
- Size of the memory array (10MB).

Unlike the previous SRAM example, the contents of the Device Information tuple does not completely characterize a flash memory array. Flash cards require an additional Device Geometry tuple to specify the block size for erasing and writing to the flash memory array.

Since no configuration table exists, the memory array described is not programmable and responds only to location 0 to 10MB in common memory address space.

Device Geometry Tuple

Flash memory cards are block oriented devices when writing to or erasing their memory arrays. As a result, the Memory Technology driver must know the block size in order to access the device correctly. The Device Geometry tuple contains the block size that is implemented by the memory array for erasing, writing and reading the flash card. Information described by the tuple includes:

- Internal bus width (always 2 bytes for release 1.0 - 2.x cards).
- Erase geometry block size.
- Read geometry block size.
- Write geometry block size.
- Partition size (indicates partition size, if the memory array is partitioned).
- Interleave size (describes whether hardware interleaving is incorporated to enhance read performance, and if so, what the interleaving size is).

Chapter 14: A Flash Card Example

JEDEC Device Identifier (ID) Tuple

Many memory devices contain the JEDEC Device ID tuple within their CIS. As its name suggests, this tuple contains the card manufacturer's JEDEC ID and incorporates device type information that specifies a corresponding programming algorithm. The Joint Electronics Device Engineering Council (JEDEC) assigns an ID to manufacturers designing programmable memory devices. All programmable memory devices should have a corresponding JEDEC identifier.

Note that for each entry in a device information (DEVICE) tuple a corresponding entry must be made in the JEDEC device identifier tuple. If a DEVICE tuple contains both programmable and non-programmable memory devices, then the JEDEC tuple entries for the non-programmable device will contain null values.

Level 1 Version / Product Information Tuple

This tuple contains the PCMCIA compliance level of the CIS (level 1 version) and ASCII characters describing the product. The data area within the flash level 1 version/production information tuple consists specifically of:

- Major version 5 (relates to PC Card February, 1995 release).
- Minor version 0 (relates to PC Card February, 1995 release).
  Note: A major version number of 5 and a minor version number of 0 indicates compliance with the PC Card 95 release.
- ASCII string indicating manufacturer and card description.
- ASCII string indicating model number of card.
- ASCII string indicating serial number of card.

The ASCII character strings contained within the product information portion of the tuple are defined by the manufacturer. The manufacturer name and card description is sometimes read and displayed by PCMCIA utilities when a card is configured. This tuple is also commonly used by PC Card enablers that are designed to identify and configure a specific card.

Configuration Tuple

The Configuration tuple identifies the type of the configuration register(s) used by the PC Card, along with their location within attribute memory space. Data entries within the Configuration tuple contain the following:

- Size of address fields—This entry defines the number of bytes used by this tuple to identify the location of the configuration registers. Since these registers can be located anywhere within attribute memory address space (0 to 64MB), the number of bytes needed to define their location depends on where they reside in the address space. In this example, the registers are mapped to location 4000h, therefore only two bytes are needed to specify their location.
- Size of configuration register mask field— Specifies the number of bytes needed by the configuration register mask field to identify the configuration registers implemented by this function. PCMCIA currently defines ten configuration registers of the 128 configuration registers that can be specified. To specify all 128 registers the configuration register mask field would require sixteen 8-bit mask registers. This example implementation uses the first two registers, therefore a single mask register is implemented. Refer to the section entitled, "Flash Card Configuration Registers" later in this chapter for details.
- Index number of the last entry in the configuration table—Since this example flash card has no configuration table this entry is zero.
- Starting (base) address of the configuration registers—In this example, a two byte field identifies the location of the configuration registers in attribute memory (location 4000h).
- Configuration register mask — A bit map that corresponds to the configuration register implemented by the PC Card function. The mask value in this example specifies that only registers corresponding to bit 0 (the Configuration Option Register) and bit 1 (the Status Register) are implemented.

Termination Tuple

The termination tuple consists only of the tuple code FFh. In this example, when processing software encounters the termination tuple, it will continue tuple processing by going to location zero in common memory. Common memory may contain additional tuple information written there by PCMCIA aware software that formats the flash memory for use as a virtual drive.

This capability stems from 1.0 compliant cards that did not require that a CIS be implemented. When processing software attempts to read the CIS, a value of FFh will be returned since no CIS is implemented. This is interpreted by software as a termination tuple. Software then reads from location zero in attribute memory where a link-target tuple will be found. The software then looks for a BIOS Parameter Block (BPB) that characterizes the size of the memory used as a virtual drive.

Flash Card Configuration Registers

The flash card in this example uses two of the configuration registers that are defined by the PCMCIA standard. These two registers are the configuration option register and the configuration status register. As implemented, these register use only a small portion of the associated functions defined by PCMCIA.

Configuration Option Register

The flash card in this example uses the configuration option register (bit 7) to permit software reset capability at the card level. The other functions associated with the configuration option register are not used.

Configuration Status Register

The flash card in this example also uses the configuration status register (bit 2) for placing the card into the power down state for power conservation. All other functions associated with the configuration status register are not used.

Chapter 15

The Previous Chapter

The previous chapter described a flash card implementation, including a functional block diagram of the card, a sample CIS, and configuration registers implemented by the card.

This Chapter

This chapter describes an example FAX/Modem implementation, including a functional block diagram, sample CIS, and related configuration registers.

The Next Chapter

The next chapter describes an PC Card ATA drive implementation, including a functional block diagram, a sample CIS, and configuration registers implemented by the card.

An Example FAX/Modem Card

Figure 15-1 illustrates the functions incorporated into a FAX/Modem PC Card. The socket interface is configured as a memory-only interface when the PC Card is first installed and reconfigured as a memory or I/O socket during the configuration process. Note that all the registers in this PC Card implementation are 8-bit registers; therefore, this PC Card does not assert the IOIS16# pin.

The modem consists of the UART (Universal Asynchronous Receiver/Transmitter), the modem controller, the modem data pump and the DAA (Data Access Arrangement).

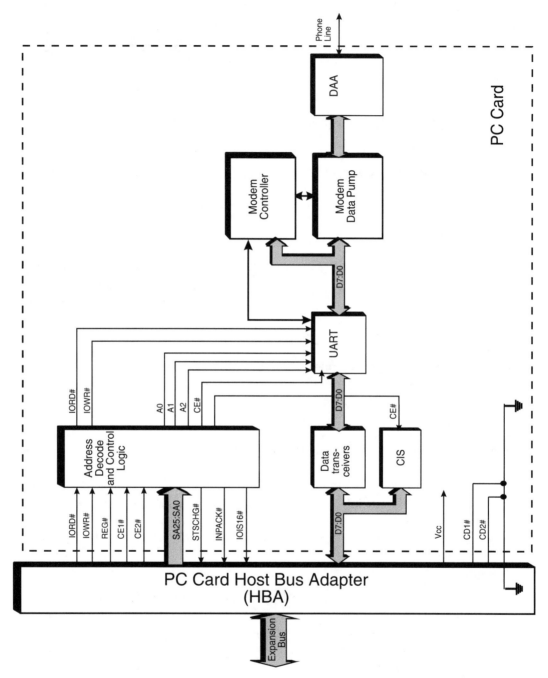

Figure 15-1. Functional Block Diagram of FAX/Modem PC Card

Chapter 15: A FAX/Modem Example

FAX/Modem Resource Requirements

FAX/Modems require I/O address space and a system IRQ line to allow the application software to communicate via a standard serial interface. In MS-DOS and Windows implementations, the serial interface has been mapped to a standardized range of addresses and associated IRQ lines. These conventional resource locations are needed because communications software typically accesses FAX/Modem hardware registers directly. Software typically expects the serial interface to be mapped to the conventional resources that are frequently referred to by the DOS device names: communications ports one through four (COM 1, COM 2, COM 3, and COM 4).

The convention location for these communications interface are:

- COM 1 = I/O addresses 3F8h-3FFh and IRQ 4
- COM 2 = I/O addresses 2F8h-2FFh and IRQ 3
- COM 3 = I/O addresses 3E8h-2EFh and IRQ 4
- COM 4 = I/O addresses 2E8h-3EFh and IRQ 3

Note that some communications software may be able to access the serial interface at other non-conventional address locations and IRQs. Specifically, PC Card aware application programs can gain access to the PC Card configuration information and determine how the PC Card has been configured by the enabler. Once the application knows how the PC Card has been configured, it can gain access to the card via the specified I/O address locations and IRQ lines without having to rely upon the conventional configurations specified above.

A FAX/Modem CIS Example

Figure 15-2 illustrates the contents of attribute memory address space for a FAX/modem. Notice that the CIS contains a configuration table. A configuration table is used by PC Cards having functions that can be configured using a variety of different system resources. The configuration table consists of entries that define different resources combinations that can be assigned to the PC Card. If one of the resource combinations are available for the PC Card's use, then it can be successfully configured. If the resource combinations required by the FAX/Modem are not available for use then the card cannot be configured.

Device Information Tuple

The Device Information tuple identifies the basic characteristics of memory cards. Since the FAX/Modem is an I/O device, the device information tuple contains no relevant information. The data portion of this tuple is zero, indicating that this card is not a memory card.

Level 1 Version / Product Information Tuple

This tuple contains the PCMCIA compliance level of the CIS (i.e. the version of CIS, recall that level 1, or layer 1 of the metaformat defines the CIS) and ASCII characters describing the product. The data area within the FAX/Modem level 1 version/production information tuple consists specifically of:

- Major version 5 (relates to PC Card February, 1995 release).
- Minor version 0 (relates to PC Card February, 1995 release).
  Note: A major version number of 4 and a minor version number of 1 indicates 2.x compliant CIS.
- ASCII string indicating manufacturer and card description.
- ASCII string indicating model number of the card.
- ASCII string indicating serial number of the card.

The ASCII character strings contained within the product information portion of the tuple are defined by the manufacturer. The manufacturer name and card description is sometimes read and displayed by PCMCIA utilities when a card is configured. This tuple is also used by client device drivers that are designed to identify a specific card.

Card Manufacturer Identification (ID) Tuple

As its name suggests, this tuple contains the PCMCIA card manufacturer's ID number. The PCMCIA organization assigns an ID to the manufacturers designing PCMCIA compliant cards.

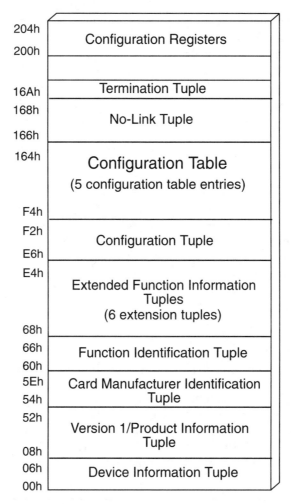

204h	Configuration Registers
200h	
16Ah	Termination Tuple
168h	No-Link Tuple
166h	
164h	**Configuration Table** (5 configuration table entries)
F4h	
F2h	Configuration Tuple
E6h	
E4h	Extended Function Information Tuples (6 extension tuples)
68h	
66h	Function Identification Tuple
60h	
5Eh	Card Manufacturer Identification Tuple
54h	
52h	Version 1/Product Information Tuple
08h	
06h	Device Information Tuple
00h	

Figure 15-2. Example of Attribute Memory Address Contents for FAX/Modem

Function Identification Tuple

The Function Identification tuple determines the type of functional device that is implemented in the PC Card. Memory cards can be specified through the Device Information tuple, whereas, I/O devices must use the Function Identification tuple. This tuple defines the following items:

- Function type code — consists of a code representing the type of device implemented in the PC Card. The function type associated with the FAX/modem is a serial port.
- Initialization byte — specifies whether this device should be configured during system initialization (also called Power-On Self Test or POST) and whether the card has a ROM containing configuration software. This is used by devices when loading the operating system. Not used by the FAX/modem.

Function Extension Tuples

Function Extension tuples are defined by PCMCIA for some types of devices, including modems. Function Extension tuples must immediately follow the Function Identification tuple to which they apply. This example consists of six different function extension tuples. Within each tuple is a code identifying it as a particular type of function extension. These extensions fall into three basic categories for serial devices:

- Data modem extensions
- FAX modem extensions
- Voice modem extensions (not used by the FAX/modem)

Each Function Extension tuple provides information related to the capabilities of the modem. This information includes items such as communications protocols, error correction protocols, and other communications parameters. This information can be used by PCMCIA aware applications to automatically configure the application based on the card's capabilities.

Configuration Tuple

The Configuration tuple identifies the type of the configuration register(s) implemented in the PC Card, along with their location within attribute memory space. This tuple also specifies the index number of the last entry within the CIS. Data entries within the Configuration tuple contain the following:

- Size of address fields — This entry defines the number of bytes used later within this tuple to identify the location of the configuration registers. Since the configuration registers can be located anywhere within attribute memory address space (0 to 64MB), the number of bytes needed to define their location depends on where they reside in the address space. In this example, the registers are mapped starting at location 200h; therefore, only two bytes are needed to specify their location.

- Size of configuration register mask field — Specifies the number of bytes needed by the configuration register mask field to identify the configuration registers implemented by this function. PCMCIA currently defines ten configuration registers out of the 128 configuration registers that can be identified. To specify all 128 registers the configuration register mask field would require sixteen 8-bit mask registers. This example implementation uses registers 0, 1, and 2 therefore a single mask register is implemented. Refer to the section entitled, "FAX/Modem Card Configuration Registers" later in this chapter for details.

- Index number of the last entry in the configuration table — This value indicates to processing software when the last entry within the card's configuration tuple has been reached.

- Starting (base) address of the configuration registers — In this example, a two byte field identifies the location of the configuration registers in attribute memory (location 0200h).

- Configuration register mask — Specifies that configuration registers zero (Configuration Option Register), one (Status Register) and two (Pin Replacement Register) are implemented.

Configuration Table

The configuration table contains the configuration option supported by the FAX/modem card. The card in this particular example contains five entries within the configuration table, each defining a different combination of system resources required to support its functions. The serial port used by the modem requires an eight byte block of contiguous I/O addresses and a system interrupt line. This device supports standard resources defined by convention in the DOS environment. The following list shows the 8-byte I/O range and IRQ line specified by each entry within the configuration table.

- COM 1—I/O base address 3F8h and IRQ 4 (entry 1)
- COM 2—I/O base address 2F8h and IRQ 3 (entry 2)
- COM 3—I/O base address 3E8h and IRQ 4 (entry 3)
- COM 4—I/O base address 2E8h and IRQ 3 (entry 4)
- Any 8-byte range of I/O addresses and any one of the IRQs: 2, 3, 4, 5, 7, 9, 10, or 15 (entry 5)

The first resource combination that can be allocated by the system will be assigned to the HBA and PC Card for its use. The index number of the configuration table entry that satisfied the resource requirements is programmed into the configuration option register. This configures the PC Card to respond to the resources specified within the selected configuration table entry.

No-Link Tuple

The no-link tuple tells processing software to terminate tuple processing when the termination tuple is reached. This prevents the implied jump to location zero of common memory.

Termination Tuple

The termination tuple consists only of the tuple code FFh. In this example, when processing software encounters the termination tuple, it will end tuple processing since the no-link tuple exists in the tuple listing.

FAX/Modem Configuration Registers

The FAX/Modem card in this example implements three of the ten configuration registers defined by the PCMCIA standard. These registers include the configuration option register, status register and pin replacement register. Their use in the fax/modem card is defined in the following sections.

Configuration Option Register

The configuration option register performs several functions related to the FAX/modem card's operation:

- Configuration Index — selects the entry within the configuration table that satisfied the card's resource requirements. This value programs the I/O address decoders on the card to respond to the correct address range.
- Interrupt Request Level — selects whether level or pulse mode interrupts should be delivered over the IREQ# pin by the PC Card.

- Software Reset — provides the ability for software to reset the PC Card. Setting this bit has the same affect on the hardware as asserting the RESET pin.

Configuration Status Register

This register performs the following functions as they relate to the FAX/modem card:

- Audio Supported — set by software to enable the PC Card to output audio information to the HBA via the speaker pin.
- Interrupt Pending — set by the PC Card to indicate that an interrupt has been asserted to the HBA and has not yet been serviced.
- Status Change — set by the PC Card to indicate that a pin replacement register has been implemented and should be checked to see if a status change has occurred.

Pin Replacement Register

The pin replacement register is used to report status change events that are supported by the PC Card. This is done in lieu of socket interface pins that are not available when the socket is configured as an I/O interface. The FAX/modem in this example implements the READY status change function and therefore implements the pin replacement register.

Chapter 16

The Previous Chapter

The previous chapter described an example FAX/Modem implementation, including a functional block diagram, sample CIS, and related configuration registers.

This Chapter

This chapter describes an example PC Card ATA drive implementation, including a functional block diagram, a sample CIS, and configuration registers implemented by the card.

The Next Chapter

The next chapter describes a multi-function PC Card design, including a functional block diagram, a multi-function CIS, and related configuration registers.

An ATA PC Card Example

Figure 16-1 illustrates the functions contained within an ATA PC Card based on rotating magnetic media. Other ATA PC Card designs are based on flash memory technology implemented as virtual disk drives that provide the same programming interface employed by standard ATA disk drives.

As with any PC Card, the initial socket interface is automatically configured as a memory-only interface when the PC Card is first installed. After the CIS is read and the ATA PC Card's enabler has detected the ATA card's presence, the enabler initiates the configuration process. As discussed in the following section an ATA PC Card can be configured to operate with the memory interface (i.e. the registers are mapped into the processor's memory address space) or with the memory or I/O interface (using standard I/O mapping).

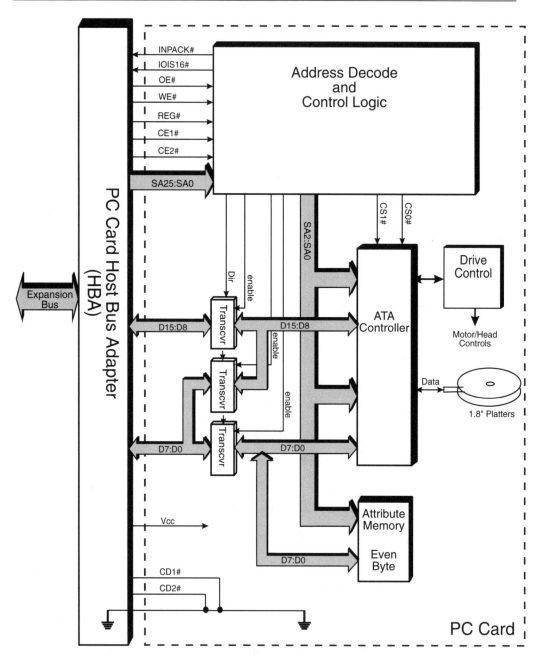

Figure 16-1. Functional Block Diagram of an ATA Disk Drive PC Card

Chapter 16: An ATA PC Card Example

ATA System Resource Requirements

ATA devices contain two register blocks called the command register block and control register block. Each of these register blocks must be assessable by the system. PC Card ATA devices support either I/O or memory-mapping using one of four addressing modes listed in table 16-1.

Standard mapping in the ISA environment includes the assignment of two separate I/O address ranges to map ATA drive registers into. If these ranges are not available, another range of I/O addresses can be used. If neither of the standard I/O address ranges are available, then a contiguous block of 16 I/O locations is requested for mapping the command and control block registers into.

Alternatively, the registers can be mapped into memory locations. When memory-mapping is chosen, a contiguous 2KB block of memory locations is used. The command and control registers are mapped into the first 16 bytes of the 2KB memory block, while the last 1KB of the block is used as a high speed buffer to transfer data to and from the PC card.

Table 16-1. ATA Addressing Options Supported by PCMCIA

Address Mode	Command Block	Control Block
I/O - Primary ATA drive address	1F0h - 1F7h	3F6h - 3F7h
I/O - Secondary ATA drive address	170h - 177h	376h - 377h
I/O - Any 16-byte contiguous range	XXX0h - XXXFh	
Memory - Any 2KB address range	Card must respond to locations 0h - Fh and 400h - 7FFh within the 2KB range	

In addition to mapping the registers, an interrupt request line must also be supported for I/O addressing. Normally IRQ 14 is used by ATA drives. When configured for memory-mapped registers, the socket interface does not define an interrupt line, therefore software polling must be used.

Supporting Two Drives

It is possible for two ATA drives to be simultaneously installed into PCMCIA sockets of the same HBA. When accessing these drives, some method must be used to individually select these drives as either drive 0 or drive 1. This is accomplished in a standard ATA environment via the daisy-chained cable with the cable-select signal or by jumpers (switches) on the drive. In the PCMCIA environment, the Socket and Copy Register, defined as one of the configuration registers, can be used to identify two ATA PC cards mapped to the same address space. The copy number programmed into the Socket and Copy Registers is used by the HBA to differentiate between drive 0 from drive 1.

The ATA Card's CIS

When an ATA card is installed, the normal process of calling client drivers that have registered with card services occurs. These client drivers attempt to identify the card installed to determine if it should be configured by them. ATA client drivers typically identify their card by interpreting one or more of the following CIS tuples:

- The JEDEC ID tuple.
- The Manufacturers ID tuple.
- The Function ID and Disk Device Function Extension tuples.

Once a PC Card has been detected as an ATA disk, the CIS can be further processed to determine the configuration options supported by the card.

The PC Card ATA specification defines Function Identification Extension tuples that are used to identify the disk as an ATA interface and to specify features supported by the ATA card. The Interface Function Extension tuple must immediately follow the Function Identification tuple that identifies the card as a disk device.

Disk Device Function Extensions

This tuple specifies additional information for disk devices. Two function extension types are currently defined. As shown in table 16-2, the first disk function extension tuple (type 01h) defines the type of interface used by the disk. An interface type of 01h indicates an ATA drive interface.

Table 16-2. Disk Function Extension Tuple Format (Type 1)

Offset	Disk Function Extension Tuple Format	
0	TPL_CODE	CISTPL_FUNCE (22H)
1	TPL_LINK	Link to next tuple
2	TPL_TYPE	Interface type extension (01h)
3	TPLFE_DATA	Interface type code (01h = ATA Interface)

A second Disk Function Extension defines additional ATA Card features as shown in table 16-3.

Table 16-3. PC Card ATA Function Extension Tuple

Offset	CIS	Tuple	Comments	Bit Fields						
00h	22h	cistpl_funce	ATA Function Extension tuple	Tuple Code						
02h	03h	link	This tuple has 3 info bytes	Link Length						
04h	02h	tplfe_type	Basic PC Card Extension tuple	PC Card ATA Basic Features						
06h	xxh	tplfe_data	PC Card ATA Features Byte 1	R	R	R	R	U	S	V
08h	xxh	tplfe_data	PC Card ATA Features Byte 2	R	I	E	N	P		

The bit fields illustrated in table 16-3 are defined in table 16-4 for normal operation and table 16-5 for low power modes.

Table 16-4. Bit Definition for Normal Operation

Name	Description	Values
V	Vpp Power	0 Not Required 1 Required for Media Modification Accesses 2 Required for all Media Accesses 3 Required Continuously
S	Silicon	0 Rotating Device 1 Silicon Device
U	Unique Drive Identifier	0 Identify Drive Model/Serial Number may not be unique 1 Identify Drive Model/Serial Number is guaranteed unique
R	Reserved	This field is reserved for future standardization. Must be 0.

Table 16-5. Bit Definition for Low Power Operation

P	Low Power Modes (Idle, Standby, Sleep)	Bit 3: 0 Low Power Mode Use Required to Minimize Power Bit 3: 1 Drive Automatically Minimizes Power. No need for host to actively power manage. Bit 2: 0 Idle Mode Not Supported Bit 2: 1 Idle Mode Supported Bit 1: 0 Standby Mode Not Supported Bit 1: 1 Standby Mode Supported Bit 0: 0 Sleep Mode Not Supported Bit 0: 1 Sleep Mode Supported
N	3F7/377 Register Inhibit Available	0 = All Primary and Secondary I/O Addressing Modes include ports 3F7 or 377. 1 = Some Primary or Secondary I/O Addressing Modes exclude 3F7 and/or 377 for floppy interference avoidance.
E	Index Emulated	0 = Index Bit is Not Emulated 1 = Index Bit is Supported or Emulated
I	IOIS16# on Twin Card	0 = IOIS16# use is Unspecified on Twin-Card Configurations 1 = IOIS16# is asserted only for Data Register on Twin-Card Configurations
R	Reserved	This field is reserved for future standardization. Must be 0.

IPL from a PCMCIA ATA Drive

To load the operating system from a PCMCIA ATA drive, the drive must be configured during main system initialization, commonly referred to as POST (power-on self test). The initialization byte within the Function Identification table specifies if a PC Card should be configured during POST.

Since in many systems PC Cards are not installed until the operating system loads, the system designer must provide PCMCIA initialization software. This software must read the CIS of all cards installed in sockets to determine if they should be configured before the operating system loads. Many of the vendors that supply socket services have a solution (i.e. ROM-based PCMCIA initialization code) that permits PC ATA cards and others requiring early configuration to be initialized during POST.

Chapter 16: An ATA PC Card Example

An Example ATA Card CIS

Figure 16-2 illustrates a memory map of the attribute memory address space used by a sample ATA card that implements rotating media. This example CIS supports all the addressing modes specified in table 16-1. Appendix D contains a detailed listing of this CIS.

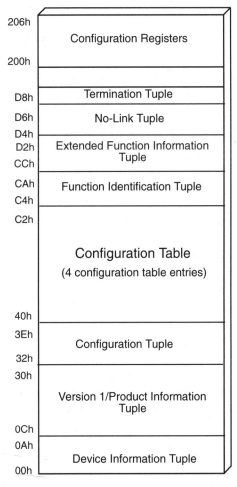

Figure 16-2. Sample ATA CIS and Configuration Register Map

Device Information Tuple

Since the ATA card contains a memory-mapped options for it registers, the Device Information tuple contains a valid memory device entry. The information described in this tuple includes:

- Memory type (specified as *function specific* memory)
- Extended memory speed defined (400ns)
- Memory size (2KB)

Level 1 Version / Product Information Tuple

This tuple contains the PCMCIA compliance level of the CIS (level 1 version) and ASCII characters describing the product. The data area within the ATA level 1 version/production information tuple consists specifically of:

- Major version 4 (indicates 2.x compliant CIS)
- Minor version 1 (indicates 2.x compliant CIS)
- ASCII string indicating manufacturer
- ASCII string indicating model information

The ASCII character strings contained within the product information portion of the tuple are left for the manufacturer to define. The manufacturer name and card description is sometimes read and displayed by PCMCIA utilities when a card is configured. This tuple is also used by client device drivers that are designed to identify a specific card.

Configuration Tuple

The Configuration tuple identifies the type of the configuration register(s) used by the PC Card, along with their location within attribute memory space. Data entries within the Configuration tuple contain the following:

- Size of address fields — this entry defines the number of bytes used by this tuple to identify the location of the configuration registers. Since these registers can be located anywhere within attribute memory address space (0 - 64MB), the number of bytes needed to define their location depends on where they reside in the address space. In this example, the registers are mapped to location 200h, therefore only two bytes are needed to specify their location.

- Size of configuration register mask field — specifies the number and mix of configuration registers implemented by the PC Card. A bit map of the configuration register identifies how many registers are implemented. PCMCIA currently defines four configuration registers, but provides expandability up to 32 configuration registers (requiring four 8-bit mask registers). This example implementation uses all four registers, therefore a signal mask register is implemented.

- Index number of the last entry in the configuration table. Since this example has four configuration entries, the index number of entry four is specified.

- Starting (base) address of the configuration registers — In this example, a two byte field identifies the location of the configuration registers in attribute memory (location 200h).

- Configuration register mask — Specifies that configuration registers zero (Configuration Option Register), one (Status Register) two (Pin Replacement Register) and three (Socket and Copy Register) are implemented.

Configuration Table

The configuration table contains the configuration option supported by the ATA card. This card in this particular example contains four entries within the configuration table, each defining a different combination of system resources required to support its functions. This card supports all four configuration options defined by the PCMCIA and ATA standards as listed in table 16-1.

Function Identification Tuple

The Function Identification tuple determines the type of functional device that is employed by the PC Card. This tuple defines the following items:

- Function type code — consists of a code representing the type of device employed by the PC Card. The function type associated with the ATA card is fixed disk.

- Initialization byte — specifies whether this device should be configured during system initialization (also called Power-On Self Test or POST) and whether the card has a ROM containing configuration software. Since the ATA drive may need to load the operating system, the POST bit is set. This indicates that the system should configure this card during POST. Refer to the section entitled, "IPL from a PCMCIA ATA Drive", discussed earlier in this chapter.

Function Extension Tuples

Two Function Extension tuples are defined by PCMCIA for ATA drives. This sample CIS includes only the type 1 disk function extension that identifies the fixed disk interface type as ATA.

No-Link Tuple

This No-Link tuple indicates that when the Termination tuple is reached that no more tuples exist within the string.

Termination Tuple

The termination tuple consists only of the tuple code FFh. In this example, when processing software encounters the checksum tuple, it terminates tuple processing since the No-Link tuple was previously encountered in this tuple string.

Configuration Registers

The ATA card in this example implements all four configuration registers defined by the PCMCIA standard. These registers include the Configuration Option Register, Status Register, Pin Replacement Register and Socket and Copy Register.

Chapter 17

The Previous Chapter

The previous chapter described an example PC Card ATA drive implementation, including a functional block diagram, a sample CIS, and configuration registers implemented by the card.

This Chapter

This chapter discusses the multiple function PC Card strategy and the mechanisms for achieving it. It also includes a functional block diagram of a multiple function PC Card, a sample multi-function CIS, related configuration registers, and multi-function interrupt handling.

The Next Chapter

The next chapter provides an overview of the PCMCIA software environment and the configuration process.

Overview

Since most systems implement a limited number of PC Card sockets (usually one or two), it is advantageous to implement cards containing multiple functions. However, prior to release of the PC Card standard PCMCIA did not offer full support for multiple function PC Cards. Only one CIS structure and only one set of configuration registers were specified for a PC Card. This meant that each function had to somehow share the single CIS and configuration registers. Several multiple function cards have been designed, but these implementations are typically vendor-specific/proprietary solutions and require vendor-specific client drivers that have been designed with knowledge of the implementation.

The PC Card standard now incorporates a multiple function card strategy that specifies how multiple functions must be implemented. This permits software solutions that are aware of the multiple function implementation to recognize and configure multiple function PC Cards. An important part of this implementation is the definition of a separate CIS and configuration registers for each function implemented within the PC Card. This chapter discusses the multiple function PC Card strategy and the mechanisms for achieving it.

An Example Multiple Function PC Card

Figure 17-1 illustrates a functional block diagram associated with a multiple function PC Card. Each function has its own CIS mapped into the PC Card's attribute memory address space, along with its own set of configuration registers. Note in this PC Card example that both functions require use of interrupts. Since a PC Card memory or I/O socket interface defines only one IREQ# pin, it is necessary to share the IREQ# pin between functions. The interrupt requests from the functions are labeled IREQ0# and IREQ1# respectively, which are inputs to the interrupt routing logic illustrated in figure 17-1. The interrupt routing logic also includes inputs named INTR0 and INTR1 from the configuration registers. These inputs represent the state of the INTR bit in the configuration status register. When the INTR bit is cleared, the interrupt routing logic knows that the corresponding interrupt request has been serviced, and that it is free to generate another IREQ# to the HBA. Interrupt sharing is discussed in the section entitled, "Shared Interrupt Handling" later in this chapter.

An Example CIS

Each function within a multiple function PC Card must have its own CIS. However, some information specified within a CIS is common to the PC Card itself (i.e. the information applies to all functions implemented by the PC Card). For this reason multiple function PC Cards contain a global CIS along with separate CISs for each function implemented. Since each function has its own CIS, it can specify the location of the configuration registers needed to support its function. Figure 17-2 illustrates a multi-function CIS structure that includes two functions.

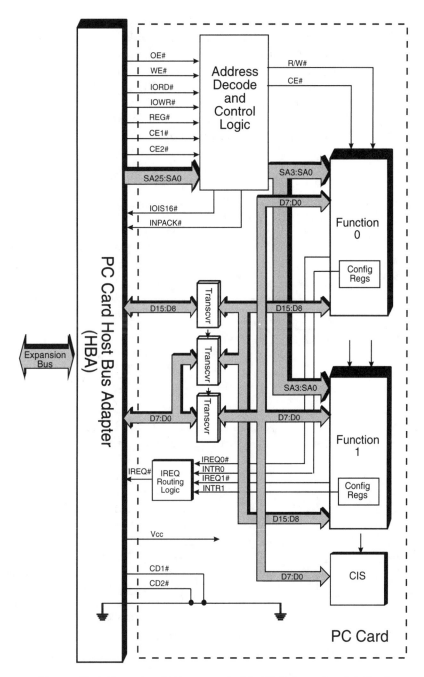

Figure 17-1. Functional Diagram of a Multiple Function PC Card

Every multiple function PC Card that is compliant with the standard must include a primary CIS that contains a LongLink_MFC tuple. This tuple specifies the location within attribute memory of the function-specific CISs that are required for each function implemented within the PC Card. Each function-specific CIS must begin with a LINKTARGET tuple to verify the start of the CIS. The standard specifies the tuples that must be included within the primary CIS, which ones are optional, and their exact order within the CIS. Table 17-1 lists these tuples in the required order.

Table 17-1. Tuples Defined for the Primary CIS (Listed in the Order)

Tuple Name	Required/Optional	Description
CISTPL_DEVICE	Required	Specifies whether memory is implemented within PC Card's common memory address space. If common memory is not used, the type code must be NULL.
CISTPL_MANFID	Optional	Only one manufacturer's ID tuple can be implemented.
CISTPL_VERS_1	Optional	May be used by enabling software to identify the PC Card.
CISTPL_LONGLINK_MFC	Required	Specifies the number of functions (i.e. the number of configuration register sets) within the PC Card, and the starting address of each function-specific CIS within attribute memory space.

The standard also specifies the order and combination of tuples required for each secondary CIS. These tuples are listed in table 17-2.

Table 17-2. Tuples Defined for each Secondary CIS (Listed in the Order)

Tuple Name	Required/Optional	Description
CISTPL_LINKTARGET	Required	Used to validate the beginning of a function-specific CIS.
CISTPL_FUNCID	Required	Must be used to identify the function.
CISTPL_FUNCE	Optional	Some functions have extensions that specify additional information about the function.
CISTPL_CONFIG	Required	Describes presence and location of Function Configuration Registers for this function.
CISTPL_ENTRY	Required	Specifies the configuration requirements of this function.

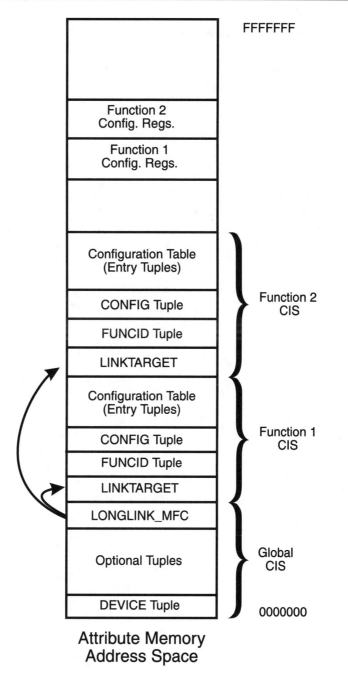

Figure 17-2. An Example CIS Structure Supporting Two Functions.

Configuration Registers

Each function contains its own set of configuration registers and may include the registers illustrated in table 17-3. The exact set of registers employed by each function depends on the requirements of the particular function being implemented. Each function that uses the I/O interface must include the Configuration Option Register, the I/O Base and typically the I/O Limit registers (the I/O Size register may be eliminated as discussed below in the section entitled "I/O Limit Register"), all other registers are optional.

Once the PC Card's enable has correctly identified the functions within the card, it must configure the HBA and PC Card. Configuring the PC Card means writing the appropriate values into the configuration registers that have been implemented. Refer to the chapter entitled "The Configuration Registers" for a detailed explanation of each register.

Table 17-3. The Configuration Registers Defined by the PC Card Standard

Offset	7	6	5	4	3	2	1	0
0	**Configuration Option Register**							
	SRESET	LevlREQ	Function Configuration Index					
2	**Configuration and Status Register**							
	Changed	SigChg	IOIS8	RFU	Audio	PwrDwn	Intr	IntrAck
4	**Pin Replacement Register**							
	CBVD1	CBVD2	CREADY	CWProt	RBVD1	RBVD2	RREADY	RWProt
6	**Socket and Copy Register**							
	RFU	Copy Number			Socket Number			
8	**Extended Status Register**							
	Event3	Event2	Event1	Req Attn	Enable3	Enable2	Enable1	Req Attn Enable
10	**I/O Base 0**							
12	**I/O Base 1**							
14	**I/O Base 2**							
16	**I/O Base 3**							
18	**I/O Limit**							

Chapter 17: A Multiple Function PC Card Example

Configuration Option Register

The configuration option register (COR) has a specific definition (different from single function PC Cards) when employed within multiple function PC Cards. Specifically, the configuration index field is different from the single function implementation. Recall that in a single function PC Card the configuration index field can be defined in any fashion that the single function card designer chooses, which specifies a given configuration for the card (i.e. a value corresponding to the index number of the configuration table entry that specifies the configuration chosen by the enabler). However, the multi-function PC Card must implement the configuration index field as specifically defined in table 17-4.

Note that the definition of the SRESET and LevlReq bits are the same as for single function cards. Each bit is defined in table 17-4.

Table 17-4. Configuration Option Register format and Definition

7	6	5	4	3	2	1	0
SRESET	LevlReq	Configuration Index					

SRESET	**Software Reset**. Setting this bit to one (1) places the card in the reset state. This is equivalent to assertion of the RESET signal except that this bit is not cleared. Returning this bit to zero (0), leaves the card in the same state that follows a hardware reset. This bit is set to zero by power up and hardware reset.
LevlReq	**Level Mode IREQ#**. Level Mode Interrupts are selected when this bit is one (1). Pulse Mode Interrupts are selected when bit is zero.
Conf Index	**Multi-function Card Index definition.** The PC Card standard specifically defines use of each bit within the configuration index. **Bit 0** — Enables/disables this function. 1=enabled; 0=disabled **Bit 1** — Specifies the number of I/O addresses used. 1=I/O function uses the number of address lines specified by the base and limit registers; 0=all host I/O address are passed to the function. (This bit is valid only when function is enable via bit 0.) **Bit 2** — Enables IREQ# routing. 1=the function will deliver interrupts to the PC Card's IREQ# line; 0=interrupts disabled for this function. (This bit is valid only when function is enabled.) **Bits 3-5** — vendor specific

Card Configuration and Status Register

Portions of the Card Configuration and Status Register (CSR) have also been redefined to support interrupt sharing on multi-function PC Cards. A new bit named IntrAck (interrupt acknowledge) specifies how the Intr bit is implemented. Refer to table 17-5

- Single function PC Cards with IntrAck reset (0) — the Intr bit remains set until the interrupt service routine is executed, at which time the Intr bit is reset.
- Multiple function PC Cards with INTRack set (1) — the Intr bit remains set even though the interrupt service routine has already serviced the interrupt request. Normally, the interrupt service routine clears an interrupt pending bit within a function specific register, causing the Intr within the CSR also to be cleared. However, to support interrupt sharing the Intr bit is not cleared until card services is ready to handle the next interrupt request. When cleared by card services, other interrupt requests that are pending can now be generated via the PC Card's IREQ# pin.

Table 17-5. Card Configuration and Status Register and Definition

7	6	5	4	3	2	1	0
Chng	SigChg	IOis8	Resrv (0)	Audio	PwrDn	Intr	IntrAck

Chng	**Status Change Detected**. This bit indicates that one or more of the Pin Replacement Register bits (CBVD1, CBVD2, CRDY, or CWProt) is set to one, normally causing the STSCHG# signal to be asserted. However, if the SigChg bit (see below) is 1 and the card is configured for an I/O interface, the STSCHG# pin is asserted when this bit is set.
SigChg	**Signal Change Enable/Disable**. This bit is set and reset by the host to enable and disable a status-change signal from the status register. When this bit is set and the card is configured for the I/O interface, the Chng bit controls pin 63 (STSCHG#). If no status change signal is desired, this bit should be set to zero and the STSCHG# signal will be held deasserted when the card is configured for I/O.
IOis8	**I/O Cycles Occur Only as 8-bit Transfers**. When the host can provide I/O cycles only using the D7:D0 data path, the PCMCIA software will set this bit to a 1. The card is guaranteed that accesses to 16-bit registers will occur as two byte accesses rather than a single 16-bit access. This information is useful when 16-bit and 8-bit registers overlap.
Resrv	Reserved bits must be 0.

Table 17-5. Card Configuration and Status Register and Definition (Continued)

7	6	5	4	3	2	1	0
Chng	SigChg	IOis8	Resrv (0)	Audio	PwrDn	Intr	IntrAck

Audio	**Audio Enable.** This bit enables audio information to be sent to the HBA via the speaker pin when configured for an I/O interface.
PwrDn	**Power Down.** This bit is set to one to request that the card enter a power-down state. PCMCIA software must not place the card into a power-down state while the card's READY pin is in the low (Busy) state.
Intr	**Interrupt Request Pending.** This bit represents the internal state of the interrupt request. This value is available whether or not interrupts have been configured. How the Intr bit is cleared is dependent of how the IntrAck bit is configured. **IntrAck=0** — Intr reflects the function's interrupt request status. If the interrupt is cleared within the function, then Intr is reset by the function. **IntrAck=1** — Intr remains set even though the interrupt condition has been cleared. It is reset by system software to indicate it is ready to receive another interrupt (implemented to support interrupt sharing).
IntrAck	**Interrupt Acknowledge.** This bit determines the response of the Intr bit. The functionality associated with the IntrAck bit permits two or more functions to share the PC Card's IREQ# pin. **IntrAck=0** — when IntrAck is reset Intr functions as described above to support a single interrupt implementation. **IntrAck=1** — This causes the Intr bit to remain set even though the interrupt service routine has already serviced the interrupt. The Intr bit is not cleared until Card Services is ready to handle the next interrupt request. When the Intr bit is cleared, the PC Card generates another interrupt request (if another interrupt request is pending from another function).

I/O Base Registers

The PC Card standard requires use of the I/O base registers by multiple function cards, and they can also be used by single function cards. These registers define the base I/O address at which the function's I/O registers will be mapped into the host processor's address space. The number of registers used depends on the address space supported by the host processor. Since Intel compatible x86 processors have 64KB of address space only the first two registers are needed to specify a base address anywhere within the entire 64KB space.

Note that in a typical single function PC Card the I/O address range is specified by the configuration index value within the configuration option register. This value identifies the configuration table entry that specifies the I/O address range that the PC Card has been configured to use.

I/O Limit Register

This register corresponds to the I/O base registers and specifies the maximum number of I/O addresses that can be mapped beginning at the base address. This register is bit mapped such that the most significant bit set within the register determines the number of address lines used to decode the address and therefore the maximum block of address space supported. The most significant bit and all bits of lesser significance must be set within the register. This results in the possible number of address lines as listed in table 17-6. Note that the largest block of I/O address space that can be defined is 256 bytes.

This register is optional and need not be implemented for each function if all functions within the PC Card use the same number of I/O address lines.

Table 17-6. Address Limit Associated with Function Base Address Register

Bit Position								Maximum
7	6	5	4	3	2	1	0	Number of
# of Address Lines Defined by Bit position								Address
8	7	6	5	4	3	2	1	Locations
0	0	0	0	0	0	0	0	Not defined
0	0	0	0	0	0	0	1	2
0	0	0	0	0	0	1	1	4
0	0	0	0	0	1	1	1	8
0	0	0	0	1	1	1	1	16
0	0	0	1	1	1	1	1	32
0	0	1	1	1	1	1	1	64
0	1	1	1	1	1	1	1	128
1	1	1	1	1	1	1	1	256

Chapter 17: A Multiple Function PC Card Example

Shared Interrupt Handling

The PC Card standard defines an interrupt sharing mechanism that allows multiple I/O functions to share the PC Card's single IREQ# pin. This mechanism requires specific hardware and software support beyond that required for single function PC Cards. The changes required are:

- Multiple Function PC Card — interrupt sharing logic required.
- HBA — no changes required.
- Socket Services — no changes required.
- Card Services — provides ISR registration, must detect IRQ, determine which PC Card function generated the interrupt, and route the request to the interrupting function's enabler.
- PC Card Enabler — must support sharing protocol.

Review of Single Function Interrupt Handling

The following discussion reviews the interrupt handling procedures typically employed in single function PC Card implementations. This discussion is based on an x86-based system operating in real mode.

IRQ Initialization

The PC Card's enabler, after having determined the configuration requirements of the PC Card, requests a specific IRQ line from card services by making the RequestIRQ function call. Card services then verifies that the IRQ line is available by successfully completing the function call. The enabler now knows that it has acquired the IRQ that it wanted and must "hook" the interrupt (i.e. place the starting address of its interrupt service routine into the interrupt table entry that corresponds to the IRQ line that it has been assigned) so that interrupt requests are directed to its interrupt service routine (ISR).

Next, the enabler requests that card services configure the HBA so that it steers the PC Card's IREQ# line to the specified IRQ line on the expansion bus (using the RequestConfiguration function call). Card services in turn makes the appropriate calls to socket services, directing it to load the appropriate registers within the HBA; thereby, setting it up to steer the PC Card's interrupt requests over the specified IRQ line.

Handling the Interrupt Request

A summary of the events that take place when a PC Card generates an IREQ# are detailed in the following paragraphs.

When a PC Card generates an interrupt request, it sets its interrupt pending bit in the CSR register and asserts the IREQ# line. The HBA steers the PC Card's IREQ# to the selected IRQ line and on to the interrupt controller. The interrupt controller responds by asserting the processor's interrupt request input (INTR). This causes the processor to cease normal program execution and to interrogate the interrupt controller to find out which interrupt has occurred. The interrupt controller responds by sending the interrupt table entry number corresponding to the IRQ line that generated the interrupt request. The processor receives the entry number (aka vector) and performs a memory read to get the starting address of the interrupt service routine from the interrupt table.

The processor temporarily stores the ISRs starting address in a special register (not named) and saves the current status of the program that was being executed when the interrupt occurred (i.e. pushes the flags, CS, and IP registers to the stack). This is done so the processor can return to the original program after the interrupt has been serviced. Once the processor saves its place, it then moves the ISRs starting address into the CS and IP registers, causing it to begin fetching and executing instructions from the PC Card's interrupt service routine.

The ISR reads the Configuration Status Register (CSR) to verify that an interrupt request is pending (i.e. the Intr bit is set). If the Intr bit is set, the ISR recognizes that an interrupt is pending and clears the Intr bit since the interrupt is now being serviced.

After clearing the interrupt within the PC Card, the ISR continues execution. Before the ISR completes it must also clear the interrupt at the interrupt controller to prevent the interrupt from being serviced again (i.e. the interrupt controller will send the same vector to the processor, causing the same ISR to be executed again). The interrupt is cleared by issuing an End Of Interrupt (EOI) command to the interrupt controller. After the EOI command has been issued and the interrupt has been serviced, the ISR executes an Interrupt Return instruction (IRET). The IRET causes the processor to restore the flags, CS, and IP registers previously saved, returning it to normal program flow.

Note: for a more in-depth discussion of x86 interrupt handling refer to the MindShare book entitled *ISA System Architecture*, published by Addison-Wesley.

Multiple Function Interrupt Handling

Each function within a multiple function PC Card has its own enabler that includes an interrupt service routine designed specifically for that function. The following sections detail the interrupt handling procedures for multi-function PC Cards.

IRQ Initialization

Multiple function IRQ initialization must be handled differently than single PC Card initialization. When a given enabler detects that its function is implemented within a multiple function PC Card it reads the function specific CIS, determines the configuration requirements of its function and initiates the configuration of the HBA and PC Card. Since a PC Card has a single IREQ# pin, all functions within the PC Card must share the same interrupt line.

Interrupt sharing is managed by card services. The interrupt sharing mechanism requires that the ISR for each function be registered with card services. The following describes the actions that would typically be taken by each function enabler during IRQ initialization.

Function Zero

When an enabler detects the presence of its function within a multi-function PC Card and determines that an interrupt is required, it must request an interrupt from card services. The multiple function enabler passes the starting address of its ISR to card services when it makes the RequestIRQ function call. It also identifies the location of its function by passing card services the logical socket number and logical function number (zero in this example) for its function.

Card services then provides a first level interrupt handler (FLIH) by hooking the interrupt table entry corresponding to the interrupt requested by the enabler. Note that multiple function enablers register their ISR with card services and do not directly hook the interrupt. When the interrupt is generated card services FLIH will be executed.

Function One

When function one's enabler detects its function within the multiple function PC Card, it must also request an interrupt (via the RequestIO service) from card services. When making the service call, the enabler passes the starting address of its interrupt service routine to card services and specifies the logical socket and function number (one in this example) of the PC Card. After the HBA and PC Card are configured, an interrupt generated by function one will cause the FLIH within card services to execute.

Handling the Interrupt Request

A summary of the events that take place when a multiple function PC Card generates an IREQ# are detailed in the following paragraphs. The example is based on an ISA platform. Refer to Figure 17-3.

When a single function within a multiple function PC Card generates an interrupt request it sets the Intr bit in its CSR register and signals the PC Card's interrupt routing logic. The routing logic in turn asserts the PC Card's IREQ# line. The HBA steers the IREQ# signal to the selected IRQ line and on to the interrupt controller. The interrupt controller responds by asserting the processor's interrupt request input. This causes the processor to cease normal program execution and to interrogate the interrupt controller to find out which interrupt has occurred. The interrupt controller responds by sending the processor an 8-bit interrupt table entry number corresponding to the IRQ line that generated the interrupt request. The processor receives the entry number (a.k.a. the vector) and performs a memory read to get the starting address of the card services FLIH from the interrupt table.

The processor temporarily stores the FLIH's starting address in a special register (not named) and saves the current status of the program that was being executed when the interrupt occurred (i.e. pushes the flags, CS, and IP registers to the stack). This is done so the processor can return to the original program after the interrupt has been serviced. Once the processor saves its place, it then moves the FLIH's starting address into the CS and IP registers, causing the processor to begin fetching and executing instructions from card services FLIH.

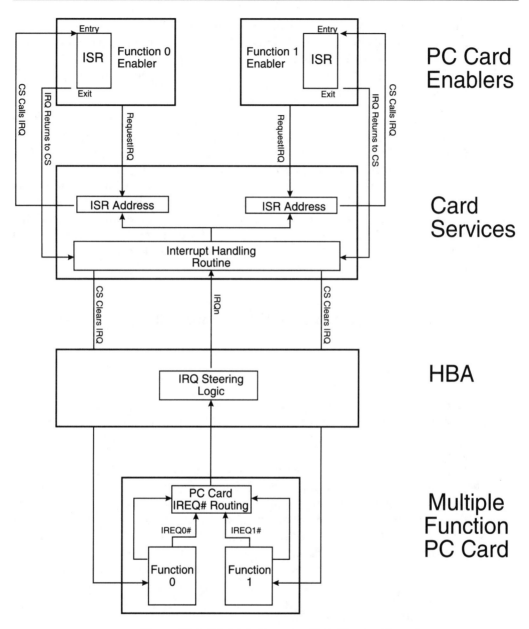

Figure 17-3. Multiple Function IRQ Sharing Procedure.

The FLIH reads the function Configuration Status Registers (CSRs) to determine which function currently has an interrupt request pending (i.e. the function whose Intr bit is set). If the Intr bit is set for one of the functions, the FLIH calls the ISR for that function, using the starting address that the enable passed to card services when the RequestIRQ function was performed.

The function's ISR does not clear the interrupt at the function's CSR, nor at the interrupt controller as single function ISRs do. When the ISR completes execution, it returns to the FLIH. Before the FLIH completes, it issues an EOI command to the interrupt controller, preventing it from servicing the same interrupt again. The FLIH also clears the Intr bit within the CSR, indicating that card services is ready to handle another interrupt request. This prompts the interrupt routing logic to issue another IREQ#, if another function within the card has signaled that it has an interrupt request pending. After the EOI command has been issued, the FLIH executes the IRET instruction, returning the processor to normal program flow.

Applications Unaware of Multiple Function Protocol

The Problem

Generic enablers for some functions (e.g. modems) request specific resources that common application program expect the function to use (e.g. many communications programs expect the modem to use the convention I/O address space and IRQ lines associated with COM1 or COM2). If two or more functions within a single PC Card require specific IRQ lines, then the interrupt sharing mechanism will not work. However, the PC Card Standard permits one of the functions within a multiple function card to request a specific IRQ that it requires to maintain compatibility with application programs. The enabler for functions that require a specific IRQ does not participate in the interrupt sharing protocol. Note however, that all other functions within the multiple function PC Card must support the interrupt sharing protocol.

An Example Solution

As an example, a generic modem enabler, being unaware that multiple function support exists, will not register its ISR with card services. Therefore, when the enabler calls the RequestIRQ function the ISR address field will be zero. (Note that card services permits only one enabler per socket to specify an ISR address field of zero.) Card services assigns the specific IRQn to the modem enabler to satisfy its configuration. The modem enabler then "hooks" the interrupt (places the starting address of its ISR into the interrupt table entry corresponding to the IRQn line that it has been assigned). Next, card services "hooks" the same interrupt by reading and saving the starting address of the modem's ISR and replacing it with the starting address of the FLIH.

Enablers for other functions within the PC Card must register their ISRs with card services. When any of the functions within a PC Card generate an interrupt request, the FLIH will be executed first (because the processor will obtain the starting address of the FLIH when it obtains the starting address of the ISR in the interrupt table). The FLIH checks the interrupt pending bits within each function to detect which has an interrupt pending.

If the modem has an interrupt pending, the FLIH jumps to the entry point of the modem's ISR (recall that card services previously read and saved the starting address of the modem's ISR when it installed the FLIH in the interrupt table). The modem's ISR executes normally by clearing the PC Card's interrupt request (for level interrupts) and performing the EOI command, and executing IRET.

Changes to Card Services Functions

To support multiple function PC Cards, many of the card services functions have been modified. For example, when accessing a single function PC Card, the function could be identified by merely specifying the logical socket number in which the PC Card resided. However, when a PC Card contains more than one function each function within the PC Card is identified by an additional logical function number. Table 17-7 lists of services that have added support for multiple function implementations.

Table 17-7. Card Services Modified for Multiple Function Support

Service Name	Code
AccessConfigurationRegister	36h
GetCardServicesInfo	0Bh
GetConfigurationInfo	04h
GetEventMask	2Eh
GetFirstClient	0Eh
GetFirstTuple	07h
GetNextClient	2Ah
GetNextTuple	0Ah
GetStatus	0Ch
GetTupleData	0Dh
ModifyConfiguration	27h
RegisterMTD	1Ah
ReleaseConfiguration	1Eh
ReleaseExclusive	2Dh
ReleaseIO	1Bh
ReleaseIRQ	1Ch
ReleaseSocketMask	2Fh
RequestConfiguration	30h
RequestExclusive	2Ch
RequestIO	1Fh
RequestIRQ	20h
RequestSocketMask	22h
ResetFunction	11h
SetEventMask	31h

Part Four

PCMCIA Software

Chapter 18

The Previous Chapter

The previous chapter discussed the multiple function PC Card strategy and the mechanisms for achieving it. It also included a functional block diagram of a multiple function PC Card, a sample multi-function CIS, related configuration registers, and multi-function interrupt handling.

This Chapter

This chapter provides an overview of the PCMCIA software environment and the configuration process. The primary role and interaction between each piece of software is established. This chapter also introduces the common software solutions provided along with the most popular suppliers.

The Next Chapter

The next chapter discusses the role of socket services and the initialization process. It also defines each function and details the calling interface.

Overview of the Configuration Process

Each PC Card must have an enabler that recognizes it, reads the CIS to determine the PC Card's resource requirements, programs the host bus adapter (HBA) and configures the card. Figure 18-1 illustrates the most common form of PC Card enabler known as the client driver. Client drivers interface directly to Card Services, which services requests from the client drivers. Client drivers call a variety of services within card services to assist it in configuring and controller accesses to its PC Card. Using card services greatly simplifies the job of enabling the PC Card, monitoring status change events, and controlling access to the card.

PCMCIA System Architecture

As illustrated in figure 18-1, card services interfaces directly to socket services to gain access to the HBA and PC Card. Socket services is designed with specific knowledge of the HBA hardware design and contains software routines that card services can call to gain access to the registers within the HBA without having to know the low-level details of the hardware interface.

Configuring a PC Card may take place when the system powers up (if the PC Card is already installed in a socket), or when a PC Card is inserted into a socket (after the system is powered up and fully operational). In either case, the PC Card must be detected by an enabler and configured. Without an enabler, a PC Card would never be recognized by the system. Once a PC Card is configured, it then responds like any other device residing on the host bus.

This configuration processor involves interaction between a client driver, card services, socket services, and the PC Card's CIS. The Role of each of these items is reviewed below.

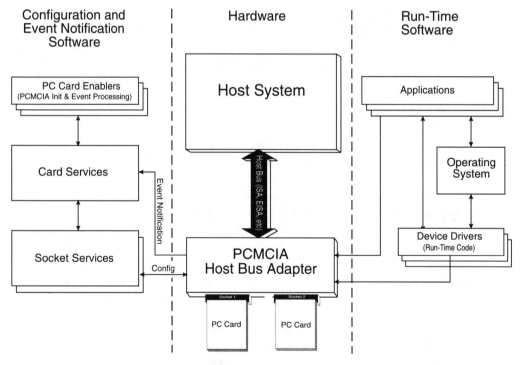

Figure 18-1. PCMCIA Software Flow

Chapter 18: The Configuration Process

The Role of the CIS

Each PC Card is required to have a Card Information Structure, or CIS to be compliant with 2.x or PC Card implementations. The CIS is a data structure that is stored in non-volatile memory, which provides a method for software to determine what kind of PC Card is installed, along with its speed, size, system resources required by the card, and other pertinent information. The CIS is mapped within the attribute memory space or alternatively can be located in common memory address space.

As illustrated in figure 18-1, the CIS is read by PC Card client drivers (via card and socket services) during card initialization to determine the configuration options supported by the card. Once the card type and resource requirements have been read from the CIS, the PC Card client driver programs the HBA and configures the PC Card, again via card and socket services. No further access is typically made to the CIS after the card has been initialized. The PC Card can now be accessed via the host expansion bus, just like any other expansion device. Note that the CIS is only accessed by programs that are PCMCIA aware. Most application programs have no knowledge that they are accessing devices implemented in PC Card packages.

The Role of the Socket Service Functions

Socket services provides a set of software routines written specifically to access the registers within a given HBA. Socket services eliminates the need for special knowledge of the HBA hardware programming interface. These routines or functions are comparable to the BIOS routines that are used in the PC environment. In practice, most client drivers seldom, if ever, directly access socket service functions, because properly designed enablers access the HBA via card services. Card services, makes calls to socket services at the HBA request.

The Role of Card Services

Card services provides a central resource available to all client drivers. Specifically, card services is a collection of service routines designed for use by programmers writing enablers for PC Cards. These services provide a software interface that permits the programmer to simplify code and helps to reduce conflicts with other client drivers and with allocating system resources for PC Cards.

A major function of card services is to provide call-back services to notify the enablers that a particular event has occurred. Each enabler must register with card services and specify which PC Card events that it wishes to be notified of. When card services detects a given event (e.g. a card has been inserted or removed) it then calls each enabler that previously registered to receive notification of card insertion or removal.

The Role of the PC Card Enabler

PC Card enablers must recognize that a PC Card has been installed and access the card's CIS to determine if it should attempt to configure the card.

Three basic types of enablers exist:

- Dedicated enablers — designed for a particular PC Card.
- Generic (Super) enablers — designed for a wide range of PC Card types.
- Point enablers — designed to configure and enable the PC Card without using card and socket services.

Note that dedicated enablers and generic enablers both interface to card services as illustrated in figure 18-1. These enablers all register with card services when they first install. The registration process permits access to card services and allows the enabler to specify the events that it wishes to be notified of. Enablers that use card services are also referred to as client drivers.

Dedicated Enablers

Dedicated enablers are typically supplied by the PC Card manufacturer to increase the probability that the card will install correctly in the absence of a generic driver. Dedicated enablers identify a specific PC Card and will typically not recognize and enabler other PC Cards of the same type. These enablers may also manage functions that are unique to a given PC Card implementation.

Chapter 18: The Configuration Process

Generic Enablers

Generic enablers are designed to handle PC Cards of a particular functional type. For example, the system manufacturer may include generic drivers for card types such as SRAM, flash ROM, Modems, and ATA drives. These enablers attempt to identify and enable cards based on a generic type without regard to the manufacturer or special features that may be incorporated into the PC Card's design.

Another class of generic enablers are the super I/O enablers. These enablers are designed to recognize and configure a wide range of I/O devices such as, modem, fax/modems, LAN controllers, etc. These enablers reduce the number of enablers that must be installed to detect the possible PC Cards that might be installed in a socket. The exact mechanism employed by these super enablers varies, but all have the same goal of enabling the most common I/O cards. Most system manufacturers supply super I/O client solutions as a part of the PCMCIA software shipped with the PC.

Point Enablers

Point enablers are dedicated enablers that bypass card and socket services. These enablers are popular in environments such as DOS where limited memory address space is available for application programs. Card and socket services take a considerable amount of memory when they install. Added to this is the space required by the enabler(s) and any TSR (terminate and stay resident programs) that might be used. As a result, too little memory is left for many application programs to run. One solution is to eliminate the PCMCIA specific software, thereby freeing up memory space that is needed to run the application programs. Point enablers are needed to configure the PC Cards that the user want to access. In the absence of card and socket services, point enablers must load the appropriate registers within the HBA to recognize and configure their PC Card.

For more information regarding enablers refer to the Chapter entitled, "PC Card Enablers."

PCMCIA Software Solutions

The entire PCMCIA software environment is typically provided by a single vendor. This software includes generic enablers, card services, a resource detection utility that builds the resource table (used by card services), and socket services. PC manufacturers license these software solutions for use in their products. PCMCIA software is available from several different vendors. The major vendor and the name of their PCMCIA software is listed in table 18-1.

Table 18-1. Major Vendors of PCMCIA Software Solutions

PCMCIA Software Vendor	Product Name
American Megatrends (AMI)	AMICARDZ
Award	CardWare
IBM	PlayAtWill (DOS & OS/2)
Microsoft	Windows95
Phoenix Technology	PCM3+
SystemSoft	CardSoft

While most PCMCIA software solutions provide the same basic functionality, many differences have existed. Some of the differences are inconsequential, such as, differences in logical drive letter assignments for various types of PC Cards, the visual and/or audible feedback provided when cards are inserted or removed, etc. However, some differences have been potentially more critical, including:

- HBAs supported
- Power management support
- Flash card support (i.e. Flash file systems and MTDs)
- Abridged versions of card services (Note that the functionality not included in card services is typically integrated directly into the enablers.)
- Resource Allocation (PC Cards mapped to different system resources)
- Generic enabler support (Types of PC Cards supported)

As the PCMCIA software has matured, the problematic differences between vendor solutions have diminished. Further, the PC Card 95 release has defined specific support for several areas that were previously the source of significant differences between vendor solutions.

Chapter 19

The Previous Chapter

The previous chapter provided an overview of the PCMCIA software environment and the configuration process. The primary role and interaction between each piece of software was established. The chapter also introduced the common software solutions provided along with the most popular suppliers.

This Chapter

This chapter discusses the role of socket services. It also describes the initialization of socket services and explains the basic purpose of the functions commonly supported in the PC environment.

The Next Chapter

The next chapter focuses on the role of card services in the PCMCIA environment. It reviews each of the functions defined by the PC Card specification that apply to 16-bit PC Cards, along with related return codes. The call back mechanism is also described and the event and call back codes are defined.

The Role of Socket Services—Making Life Easier

Before the development of socket services, a PC Card's client driver was responsible for ensuring that its card satisfied the requirements of the PC Card plug and play environment. Plug and play means that the PC Card can be automatically configured after being installed in a system, without requiring user intervention. In the PC Card environment this responsibility includes:

- Accessing registers within the HBA to open an attribute memory window, allowing access to the card's CIS.
- Interpreting the CIS to determine the configuration requirements of the card.

- Determining if the resources needed by the card are available (not already in use by other system devices).
- Loading HBA registers with the specified configuration values that permit host software to access the PC Card.
- Polling HBA registers to monitor socket status change events (e.g. card removal).
- Releasing system resources by clearing registers in the HBA when a card removal event occurs.
- Providing the ability to perform these functions regardless of the HBA design.

These requirements make it clear that developing PC Card client driver prior to the introduction of socket services required detailed knowledge of the particular HBA's hardware interface. Furthermore, HBA design changes could lead to heavy revision and update of the client driver.

As shown in figure 19-1, today's client drivers can configure a PC Card with relative ease by accessing the PCMCIA configuration software that is comprised of card and socket services. This chapter focuses on the role of socket services, which eliminates the need for client drivers to know the details of the HBA hardware.

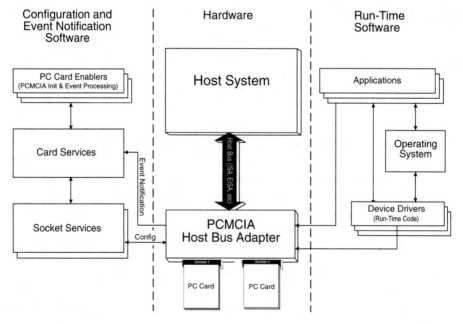

Figure 19-1. Relationship of Socket Services to the Rest of the System.

Chapter 19: Socket Services

Socket services provides a set of functions that can be called by client drivers (typically card services), eliminating the need for special knowledge of the HBA hardware programming interface. These functions can be compared to the BIOS routines that are used in the PC environment. In practice, most client drivers seldom, if ever, directly access socket service functions, because client drivers typically access the HBA via card services. Card services, makes calls to socket services at the client drivers request. In fact, card services blocks access attempts to socket services that are made by client drivers.

Installation and Initialization

Socket services can be contained in ROM, can be loaded into system memory via an installable device driver, or can be incorporated as extensions to the operating system. In the PC environment socket services are typically installed via a device driver and must be loaded into the system before card services and other client drivers (i.e. any software that requires socket services). Without socket services being present card services and PC Card client drivers will not install.

The method used to install socket services and the protocol used to call the functions is platform dependent. The PCMCIA standard currently defines the socket services function call interface only for the Intel x86 platform. Refer to the section entitled, "Socket Services Calling Convention" later in this chapter.

Socket Services Functions

As discussed in the chapter entitled, "The Host Bus Adapter", the HBA must be programmed to allow system access to the PC Card and to manage a variety of HBA functions including:

- Specifying the socket interface type (memory or I/O).
- Programming memory address windows.
- Programming I/O address windows.
- Steering each PC Card's IREQ# signal to the selected system interrupt line.
- Steering the HBA's status change interrupt to the selected system interrupt line.
- Controlling socket power switching.
- Enabling power conservation features.
- Controlling EDC generators.

Socket services controls these functions through a defined set of function calls, each related to objects managed by the adapter. Table 19-1 lists the functions according to the object-based grouping defined below:

- **Adapter Functions** — Those functions that affect all sockets that are controlled by the HBA (i.e., setting Vcc to 3.3 volts for one socket causes all other sockets to also receive 3.3 volts). Adapter functions also pertain to items such as the single status change interrupt, which reports status changes for all sockets.
- **Socket Functions** — Those functions controlled individually at the socket level (i.e., setting Vcc to 3.3 volts for a given socket affects only that socket).
- **Window Functions** — Those functions that control the memory and I/O address windows.
- **Error Detection and Correction (EDC) Functions** — Those functions used to interact with the EDC generators.

Table 19-1. Socket Services Functions

ADAPTER Functions	WINDOW Functions
AcknowledgeInterrupt	GetPage
GetAccessOffsets	GetWindow
GetAdapter	InquireWindow
GetAdapterCount	SetPage
GetSetPriorHandler	SetWindow
GetSetSSAddr	
GetSSInfo	**EDC Functions**
GetVendorInfo	GetEDC
InquireAdapter	InquireEDC
SetAdapter	PauseEDC
VendorSpecific	ReadEDC
	ResumeEDC
SOCKET Functions	SetEDC
GetSocket	StartEDC
GetStatus	StopEDC
InquireSocket	
ResetSocket	
SetSocket	

Note that three new socket service functions were added to the PC Card 95 Standard. These functions support CardBus bridge implementations and are not included in this book. For information regarding CardBus, see Mind-Share's *CardBus System Architecture* book, published by Addison-Wesley.

Socket services has also been designed to permit ease of use. Within each functional group shown in table 19-1, there is are "inquire," "get," and "set" functions, defined below:

- **Inquire functions** — used to report the capabilities of each object defined.
- **Get functions** — used to report the current parameter settings associated with the object.
- **Set functions** — used to set the parameters associated with the object.

The "get" and "set" functions for a specific item have the same basic data structure format, allowing easy modification of parameters. For example, if some parameter within the adapter must be modified, the GetAdapter function can be called to obtain the current adapter settings. This adapter setting information can be written back to the adapter registers using the SetAdapter function once the specific parameter has been changed. This technique permits easy read/modify/write operations to modify individual parameters without having to build the entire data structure that must be passed to socket services when the function is called.

Socket Services Calling Convention

The method used for calling functions depends on the specific platform. Currently, the PCMCIA specification details the programming interface or socket services binding, for Intel x86-compatible systems. The binding specifies use of software interrupt 1Ah to call socket service functions (real mode). This interrupt is typically used by the real-time clock BIOS functions. Therefore socket services shares entry 1Ah in the interrupt table with the real-time clock.

When in protected mode the method of calling socket service functions is operating system specific.

When socket services installs it hooks interrupt 1Ah. This is done by reading and saving the current value of entry 1Ah within the interrupt table (the real time clock BIOS entry pointer) and replacing it with an entry point for its own functions. Socket services functions can then be called using the INT 1Ah instruction. The function numbers are defined in table 19-2 and the general register usage is defined as follows. The exact register content defined for each function can be found in the PCMCIA specification:

Entry:	[AH]	Function number desired in hex
	[AL]	HBA number
	[BH]	Window number
	[BL]	Page or Socket (depending on function)
	[CX]	Counts
	[DX]	Attributes
	[DS]:[(E)SI]	Reserved in ROM BIOS Int 1Ah interface
	[ES]:[(E)DI]	Pointer to socket services client buffer
	[DI]	Offset in 4 KB units
Exit:	[CF]	Status (carry set = error, reset = success)
	[AH]	Success or failure return code depending on Carry Flag value.

If the value in the AH register does not match one of the socket services functions, socket services will pass the call on to the Real Time Clock function, whose entry point was saved during initialization of socket services.

Note that the last function number within socket services is for card services (function 0AFh). Card services also installs into entry 1Ah in the interrupt table and therefore will be called before socket services. Card service functions are called using the 0AFh value in the AH register, allowing definition of the call as a CS function. CS then checks the AL register to identify which CS function is being called. If, however, a socket services function is called, then the AH register contains a value other than 0AFh and CS will not pass the function to socket services. This prevents client drivers from accessing socket services directly and changing HBA settings without CS being notified. See the chapter entitled "PC Card Configuration: Card Services and Client Drivers" for additional information.

Upon exit from a socket services routine, a return (or completion) code is placed in the AH register. The state of the carry flag determines whether the socket service function incurred an error or executed successfully. Table 19-3 lists the return codes.

Table 19-2. Socket Services Function Code Listing

SS Functions Arranged Alphabetically		SS Functions Arranged Numerically	
Function	**Code**	**Code**	**Function**
ACCESS_OFFSETS	0A1h	80h	GET_ADP_CNT
ACK_INTERRUPT	9Eh	81h and 82h	Reserved
CARD_SERVICES	0AFh	83h	GET_SS_INFO
GET_ADAPTER	85h	84h	INQ_ADAPTER
GET_ADP_CNT	80h	85h	GET_ADAPTER
GET_EDC	96h	86h	SET_ADAPTER
GET_PAGE	8Ah	87h	INQ_WINDOW
GET_SOCKET	8Dh	88h	GET_WINDOW
GET_SS_INFO	83h	89h	SET_WINDOW
GET_STATUS	8Fh	8Ah	GET_PAGE
GET_VENDOR_INFO	9Dh	8Bh	SET_PAGE
GET_WINDOW	88h	8Ch	INQ_SOCKET
INQ_ADAPTER	84h	8Dh	GET_SOCKET
INQ_EDC	95h	8Eh	SET_SOCKET
INQ_SOCKET	8Ch	8Fh	GET_STATUS
INQ_WINDOW	87h	90h	RESET_SOCKET
PAUSE_EDC	99h	91h thru 94h	Reserved
PRIOR_HANDLER	9Fh	95h	INQ_EDC
READ_EDC	9Ch	96h	GET_EDC
Reserved	81h and 82h	97h	SET_EDC
Reserved	91h thru 94h	98h	START_EDC
Reserved for expansion	A2h thru ADh	99h	PAUSE_EDC
RESET_SOCKET	90h	9Ah	RESUME_EDC
RESUME_EDC	9Ah	9Bh	STOP_EDC
SET_ADAPTER	86h	9Ch	READ_EDC
SET_EDC	97h	9Dh	GET_VENDOR_INFO
SET_PAGE	8Bh	9Eh	ACK_INTERRUPT
SET_SOCKET	8Eh	9Fh	PRIOR_HANDLER
SET_WINDOW	89h	0A0h	SS_ADDR
SS_ADDR	0A0h	0A1h	ACCESS_OFFSETS
START_EDC	98h	A2h thru ADh	Reserved for expansion
STOP_EDC	9Bh	0AEh	VEND_SPECIFIC
VEND_SPECIFIC	0AEh	0AFh	CARD_SERVICES

Table 19-3. Socket Services Return Codes

Return Codes listed alphabetically		Return Codes listed numerically	
Name of Return Code	Code	Code	Name of Return Code
BAD_ADAPTER	01h	00h	Success
BAD_ATTRIBUTE	02h	01h	BAD_ADAPTER
BAD_BASE	03h	02h	BAD_ATTRIBUTE
BAD_EDC	04h	03h	BAD_BASE
BAD_IRQ	06h	04h	BAD_EDC
BAD_MODE	16h	05h	reserved
BAD_OFFSET	07h	06h	BAD_IRQ
BAD_PAGE	08h	07h	BAD_OFFSET
BAD_SERVICE	15h	08h	BAD_PAGE
BAD_SIZE	0Ah	09h	READ_FAILURE
BAD_SOCKET	0Bh	0Ah	BAD_SIZE
BAD_SPEED	17h	0Bh	BAD_SOCKET
BAD_TYPE	0Dh	0Ch	reserved
BAD_VCC	0Eh	0Dh	BAD_TYPE
BAD_VPP	0Fh	0Eh	BAD_VCC
BAD_WINDOW	11h	0Fh	BAD_VPP
BUSY	18h	10h	reserved
NO_CARD	14h	11h	BAD_WINDOW
READ_FAILURE	09h	12h	WRITE_FAILURE
reserved	05h	13h	reserved
reserved	0Ch	14h	NO_CARD
reserved	10h	15h	BAD_SERVICE
reserved	13h	16h	BAD_MODE
reserved	19h-FFh	17h	BAD_SPEED
Success	00h	18h	BUSY
WRITE_FAILURE	12h	19h-FFh	reserved

Adapter Functions

The adapter functions can be categorized into four classes:

- Functions used to identify the number of adapters within the system and to assign socket services to a specific adapter or adapters. Note that in some cases multiple adapters having different hardware interfaces may be installed in the system. This would require multiple versions of socket services be installed to handle the various adapters.
- Functions that control adapter parameters via the inquire, get and set functions.
- A function used to support status change interrupt processing.
- Low-level access and protected-mode support functions.

Verifying SS is installed (GetAdapterCount)

The Get Adapter Count (GetAdapterCount) function is used by the socket service client (typically Card Services) to determine if socket services is installed and to determine the number of HBAs in the system. This function is typically the first function called and returns the following information to the client.

- the number of adapters that are detected by socket services
- the ASCII string "SS" that verifies that socket services is installed.

Once the client detects that one or more adapters are installed, socket services must be assigned to a given adapter or adapters.

Getting Information from Socket Services (GetSSInfo)

A socket service client calls Get Socket Services Information (GetSSInfo) to determine among other things the number of adapters discovered and controlled by a given set of socket services. When making the GetSSInfo call, the client passes a logical HBA number to socket services as an input. This logical number will be used by the client when it wants to access the HBA in the future. Socket services must remember the logical HBA number and use it to identify accesses to an HBA. Socket services will assign the logical HBA number to the first HBA that it discovers. If socket services discovers more than one HBA, it will assign the next logical number to the second HBA it discovers, etc. Socket services returns the total number of adapters that it has discovered, telling the client the number of adapters this particular set of socket services controls, and therefore the range of logical adapters that it will respond to in the future.

Note that the first adapter detected by the first set of socket services installed is assigned as adapter "0". The client will continue making GetSSInfo calls until all HBAs have been located. This means that one GetSSInfo call will be make by the client for each set of socket services installed. Normally only one set of socket services will be installed.

The following information is returned by the GetSSInfo function:

- Compliance level of adapter. Returned as BCD (Binary Coded Decimal) value. (i.e. 0500h = PC Card Standard, February 1995).
- Number of adapters supported or found by this set of socket services. If socket services recognizes more than one adapter in the system, it returns the total number that it finds and therefore the number it can control.
- First adapter number supported. Note that the first socket services installed always controls adapter zero. The adapter numbers are assigned sequentially starting with zero.

The GetSSInfo function must be run once for each set of socket services installed, thereby assigning logical adapter numbers to all adapters controlled by a particular copy of socket services.

When Two or More Socket Services Are Needed (GetSetPriorHandle)

Some users may want to add more PCMCIA sockets to their system, resulting in two or more different HBA implementations. For example, consider a notebook system with two sockets. When the system is installed in a docking station, more sockets can be added via an additional HBA inserted in an expansion card slot. The additional HBA may have a different hardware interface, requiring its own set of socket services.

PCMCIA can accommodate multiple sets of socket services to support a variety of different HBA implementations. During the initialization process, a socket services client (the SS initialization routine) detects existing HBAs and identifies those that it is compatible with, using the GetAdapterCount and GetSSInfo (as discussed earlier). When installed, additional socket services will also initialize and attempt to identify HBAs that they are compatible with.

When an additional copy of socket services is installed, the client must determine which adapter numbers have already been assigned by previous copies of socket services. The new socket services initialization code can then call the GetSSInfo, to ascertain the first adapter that this new socket services will control.

When a socket services client (card services) makes a call, it specifies a target adapter number or a target socket residing within a particular adapter. The socket services copy receiving the call will be the last installed. If the target adapter or socket is not controlled by this set of socket services, it must pass the call to the next socket services in the chain. This means that some method of linking copies of socket services must be employed. The exact method used to link all copies of socket services together depends on the implementation used by a given architecture.

Some architectures may use the socket services function GetSetPriorHandle to link together multiple copies of socket services. The GetSetPriorHandle function retrieves the handle (entry point address) at which the previous socket services resides. In this way, a linked list of entry points can be maintained such that each socket services passes the call to the next until the target adapter is located. The socket services chain can also be modified (set), allowing a new socket services to supersede or replace an existing copy.

The Intel X86 architecture uses a software interrupt, 1Ah, to call socket services. When the first set of socket services installs, it first reads and saves the existing value in entry 1Ah of the interrupt table and then replaces it with its entry point. If another socket services installs, it also uses entry 1A, by reading and saving the previous pointer (belonging to the current socket services) and replacing it with its own pointer. In this way, each subsequent socket services that installs obtains the pointer to the previous socket services, creating a linked list. Calls to a particular adapter will then be passed from one socket services to the next until the target adapter is located.

Controlling HBA Parameters (InquireAdapter, GetAdapter, SetAdapter)

Before configuring the HBA, the programmer must first determine a specific HBA's capabilities using the InquireAdapter function. Once its capabilities are determined, the HBA configuration parameters can be set using the SetAdapter function. If necessary, the client can check the current adapter settings using the GetAdapter function.

InquireAdapter Function. This function requires the following input parameters be specified: the target adapter number and the location of a memory buffer. The function returns information to the processor's registers and to the specified memory buffer. Parameters returned to the processor's registers include:

- Number of sockets
- Number of address windows
- Number of EDC generators

Parameters returned in memory buffer provide additional information regarding the capabilities of the adapter. The memory buffer format is defined by the socket services specification and can be categorized into two separate parts as shown in table 19-4.

Table 19-4. Adapter Information Structure Definition

Adapter Information Structure	
Adapter Characteristics Structure	**Indicators** — If indicator bit is set, indicators for write protect, battery status, busy status and XIP (Execute-in-place) status are shared for all sockets on the adapter. If reset, indicators exist for individual sockets.
	Power Level — If power level bit is set, the adapter applies the same power level to all sockets. When a SetSocket function is used to set the power for a specific socket, that setting is reflected at all sockets. If power level bit is reset, the adapter can apply power to sockets individually in response to the SetSocket function.
	Data Bus Width — When data bus width bit is set, all adapter address windows use the same data width. If data bus width bit is reset, data width can be assigned to individual windows within the adapter.
	Status Interrupts (High Level) — Bit map of system interrupts to which status interrupts can be steered using an active high state.
	Status Interrupts (Low Level) — Bit map of system interrupts to which status interrupts can be steered using an active low state.
Power Entry Structure	**Number of Power Entries**
	Power Entries — Each entry specifies a voltage level supported and the socket pins (Vcc, Vpp1 and Vpp2) to which the voltage level applies. The voltage level is specified as a DC voltage in tenth of a volt increments. Flag bits are set to indicate the voltage is valid for the specified supply.

GetAdapter Function. The GetAdapter function returns the current status of the HBA settings. When the GetAdapter function is called, the socket services client must pass the physical adapter number to socket services. Adapter parameter states returned by this function include:

- **Powerdown state** — If the bit is set, the adapter is in power conservation state and the SetAdapter function should be used to restore full power before using the adapter. If the bit is reset, full power is applied and the adapter is fully functional.
- **Maintain state** — If this bit is set, configuration information is retained by the adapter hardware during power conservation mode. If reset, the client is responsible for maintaining adapter configuration information during power conservation.
- **Status Change Interrupt Steering** — Returns the system interrupt line, to which status change interrupts are directed.
- **Status Change Interrupt Level** — If set, the status change interrupt is active high. If reset, the interrupt is active low.
- **Status Change Interrupt Enable/Disable State** — The status change interrupt is enabled when set and disabled when reset.

SetAdapter Function. HBA parameters can be set using the SetAdapter function. The exact same parameter mapping is used for the SetAdapter function as for the GetAdapter function. This allows for easy read-modify-write operations when a specific parameter must be changed.

For example, to place the adapter into power conservation mode, the GetAdapter function can be called and the powerdown bit can be toggled. Next the SetAdapter call can be made, causing the powerdown bit to be set within the adapter.

Vendor Functions (GetVendorInfo, VendorSpecific)

The GetVendorInfo function returns information about the vendor that implemented the socket services for a particular adapter in the system. Input parameters to socket services for this call include:

- HBA number
- Type of vendor information requested — a code type of zero indicates that the programmer is requesting the vendor information as an ASCIIZ string (only code currently defined).

- Pointer to the buffer where the ASCIIZ string is to be returned. The buffer format is specified in the socket services standard.

The function returns the ASCIIZ string to the buffer specified, indicating the version number of this particular release of socket services. The vendor's first release of socket services must use a version number of 0100h (release 1.00).

The optional VendorSpecific function is left up to the vendor to implement. The adapter number is specified as an input parameter to socket services when the call is made. The functions supported and the function identification numbers are defined by the vendor to support capabilities beyond the scope of the specification.

Indirect Access to PC Card Memory (GetAccessOffsets)

Some HBAs may access memory cards via I/O registers rather than via memory-mapped address ranges. This eliminates memory address conflicts that might otherwise occur when mapping a PC Card into the system memory address space. These HBAs define a command set that is used when accessing the cards. The client driver uses the GetAccessOffsets function to locate the code that performs these commands. These memory client drivers are HBA specific.

Determining What Card Caused a Status Change Interrupt (AcknowledgeInterrupt)

When a status change event occurs at one of the HBAs sockets, an interrupt request is generated by the HBA. The socket services client (typically card services) is notified of the event via a system interrupt. When the client receives the interrupt, it has no knowledge of which socket encountered the status change event or what the specific event was. The client must determine which socket has experienced a status change event by calling the AcknowledgeInterrupt function. Once the socket (or sockets) that has experienced a status change has been determined, then the GetStatus function is called to determine which event caused the interrupt.

The AcknowledgeInterrupt function must be called once for each HBA in the system. The client supplies the HBA number to socket services when the AcknowledgeInterrupt function is called and socket services returns a bit map of the sockets within the HBA that have experienced a status change. When obtaining status information from the HBA, socket services also prepares the adapter to generate another status change interrupt when one occurs.

In the interrupt service routine, the sockets that have experienced a status change are determined using the AcknowledgeInterrupt function. After the interrupt service routine completes, the client then calls the GetStatus function, specifying the socket that experienced the status change. Most HBAs preserve the state of the status change so that the status change event that caused the interrupt can be determined using the GetStatus function. If the HBA does not preserve this state information, then socket services must.

Note that the AcknowledgeInterrupt function is called by the status change interrupt service routine. Socket services must not re-enable interrupts while processing a status change interrupt service routine. This could cause nesting of status change interrupts to itself, a situation that socket services is unprepared to manage.

Socket Functions

Socket functions deal with parameters that can be controlled on a socket-by-socket basis. These calls require that a particular socket number be specified, whereas adapter functions require an HBA number. The following sections discuss each function in the socket group.

Controlling Individual Sockets (InquireSocket, SetSocket, GetSocket)

Functions used to control a socket are similar to the adapter functions that are used to control HBA functionality. The adapter functions control parameters that apply to all sockets supported by a specific HBA, whereas the socket functions control parameters that apply individually to each of the HBA's sockets.

InquireSocket. This function requires that a target socket number be specified along with the address of a memory buffer. This function returns the following information:

- Events that can trigger a status change interrupt. These events can be a combination of the following items:

  - PC Card write-protect (WP) signal.
  - A signal (from card interlock logic) indicating the state of a card lock mechanism.
  - A signal (from the card interlock logic) indicating a request to eject a PC Card from the socket.
  - A signal indicating a request to insert a card into the socket.
  - PC Card BVD1 signal indicating that the card's battery is completely discharged.
  - PC Card BVD2 signal indicating the card's battery is weak.
  - PC Card READY signal, indicating a change in the card's ready state.
  - PC Card Detect Signals.

- Bit map of status change events that are reported via the GetStatus function. This bit map includes all the items that can generate a status change interrupt (listed above), plus other events that do not generate an interrupt but whose status is returned to the socket services client driver by the GetStatus function.

- Bit map of items for which there is a control or an indicator supported at the socket level. Indicators are items such as LED indicators that the HBA provides which shows the status of given events. These items may include:

  - Indicator for WP signal.
  - Indicator for state of card lock mechanism.
  - Control for motor to eject card from socket.
  - Control for motor to insert card into socket.
  - Control to establish a card lock.
  - Indicator for BVD1 and BVD2 state.
  - Indicator showing when card is in use.
  - Indicator for execute-in-place (XIP) application is progress.

- The Socket Information Structure is returned to a memory buffer supplied by the socket services client. The memory buffer format is defined by the socket services as shown in table 19-5.

Table 19-5. Socket Information Structure Definition

Socket Information Structure	
Socket Characteristics Structure	**Socket Interface Type**—If interface bit is set, the socket is a memory only interface. If reset, the socket interface is memory or I/O.
	PC Card Interrupts (High Level)—Bit map of system interrupts to which PC Card interrupts can be steered using an active high state.
	PC Card Interrupts (Low Level)—Bit map of system interrupts to which PC Card interrupts can be steered using an active low state.

GetSocket Function. The GetSocket function returns the current status of the HBA socket settings. When the GetSocket function is called, the socket services client must pass the adapter and socket number to socket services. The parameter's returned by this function are:

- **Status Change Mask** — Returns the current setting of the events that cause a status change interrupt from the socket.
- **Vcc Level** — Returns the current supply voltage applied to the socket on the Vcc pin.
- **Vpp Levels** — Returns the current supply voltage applied to the socket on the Vpp pins. Separate values are returned for Vpp1 and Vpp2.
- **State Change**. Returns the latched values of the status change events that have occurred at the socket.
- **Socket Controls and Indicators** — Returns a bit map of socket controls and indicators that are in use. Bits that are set indicate the control or indicator is activated.
- **IREQ Routing** — Returns the system interrupt line to which the card's IREQ# signal is directed. Optionally, an additional bit can specify whether the IREQ# signal should be inverted or not, and another optional bit can enable or disable interrupt routing.
- **Interface Type** — Returns the interface setting. Only one of the following selections can be set; a "Memory-Only" interface and a "Memory or I/O" interface

SetSocket Function. Socket parameters are set using the SetSocket function. The exact same parameter mapping is used for the SetSocket function as for the GetSocket function. That is, the data structure format for the SetSocket function mirrors the definition of the GetSocket function's data structure format listed earlier. This simplifies read-modify-write operations when a specific parameter must be changed.

Determining the Current Status of the Socket and PC Card (GetStatus)

This function is intended to be called by the socket services client to determine what event(s) have caused a status change interrupt. This call should not be made during hardware interrupt processing of the status change interrupt, but rather after the interrupt has been processed and the socket(s) experiencing a status change event has been identified. The socket services client can then call the GetStatus function to determine which event caused the status change interrupt.

The information returned reflects the current state of the parameters set within the HBA:

- Returns the current state of the events that can cause a status change interrupt (as defined by the InquireSocket function) and the current state of the socket control and indicators (also defined in the InquireSocket function).
- Returns the current bit map of parameters or events that cause a status change interrupt. These events are defined in the GetSocket function's status change mask.
- Returns a bit map of Socket control and indicator bits supported by HBA.
- Returns the current settings of the IREQ Routing parameters.
- Returns the current Interface Type setting.

Resetting the Socket Under Software Control (ResetSocket)

This function provides a software reset to the PC Card and resets the socket hardware interface to its power-on default condition as follows:

- Socket interface is reset to memory only.
- IREQ routing is disabled.
- All socket supplies (Vcc, Vpp1, and Vpp2) are set to 5vdc.
- All address windows are disabled.
- All EDC Generators are disabled.

Window Functions

Window functions, like the adapter and socket functions, include the inquire, get, and set functions, as well as page functions that allow memory windows to be divided into multiple pages. Memory locations within a window can be segmented into 16KB pages.

Controlling Windows (InquireWindow, GetWindow and Set-Window)

The window functions are designed for flexibility, such that they can be used for common memory, attribute memory, or I/O. Despite this flexibility provided by socket services, a given hardware implementation of the HBA may be more restrictive. The capabilities for each window is obtained when the socket services client calls the InquireWindow function for each window detected by the InquireAdapter function.

The characteristics of a given window extend far beyond whether they can be used for memory, I/O or both. Many other parameters such as the base address, window size, fastest and slowest devices supported, etc., must be characterized for each window. Once the characteristics of the window is determined then it can be programmed by the socket services client at the request of the PC Card's driver.

InquireWindow Function. When the InquireWindow function is called, the HBA number and window number are passed to socket services, along with a pointer to a memory buffer supplied by the socket services client. Information is returned to the processor's registers and to the specified memory buffer. The total set of information returned to the socket services client includes the following:

- **Window Type** — Returns the characteristics of the window selected with the HBA and window parameters. A single window may be designed to provide support for any or all of the following:

    - A window can be used as a common memory window.
    - A window can be used as an attribute memory window.
    - A window can be used as an I/O window.
    - A window can specify that the WAIT# signal from the PC Card to is used to generate additional wait states during a socket data transfer.

- Note that even though socket services allows a window to be used as both an I/O window and a memory window, this usually is not the case. More typically, hardware designs restrict a given window to either I/O addresses or memory addresses, but not both.

- **Socket Assignment** — Returns a bit map of sockets that a window can be assigned to. Bit zero refers to socket zero and bit N refers to the maximum socket number. The size of this bit map restricts the number of sockets that can be supported by a given HBA. In the x86 environment, socket services has a 16-bit field, permitting a maximum of 16 sockets per HBA.

- **Window Characteristics Structure** — Returns a variety of windows parameters to a memory buffer supplied by the socket services client. Two types of window characteristics structures are defined: one for memory windows and one for I/O windows. As mentioned earlier, a given adapter may be designed to permit a given window to support memory addresses only, I/O addresses only, or both memory or I/O. A window characteristics structure is returned for each window type supported by the target address window.

Table 19-6 lists the parameters defined within a memory window characteristics structure, and table 19-7 lists parameters defined within a I/O window structure. The parameter definition for many of the entries within both structures are identical; however, some important differences exist. Parameters that differ are highlighted in tables 19-6 and 19-7.

Table 19-6. Memory Window Characteristics Structure Definition

Memory Characteristics Structure		
Mem Window Capabilities		Consists of flag bits that specify any of the parameters listed below.
	Base Address	Determines if the base address is programmable (bit is set) or is fixed (bit is reset) in the host's address space. If programmable, the base address must be within the range specified by the FirstByte and LastByte entries, and if fixed, the base address location is specified by the value of the FirstByte entry and the LastByte entry has no meaning.
	Window Size	Determines if the memory window size is programmable (bit is set) or is fixed (bit is reset). If programmable, the size can be any value within the range specified by the Minimum Size and Maximum Size entries. If fixed, the window size is determined by the value of the Minimum Size entry and the Maximum Size entry should be set to the same value and the Minimum Size.
	Window Enable	Determines if the HBA will preserve window state information when the window is disabled (bit is set), or whether software must be responsible for preserving the state information (bit is reset). This means that when the window is re-enabled, it must be reprogrammed by the client if the HBA does not preserve the information.
	8-Bit Data Width	Determines whether the memory window supports 8-bit data transfers to the socket required (8-bit hosts). If set, 8-bit transfers are supported and if reset, they are not supported.
	16-Bit Data Width	Determines whether the memory window supports 16-bit data transfers to the socket required (16-bit hosts). If set, 16-bit transfers are supported and if reset, they are not supported.
	Base Address Alignment	If set, the base address must be programmed to start at an address aligned on the size of the window. If reset, the base address can be programmed to start anywhere within the window's address range, consistent with the "Base Address Alignment" value (defined later).
	Window Size Increments	Determines if windows supporting a programmable size must be sized in "powers of two" increments consistent with the "Window Size Granularity" value defined later (bit is set). If the granularity is 4KB, then the window size can be 4KB, 8KB, 16KB, 32KB, ... up to the maximum size of the window. If bit is reset, window sizes can be any multiple of the "Window Size Granularity" value -- 4KB, 8KB, 12KB, 16KB, 20KB .... up to the maximum window size.
	Window Page Boundaries.	Specifies whether offsets specified to Set Page must be on boundaries equal to the size of the window (bit is set), or if page offset can be set without relation to the window size (bit is reset).

Table 19-6. Memory Window Characteristics Structure Definition(Continued)

Memory Characteristics Structure	
Mem Window Capabilities	Consists of flag bits that specify any of the parameters listed below.
Window Page Support	Determines if window hardware supports dividing a window into multiple pages (bit set), or does not support window paging (bit is reset).
Page Sharing	If set, the window paging hardware is shared with another window and care must be taken to ensure that no conflicts arise due to resource sharing. If reset, paging hardware is dedicated to the window.
Page Enable.	If set, the HBA preserves the paging characteristics when the page is disabled. If reset, the software must preserve the settings and reprogram the paging hardware when the page is enabled again.
Write-Protect.	Determines if the window can be write-protected (bit is set) or not (bit is reset).
FirstByte	The first byte in the host system's addressable memory space that can be programmed for the window's base address. Note that if the base address register is not programmable, the value is the fixed address for the window's base address.
LastByte	The last byte in the host system's memory address space that the window can be programmed to.
Minimum Window Size	Defines minimum size that the window can be programmed to.
Maximum Window Size	Maximum size that window can be programmed to.
Window Size Granularity	Window size granularity determines the minimum size that a window can be programmed to based on the hardware implementation. For example, if lower address lines A11:A0 go directly to the PC Card socket, then the window size that can be programmed is based on 4KB intervals.
Base Address Alignment	Specifies the base address alignment value for the window.
Window Offset Alignment	Specifies the alignment boundaries that the window offset can be programmed to for remapping the system address to PCMCIA memory.
Selected Access Speed	Specifies the slowest access speed supported for devices accessed through this window.
Fastest Access Speed	Specifies the fastest access speed supported for devices accessed through this window.

Table 19-7. I/O Window Information Structure Definition

I/O Window Information Structure		
I/O Window Capabilities		Consists of flag bits that specify any combination of the parameters below.
	Base Address	Determines if the base address is programmable (bit is set) or is fixed (bit is reset) in the host's address space. If programmable, the base address must be within the range specified by the FirstByte and Last-Byte entries, and if fixed, the base address location is specified by the value of the FirstByte entry and the LastByte entry has no meaning.
	Window Size	Determines if the I/O window size is programmable (bit is set) or is fixed (bit is reset). If programmable, the size can be any value within the range specified by the Minimum Size and Maximum Size entries. If fixed, the window size is determined by the value of the Minimum Size entry and the Maximum Size entry should be set to the same value and the Minimum Size.
	Window Enable	Determines if the HBA will preserve window state information when the window is disabled (bit is set), or whether the client must be responsible for preserving the state information (bit is reset). This means that the window must be reprogrammed by the client when re-enabled if the HBA does not preserve the information.
	8-Bit Data Width	Determines whether the I/O window supports 8-bit data transfers to the socket required by 8-bit hosts. If set, 8-bit transfers are supported and if reset, they are not supported.
	16-Bit Data Width	Determines whether the I/O window supports 16-bit data transfers to the socket (16-bit hosts). If set, 16-bit transfers are supported and if reset, they are not supported (8-bit hosts).
	Base Address Alignment	If set, the base address must be programmed to start at address locations equal to the size of the window. If reset, the base address can be programmed to start anywhere within the window's address range, consistent with the "Base Address Alignment" value defined later.
	Window Size Increments	Determines if windows supporting a programmable size must sized in "powers of two" increments consistent with the "Window Size Granularity", or if the windows size can be any multiple of the "Window Size Granularity" value.
	INPACK Signal Support	Specifies whether the adapter supports the Input Port Acknowledge (INPACK) signal or not. The INPACK signal permits an I/O window to overlap address space mapped elsewhere in the system.
	EISA Slot Specific I/O Address Support	Indicates support for EISA compatible addressing. In this case, the HBA in this case should respond to I/O addresses consistent with the slot specific addressing protocol required by EISA systems. See the MindShare publication, "EISA System Architecture" for details.

Table 19-7. I/O Window Information Structure Definition (Continued)

I/O Window Information Structure		
I/O Window Capabilities		Consists of flag bits that specify any combination of the parameters below.
	Ignore EISA-Defined alias (ISA) I/O Accesses.	Determines whether accesses to ISA address alias ranges should be ignored or not when slot-specific EISA I/O addressing is used.
FirstByte		The first byte in the host system's addressable I/O space that can be programmed for the window's base address. Note that if the base address register is not programmable the value is the fixed address for the window's base address.
LastByte		The last byte in the host system's I/O address space that the window can be programmed to.
Minimum Window Size		Defines minimum size that window can be programmed to.
Maximum Window Size		Maximum size that window can be programmed to.
Window Size Granularity		Describes the size interval that the window can be programmed to.
Base Address Alignment		Specifies the base address alignment value.
Number of Address Lines Decoded		Specifies the number of address lines decoded by the window.
EISA Slot Addressing		Specifies the upper nibble (A15:A12) of an x86 I/O address when EISA addressing is supported.
Fastest Access Speed		Specifies the fastest access speed supported for devices accessed through this window.

GetWindow Function. The Get Window function returns the current setting of the window specified by the programmer. The programmer passes the HBA and window numbers to the function. The function returns the following information:

- **Socket to which window is assigned.**

- **Window size.**

- **Current State of window hardware**—Returns the current setting of other window parameters. The value can be a combination of the following:

  - **Memory or I/O mapped.** This bit specifies whether the window is mapped into the host system's memory address space or I/O address space.
  - **Enabled or disabled.** Specifies whether the window is currently enabled or disabled.

- **Window data width**. Specifies whether the window is programmed for 16-bit data width or 8-bit data width.
- **Memory window pages used** (memory windows only). This parameter indicates if memory window pages are in use, indicating that this window is subdivided into multiple 16KB pages and that the GetPage and SetPage functions can be used for accessing individual pages within the window.
- **EISA I/O Mapping used**.
- **Card access permitted during EISA I/O accesses**. If this bit is set and EISA mapping is used, accesses to standard ISA addresses result in PC Card accesses. If reset, accesses to ISA addresses are ignored.

- **Access Speed**. Indicates the current access speed programmed into the memory window.

- **Window's Base Address**.

SetWindow Function. This function uses the same mapping as the GetWindow function. The definition of the parameters are the same, allowing the GetWindow function to be called to obtain the current window settings. Parameters requiring modification can then be changed from the current settings and the SetWindow function called to update the window's settings.

EDC Functions

Error Detection/Correction Generators are optional for PCMCIA HBAs. These functions are designed to enable and control EDC generators implemented by HBAs. However, card services provides no support for EDC functions. Furthermore, to the author's knowledge no current HBA designs employ EDC generators. Based on these issues discussion of the socket services EDC functions has been omitted from this book.

Maximum Number of Sockets Per HBA

The maximum number of sockets that a single adapter can support under control of socket services is limited by the **InquireWindow** function. A bit-map of assignable sockets is returned by this function. The size of this bit-mapped socket selection field defines the maximum number of sockets supported by each adapter. The field size is not defined by PCMCIA and depends on the socket services implementation. The Intel x86 socket services definition defines a 16-bit socket selection field, permitting 16 sockets per HBA.

Maximum Number of HBAs Supported by Socket Services

The maximum number of adapters supported by socket services depends on several factors, including:

- Limitations associated with the implementation of socket services for a given platform. For example, the field size used to specify a target adapter can vary with a particular implementation. Note that the x86 implementation uses an 8-bit field, permitting 256 adapters to be specified (clearly not a meaningful limitation).
- Constraints related to available space when implementing socket services in ROM.
- Constraints related to available memory space required by multiple sets of socket services required to support numerous adapters.

Chapter 20

The Previous Chapter

The previous chapter discussed the role of socket services. It also described the initialization of socket services and explained the basic purpose of the functions commonly supported in the PC environment.

This Chapter

This chapter focuses on the role of card services in the PCMCIA environment. It also reviews each of the functions defined by the PC Card specification that apply to 16-bit PC Cards, along with related return codes. The call-back mechanism is also described and the event and call-back codes are defined.

The Next Chapter

The next chapter discusses the three basic types of enablers: point enablers, device specific enablers, and super enablers. The chapter also discusses the specific jobs performed by several different device specific enablers including SRAM enablers, FLASH enablers, I/O device enablers, and ATA enablers.

Overview

Each PC Card must have a client driver that recognizes it, reads the CIS to determine its resource requirements, programs the host bus adapter (HBA) and configures the PC Card. As illustrated in figure 20-1, PC Card client drivers interface directly to Card Services. Card services simplifies the job of configuring a PC Card and monitoring status change events.

PCMCIA System Architecture

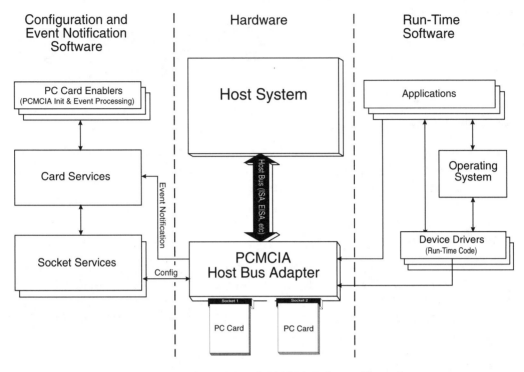

Figure 20-1. PCMCIA Software Flow

Configuring a PC Card may take place when the system powers up (if the PC Card is already installed in a socket), or when a PC Card is inserted into a socket (after the system is powered up and fully operational). In either case, the PC Card must be detected and configured by an enabler. Without an enabler, a PC Card would never be recognized by the system. However, once a PC Card is recognized and configured by the enabler, it then responds like any other device residing on the host bus.

Enablers that use card services are called card services client drivers. The term client driver is used because card services and the enablers perform their functions based on the client/server model. Card services exists to serve the needs of its clients (i.e. the enablers) as they attempt to configure and access their PC Cards. Two basic types of client drivers exist:

- Dedicated client drivers — designed for a particular PC Card.
- Generic or super client drivers — designed for a wide range of PC Cards.

Dedicated client drivers are typically supplied by the PC Card manufacturer to increase the probability that its card will be recognized and configured correctly in the absence of a generic driver. Dedicated client drivers may also manage functions that are unique to a given manufacturer's implementation.

Generic client drivers are frequently designed to handle PC Cards of a particular functional type. For example, the system manufacturer may include generic drivers for card types such as SRAM, flash ROM, Modems, and ATA drives. Ideally, a single super client driver could detect and configure all PC Cards regardless of type.

Enabling PC Cards Before Card Services

Prior to the release of card services, the enabler was burdened with recognizing when a card was inserted into a socket, reading its CIS, programming the HBA and configuring the PC Card so that it responded to a given system address range. The PC Card's enabler also had to continually monitor the socket to detect if the PC Card was removed. If removed, the enabler would deallocate the system resources the card was using by clearing registers in the HBA. In this way, the HBA would no longer respond to addresses previously assigned to the PC Card.

To configure a card, an enabler also had to determine what address ranges were available within the system (not in use by other devices) for allocation to its card. This was an almost impossible job for enablers since they had no knowledge of the other devices incorporated into the system or of other installed PC Cards. Assumptions had to be made by the programmer based on what resources were likely available so that contention with other devices was (hopefully) avoided.

It is also possible that other software applications or utility programs written by other programmers may want to share access to a given PC Card. These various programs will not be aware of each other and, as a result, conflicts may occur.

In summary, PC Card enablers that are compliant with PCMCIA releases prior to 2.0 each act independently, unaware of the existence of each other. Furthermore, they have no knowledge of the resources available within the system that could safely be allocated to their associated PC Card.

The Role of Card Services

Card services provides a central resource available to all client drivers. Specifically, card services is a collection of functions designed for use by programmers writing client drivers for PC Cards. These functions provide a software interface that permits the programmer to simplify code and helps to reduce conflicts with other client drivers and system resources. Card services is divided into five functional groupings by the PCMCIA specification:

- **Client Services**—Provides a registration facility that permits client drivers to register and be notified by card services when specific socket events occur (such as card insertion or removal).
- **Resource Management**—Allows client drivers to request the use of system resources required by the PC Card they are enabling. If the resources are granted, addition resource management functions can be used to assign these resources by programming the HBA (via socket services) and configuring the PC Card (by writing to the PC Card's configuration registers).
- **Client Utilities**—Provides a set of functions that allow the client driver to perform common jobs with ease. For example, the functions include accessing the PC Card's CIS, thereby simplifying tuple processing code.
- **Bulk Memory Services**—Provides block memory functions to read, write, copy and erase blocks of data within memory cards (without knowledge of the specific memory technology). These functions are passed to the appropriate Memory Technology Driver (MTD) that understands the hardware protocol necessary to erase or write to devices such as flash memory. (See the next chapter "PC Card Enablers" for details regarding memory technology drivers.)
- **Advanced Client Services**—Provides specialized functions that may be needed by some client drivers.

Only one copy of card services is required (and permitted), since it controls access to all sockets (whether associated with a single adapter or multiple adapters). Once a PC Card has been configured, it responds like any other host bus device. As a result, application programs designed to access a particular function need not even be aware of the existence of card and socket services. Card services and socket services are employed by enablers during:

- PC Card initialization and configuration (client driver makes calls).
- PC Card event notification (interrupt driven calls).

- Block transfers to/from memory card (memory client driver makes calls during run-time).

During other times, card and socket services remain in memory, but are not used. The following sections discuss typical uses of the card services functions. The information included in this chapter is not intended for reference purposes. The function descriptions provide only a basic description of the function's purpose. Refer to the PCMCIA Card Services standard for the exact calling parameters, format, field sizes, etc., of each function.

Initialization of Card Services

Card Services is designed as an operating system dependent extension that provides client services for the PC Card environment. Card services may come with the operation system as a built-in extension (e.g. OS/2 and Windows 95). In the MS-DOS environment, card services is typically implemented as an installable device driver.

In the DOS environment card services are called using an INT 1A instruction, requiring that card services "hook" entry 1Ah within the interrupt table. Also card services hooks the hardware interrupt used by the HBA to report status change events. This allows card services to be notified when a status change event occurs at the socket level.

Verifying the Presence of Socket Services

Since card services utilizes socket services to fulfill client driver requests, it must install after socket services installs. Socket services may reside in ROM on the system, or may be installed as a loadable device driver when the operating system loads. If socket services installs as a device driver, card services must be placed in the config.sys so that it installs after socket services.

Before card services installs it must verify that socket services are resident. This is done by calling the GetAdapterCount function within socket services. This function returns the total number of HBAs detected in the system and which returns the ASCII string "SS" verifying that socket services is present. If "SS" is detected, then card services proceeds with its installation.

After card services installs, it blocks access to socket services. If a client driver attempts to call socket services directly, card services will not pass the call on to socket services, but will return failure to the client driver. This prevents a client driver from using socket services to access the adapter hardware directly and perhaps allocating resources or modifying the HBA's programming without the knowledge of card services. Since this would result in card services becoming desynchronized with regard to the actual adapter hardware, attempts to access socket services without going through card services are prevented.

Note that card services does include a function (ReturnSSEntry) that can be called by a client driver that returns the entry point of socket services. This allows a client driver to gain direct access to socket services, but it must not perform any socket service function that causes card services to become desynchronized with the HBA.

Verifying that Card Services Installed

Initialization code used to install card services also includes code that actually calls card services to validate that the installation of card services was successful. This is accomplished by calling the GetCSInfo service, which returns information about this version of card services and the ASCII values "CS" to verify that card services are present. If card services installed correctly, the initialization code can make additional service call to prepare card services for access by a PC Card client driver.

Determining Availability of System Resources

One of the major functions performed by card services is to allocate available system resources to PC Cards. Resource management services are called by a PC Card's client driver in an attempt to acquire the resources (i.e. the I/O address space, memory address space, IRQ line, and DMA channels) that will satisfy the card's configuration requirements. Card services must check the available system resources to verify that the requested resources are not already used by the system.

Since card services is an extension to the operation system, in many operating environments it will have no specific knowledge of the resources that are already being used by other devices installed into the system. As a result, some method must be employed by card services (or by other platform specific software) that can detect free resources that can be allocated and assigned to PC Cards. The exact method used is operating system and hardware platform specific.

In x86 DOS compatible systems, a utility program is typically used to scan the host system in an attempt to detect the presence of devices that use system resources. The utility program builds a table of system resources that are not in use and passes the table to card services. Card services then manages the resources table as resources are requested and released by the client drivers as PC Cards are inserted and removed from sockets. This program is either embedded within card services initialization code or is implemented as a separate installable device driver that executes immediately after card services has installed (e.g. listed in the config.sys file immediately following the card services device driver) and before the PC Card enablers.

Power Management Support

Power management support was added to the PC Card standard (95 release). Card service defines power management (PM) support via power management call-back events. Card services can be designed to detect the presence of a power management facility within the PC platform and register to receive notification of power management events. When card services receives the power management notification, it calls-back all client drivers that registered to receive the PM events.

Card Services Calling Conventions

When a client calls card services, the binding used in a given environment will differ. The PC Card specification specifies a card services programming interface (binding) for x86 real mode (DOS), Intel 80286 Protected Mode (Windows), Intel 80286 Protected Mode (OS/2), and Intel 80386 Flat Address Model (Windows VxD Clients). Each binding specifies the register usage for calling card services functions and the register usage employed when the call-back handler is invoked. An example of the binding specified for the Intel X86 Real Mode environment follows. Refer to the card services specification for additional information.

Input:

[AH]	AFh (specifies card services function)
[AL]	Service Desired (service code number)
[DX]	Handle
[DI]:[SI]	Pointer argument
	[DI]=16-bit segment, [SI]=16-bit offset
[CX]	Argument Length (total length of argument packet)
[ES]:[BX]	Pointer to argument packet (used when additional address space is required to pass parameters and data)
	[ES]=16-bit segment, [BX]=16-bit offset

Output:

[AX]	Return Code
[CF]	Success when clear, failure when set

Specifying the Service

The AH register must contain a value of AFh to specify that this card is meant for card services. The AL register then specifies the service code number of the service being requested.

Table 20-1 lists all of the services (listed in alphabetical order) defined by the PC Card Standard along with their associated service number. Table 20-2 lists the services and their service number in ascending numerical order. Note that the services in shaded boxes were added by the PC Card 95 release.

The value placed in the AH register permits card services to block access to socket services functions made by enablers. Note that AFh is the last function number within socket services (function 0AFh) and is defined for use by card services.

When card services initializes, it hooks entry 1Ah in the interrupt table. Card services saves the current value of entry 1Ah (pointing to socket services) before installing its own. As a result, card services knows the entry point for socket services. INT 1Ah calls now access card services, which verifies that the call is a card services call by checking for the value AFh in the AH register. If verified, the card services function call specified in the AL register is then processed.

If card services finds a value other than 0AFh, it then checks to determine if the value represents a valid socket services function. If it is a valid socket services function, card services blocks access and returns failure to the calling program. This prevents client drivers from accessing socket services directly and changing HBA settings without card services being notified.

If the value in the AH register is for neither card services nor socket services, then card services passes the call to socket services, knowing it will not recognize the call. Socket services then passes the call to the previous interrupt service routine in the chain. Interrupt table entry 1Ah is used by the real-time clock functions in DOS compatible machines, therefore, card and socket services shares INT 1Ah with the real-time clock functions.

The Handle

A handle may specify the client making the service call or a particular resource that is being targeted by the function. The client handle is returned to the client during the registration process. This handle is used by the client when requesting many services. For example, a memory client may choose to Open a region of memory within a memory card for use with other memory services (i.e. read, write, or erase services). The client must specify its client handle in the DX register as an input and card services returns a memory handle (to identify the region of memory) to the DX register. The client later uses memory handle as an input when calling the read, write, or erase memory services.

Table 20-1. *Card Services Listed in Alphabetical Order*

Function	Code
AccessConfigReg	36h
AddSocketServices	32h
AdjustResourceInfo	35h
CheckEraseQueue	26h
CloseMemory	00h
CopyMemory	01h
DeregisterClient	02h
DeregisterEraseQueue	25h
GetCardServicesInfo	0Bh
GetClientInfo	03h
GetConfigurationInfo	04h
GetEvenMask	2Eh
GetFirstClient	0Eh
GetFirstPartition	05h
GetFirstRegion	06h
GetFirstTuple	07h
GetFirstWindow	37h
GetMemPage	39h
GetNextClient	2Ah
GetNextPartition	08h
GetNextRegion	09h
GetNextTuple	0Ah
GetNextWindow	38h
GetStatus	0Ch
GetTupleData	0Dh
MapLogSocket	12h
MapLogWindow	13h
MapMemPage	14h
MapPhySocket	15h
MapPhyWindow	16h

Function	Code
ModifyConfiguration	27h
ModifyWindow	17h
OpenMemory	18h
ReadMemory	19h
RegisterClient	10h
RegisterEraseQueue	0Fh
RegisterMTD	1Ah
RegisterTimer	28h
ReleaseConfiguration	1Eh
ReleaseDMA	3Bh
ReleaseExclusive	2Dh
ReleaseIO	1Bh
ReleaseIRQ	1Ch
ReleaseSocketMask	2Fh
ReleaseWindow	1Dh
ReplaceSocket Services	33h
RequestConfiguration	30h
RequestDMA	3Ah
RequestExclusive	2Ch
RequestIO	1Fh
RequestIRQ	20h
RequestSocketMask	22h
RequestWindow	21h
ResetCard	11h
ReturnSSEntry	23h
SetEvenMask	31h
SetRegion	29h
ValidateCIS	2Bh
VendorSpecific	34h
WriteMemory	24h

Table 20-2. Card Services Function Codes Listed in Numerical Order

Code	Function
00h	CloseMemory
01h	CopyMemory
02h	DeregisterClient
03h	GetClientInfo
04h	GetConfigurationInfo
05h	GetFirstPartition
06h	GetFirstRegion
07h	GetFirstTuple
08h	GetNextPartition
09h	GetNextRegion
0Ah	GetNextTuple
0Bh	GetCardServicesInfo
0Ch	GetStatus
0Dh	GetTupleData
0Eh	GetFirstClient
0Fh	RegisterEraseQueue
10h	RegisterClient
11h	ResetFunction
12h	MapLogSocket
13h	MapLogWindow
14h	MapMemPage
15h	MapPhySocket
16h	MapPhyWindow
17h	ModifyWindow
18h	OpenMemory
19h	ReadMemory
1Ah	RegisterMTD
1Bh	ReleaseIO
1Ch	ReleaseIRQ
1Dh	ReleaseWindow

Code	Function
1Eh	ReleaseConfiguration
1Fh	RequestIO
20h	RequestIRQ
21h	RequestWindow
22h	RequestSocketMask
23h	ReturnSSEntry
24h	WriteMemory
25h	DeregisterEraseQueue
26h	CheckEraseQueue
27h	ModifyConfiguration
28h	RegisterTimer
29h	SetRegion
2Ah	GetNextClient
2Bh	ValidateCIS
2Ch	RequestExclusive
2Dh	ReleaseExclusive
2Eh	GetEvenMask
2Fh	ReleaseSocketMask
30h	RequestConfiguration
31h	SetEvenMask
32h	AddSocketServices
33h	ReplaceSocket Services
34h	VendorSpecific
35h	AdjustResourceInfo
36h	AccessConfigReg
37h	GetFirstWindow
38h	GetNextWindow
39h	GetMemPage
3Ah	RequestDMA
3Bh	ReleaseDMA

The Argument Packet

Some services require that the client provide a memory buffer to pass parameters. Functions requiring a large data area for passing parameters use an argument packet. The pointer to the argument packet specifies the start memory location of the buffer, while the argument length specifies the size of the buffer (i.e. length of argument packet). The size and format of the argument packet is typically depends of the individual function.

Not all of the generic arguments just defined are used when calling a given service. Many functions require only a function code, handle and the pointer argument to pass all of the required parameters. Some service require the pointer argument, while other require use of the argument packet.

Return Codes

A variety of codes may be returned by card services into the processor's AX register. The return codes specify the results of the service. Table 20-3 lists and defines each of the return codes in alphabetical order. Table 20-4 lists the return codes in numerical order.

The Pointer Argument

Some services require a read/write buffer to pass input and output information between the client and card services. The pointer argument value placed in the DI and SI registers specifies the location of the memory buffer. These same buffer is used by card services to return data to the client. DI:SI are also used to specify the memory location the call-back buffer.

Table 20-3. Card Services Return Codes Listed in Alphabetical Order

Return Code	Value	Description
BAD_ADAPTER	01h	Specified adapter is invalid
BAD_ARG_LENGTH	1Bh	ArgLength argument is invalid
BAD_ARGS	1Ch	Values in Argument Packet are invalid
BAD_ATTRIBUTE	02h	Value specified for attributes field is invalid
BAD_BASE	03h	Specified base system memory address is invalid
BAD_EDC	04h	Specified EDC generator is invalid
BAD_HANDLE	21h	ClientHandle is invalid
BAD_IRQ	06h	Specified IRQ level is invalid
BAD_OFFSET	07h	Specified PC Card memory array offset is invalid
BAD_PAGE	08h	Specified page is invalid
BAD_SIZE	0Ah	Specified size is invalid
BAD_SOCKET	0Bh	Specified socket is invalid (logical or physical)
BAD_SPEED	17h	Specified speed is unavailable
BAD_TYPE	0Dh	Window or interface type specified is invalid
BAD_VCC	0Eh	Specified Vcc power level index is invalid
BAD_VERSION	22h	Client version is unsupported
BAD_VPP	0Fh	Specified VPP1 or VPP2 power level index is invalid
BAD_WINDOW	11h	Specified window is invalid
BUSY	18h	Unable to process request at this time - retry later
CONFIGURATION_LOCKED	1Dh	A configuration has already been locked
GENERAL_FAILURE	19h	An undefined error has occurred
IN_USE	1Eh	Requested resource is being used by a client
NO_CARD	14h	No PC Card in socket
NO_MORE_ITEMS	1Fh	There are no more of the requested item
OUT_OF_RESOURCE	20h	Card Services has exhausted resource
READ_FAILURE	09h	Unable to complete read request
Reserved	05, 0C, 10, 13h	Reserved for historical purposes
SUCCESS	00h	The request succeeded
UNSUPPORTED_MODE	16h	Processor mode is not supported
UNSUPPORTED_SERVICE	15h	Implementation does not support service
WRITE_FAILURE	12h	Unable to complete write request
WRITE_PROTECTED	1Ah	Media is write-protected

Table 20-4. Card Services Return Codes Listed in Numerical Order

Value	Return Code	Description
00h	SUCCESS	The request succeeded
01h	BAD_ADAPTER	Specified adapter is invalid
02h	BAD_ATTRIBUTE	Value specified for attributes field is invalid
03h	BAD_BASE	Specified base system memory address is invalid
04h	BAD_EDC	Specified EDC generator is invalid
05h	*Reserved*	Reserved for historical purposes
06h	BAD_IRQ	Specified IRQ level is invalid
07h	BAD_OFFSET	Specified PC Card memory array offset is invalid
08h	BAD_PAGE	Specified page is invalid
09h	READ_FAILURE	Unable to complete read request
0Ah	BAD_SIZE	Specified size is invalid
0Bh	BAD_SOCKET	Specified socket is invalid (logical or physical)
0Ch	*Reserved*	Reserved for historical purposes
0Dh	BAD_TYPE	Window or interface type specified is invalid
0Eh	BAD_VCC	Specified Vcc power level index is invalid
0Fh	BAD_VPP	Specified VPP1 or VPP2 power level index is invalid
10h	*Reserved*	Reserved for historical purposes
11h	BAD_WINDOW	Specified window is invalid
12h	WRITE_FAILURE	Unable to complete write request
13h	*Reserved*	Reserved for historical purposes
14h	NO_CARD	No PC Card in socket
15h	UNSUPPORTED_SERVICE	Implementation does not support service
16h	UNSUPPORTED_MODE	Processor mode is not supported
17h	BAD_SPEED	Specified speed is unavailable
18h	BUSY	Unable to process request at this time - retry later
19h	GENERAL_FAILURE	An undefined error has occurred
1Ah	WRITE_PROTECTED	Media is write-protected
1Bh	BAD_ARG_LENGTH	ArgLength argument is invalid
1Ch	BAD_ARGS	Values in Argument Packet are invalid
1Dh	CONFIGURATION_LOCKED	A configuration has already been locked
1Eh	IN_USE	Requested resource is being used by a client
1Fh	NO_MORE_ITEMS	There are no more of the requested item
20h	OUT_OF_RESOURCE	Card Services has exhausted resource
21h	BAD_HANDLE	ClientHandle is invalid
22h	BAD_VERSION	Client version is unsupported

Client Services (Client Registration and Support)

The category of card services defined as "client services functions" are those typically used when a card services client driver performs device initialization. Other services within this category provide basic card support. Table 20-5 lists the card services functions typically used during the registration process. The sections following the table discuss the registration process and discuss the use of each function listed.

Table 20-5. Client Services Functions

Client Services Functions	
Tuple Name	Description
GetCardServicesInfo	Determines if a valid copy of card services is installed and reports information regarding this copy of card services, including its revision and compliance level.
RegisterClient	Used by the client to register with card services as either a memory, MTD or I/O client. The client driver also specifies which card status events (such as card removal) it wishes to be notified of by card services. The client can also request that card services generate artificial card insertion events for all PC Cards that are currently installed, allowing the client to configure PC Cards it wishes to use.
DeregisterClient	Allows the client to notify card services that it no longer requires notification of status change events.
GetStatus	Returns the current status of the PC Card and its socket. It returns the same information obtained with the socket services GetStatus function.
ResetCard	This function resets the PC Card specified in the input argument, providing that all other clients that are using the same PC Card agree. Since more that one client may use a card, the ResetCard function will not be satisfied until all other clients agree to the reset. Card services generates Reset Request call-back events to all registered clients. Once all client drivers have responded to the call-back, card services calls the client that initiated the request via a Reset Complete call-back to inform the client whether the reset succeeded or failed.
SetEventMask	Used by the client to indicate the events it wishes to receive call-backs for. During registration, a client driver can specify which PC Card events that it wants to be notified of. This function can be used after registration to change the global event mask, originally set during RegisterClient. This function can also be used to change the SocketEvent mask originally set during Request-SocketMask (see table 20-8), but only if the RequestSocketMask function has been previously called by the client.
GetEventMask	Allows the client to obtain the current values of either the global or socket event mask.

Determining If Card Services Is Installed (GetCardServicesInfo)

The registration process begins with the card services client verifying that a valid copy of card services is installed and determining the compliance level of this particular version of card services. The GetCardServicesInfo function performs this task. When the card services client calls the GetCardServicesInfo function, it specifies a buffer size and pointer to the buffer where card services data is to be returned. Information returned by the GetCardServicesInfo function:

- **Length of data returned by card services**.
- **Card services signature**—Two consecutive bytes containing the ASCII characters "CS" verify the validity of the returned data.
- **Number of sockets**—Returns the number of sockets in the system.
- **Card services revision**—Indicates the vendor's revision level.
- **Card services compliance level**—Indicates the PCMCIA compliance level of card services. The compliance level is the PCMCIA release number upon which this socket services was based.
- **Location of vendor string**—Optional information can be provided by the card services vendor. This field specifies the start location within the buffer where the vendor information can be found. See "Vendor String" below.
- **Vendor string length**—Specifies the length of the vendor string.
- **Vendor string**—A vendor-defined string comprised of ASCIIZ characters.

Signing Up with Card Services (RegisterClient)

Once the card services client determines that an appropriate copy of card services exists, it then can register with card services using the RegisterClient function. A card services client driver registers with card services for notification of selected events generated by PC Cards. This function can also be used by the card services client to request that card services notify it of all PC Cards currently installed. This gives the card services client driver an opportunity to identify and configure the PC Cards that it requires access to.

In summary, the card services client registers with card services for the following reasons:

- To receive notification of specified PC Card status change events.
- To specify the type of client (memory, I/O or MTD) that is registering.
- To receive notification of PC Cards already installed in sockets (artificial card insertion events).

Note that card services returns a handle to the client upon return from the RegisterClient function. The client driver uses this handle to identify itself when calling other card services functions. Note that card services returns to the client drivers without having fully completed the registration process. Card services attempts to complete the registration process in the background and notifies the client driver that registration has been completed via the RegistrationComplete call-back.

Receiving Notification of Status Change Events

To receive notification of status change events occurring at the PC Card, the client driver must specify the events that it wishes to be notified of. This is accomplished by the card services calling a routine within the client when a card status change event occurs. This routine is referred to as the client's call-back routine. The card services client driver must specify the entry point of its call-back routine and the start address of a data buffer to deposit the change event into. Note that an event mask is passed to card services when the RegisterClient function is called, indicating to card services the events for which the client wants to be notified. Events that can be specified include the following (Refer to the section later in this chapter entitled "The Call-Back Process" for additional information):

- Write Protect change.
- Card Lock change (from HBAs that support a card interlock mechanism).
- Card Ejection request (HBAs supporting a card interlock mechanism).
- Card Insertion request (HBAs supporting a card interlock mechanism).
- Battery Dead.
- Ready Change.
- Card Detect Change.
- Power Management Change.
- PC Card reset request by another client.
- Socket Services Updated.

A given client determines which of the events it wants to be notified of during the registration process. For example, if the client driver so specifies, it can register with card services to receive card insertion events. This allows the client driver to be notified when a PC Card is inserted, permitting it to then check the PC Card to determine if it should configure the card.

The card insertion callback is triggered when a PC Card is inserted. Card services is notified via a status change interrupt generated by the HBA. Card services then interrogates the HBA to determine the cause of interrupt and calls back all client drivers that have registered to be notified of the card insertion event. When called-back each client driver then reads the card's CIS to determine if it should configure the card.

When call-backs occur, card services passes event information to the clients call-back buffer. The information passed typically includes an event code, logical socket number and information specific to the event. The exact information returned to the client depends on the specific event. Refer to the PCMCIA Card Services standard for details.

Note that the GetEventMask function can be used by the client driver to read the current setting of its event mask. The client passes its card services handle to identify itself, and card services returns the event mask indicating which status change events the client is currently registered to receive. Similarly, a client driver can call the card service's SetEventMask function to change the events for which it wants to be notified.

Determining the Order of Call-Backs: Client Driver Type

When a client driver registers with card services, it must also specify its driver type. For example, if a PC Card contains SRAM, flash memory, and I/O registers, the client driver that configures the card must contain a separate client driver for each group, and must register with card services three separate times as defined below:

- I/O client driver.
- Memory technology client driver (MTD) for Flash memory.
- Memory client driver.

The client driver type determines the order in which clients are called-back when a status change event occurs. I/O clients are called first on a Last In First Out (LIFO) basis; that is, the last I/O client registered is the first to be called. This is done on the premise that the last I/O client installed likely supersedes client drivers installed previously. MTD drivers are called next on a FIFO basis (the first to register is the first to be called). Finally, the memory client drivers receive the call-back last, also in a FIFO order.

Artificial Card Insertion Events

A client driver may also register with card services to have artificial card insertion events generated during the registration process. Card services can create a call-back to the client driver for each card currently installed in the system. In this way, the client driver's call-back routine can determine which of the cards already installed it should attempt to configure.

A client driver determines whether it should configure a card based on reading the CIS to determine if it recognizes the card. For example, a client driver may be designed to recognize a specific card (usually a client driver written by a manufacturer for only its card), or it may recognize any card within a given group (usually a client driver written for example to recognize all modem cards). When recognizing a card that it has been designed to configure and monitor, it then attempts to configure the card when an card insertion event occurs, providing that the card has not already been configured.

When artificial insertion notifications have been made for all PC Cards installed in sockets, card services generates a RegistrationComplete event. This event informs the client driver that the call-back process is complete. Note that when card services returns from the initial RegisterClient service, the registration process is not complete. Card services attempts to complete the registration process in the background; and therefore, the client is not fully registered until the RegistrationComplete call-back is received.

When processing the artificial card insertion events, the client driver may or may not recognize any PC Cards currently installed that it can configure. The client driver having registered with card services to receive card insertion events, will remain in memory and be called-back when a another PC Card is inserted sometime later. The client driver then checks to see if it can the configure this card.

Telling Card Services You're Leaving (DeregisterClient)

If a client driver will no longer be available at the call-back entry point (for example a driver that is transient), it must deregister with card services by passing its card services handle to card services and calling the DeregisterClient function. This tells card services that the client driver will no longer require call-backs.

Client Utility Services (Detecting a PC Card)

During the configuration process, the client driver must determine if it wishes to enable the PC Card, and if so, should attempt to configure it for operation. Once the client driver establishes that it will attempt to configure the PC Card, it may also be necessary to read additional information from the card to determine the specific resources it requires.

The GetConfigurationInfo function may be sufficient for many client drivers to determine if they should configure the PC Card. Other client drivers may need to further process the CIS to determine if it should attempt to configure the card. Card services assists with this by providing a group of utility functions that the client driver can use to obtain additional configuration information from the PC Card's CIS. These functions are listed in table 20-6.

Table 20-6. Client Utility Functions Used by the Client Driver to Access PC Card Information

Client Utility Functions	
Function Name	Description
AccessConfigRegisters	Used to access a PC Card configuration registers.
GetConfigurationInfo	Provides the client with information about a specified socket and the PC Card installed. This information can be used to determine the configuration requirements of the PC Card installed.
GetFirstTuple	Permits the client to specify a given tuple code and find the first occurrence of that tuple within the PC Card's CIS.
GetNextTuple	Requests that card services find the next occurrence of the tuple code that was previously specified for the GetFirstTuple function.
GetTupleData	Requests the contents of the specified tuple, once it has been located using GetFirst/NextTuple.

Table 20-6. Client Utility Functions Used by the Client Driver to Access PC Card Information (Continued)

Client Utility Functions	
Function Name	Description
GetFirstRegion	Used by memory technology client drivers (MTDs) to get device information for devices defined for the first region within the PC Card (as defined in the card's CIS). Information received by the client includes: location of region within the card, size of region, speed of devices within region, memory type (attribute or common), erase/write capabilities, etc.
GetNextRegion	Finds the device information for the next region within the card.
GetFirstPartition	Similar to the GetFirstRegion function, this function returns information for the first partition on the card based on information contained in the PC Card's CIS. If a PC Card has no partition information defined in its CIS, then card services may be able to determine partition information based on a given file system structure (such as the BIOS parameter block (BPB)/FAT structure used by DOS).
GetNextPartition	Finds device information for the next partition.

Client drivers can use these utility functions to obtain information regarding the configuration of the PC Card in a given socket, or to scan the CIS itself to determine the exact configuration requirements of the PC Card. If the client driver is a memory drive, the job of determining the configuration requirements can be quite simple, since it is likely that the first tuple (Device Information Tuple) within the CIS will provide the client driver with much (if not all) of the information it needs to configure the card. Tuple processing for I/O devices can be considerably more challenging due to the resource combinations that may be required.

Evaluating the PC Card and Socket (GetConfigurationInfo)

The GetConfigurationInfo service provides the enabler with information about the specified socket and card. An enabler may call this function to determine if the card installed into the socket has already been configured. If not configured the information returned to the enabler provides a general view of the card installed in the socket. Refer to table 20-7 for a list of the information returned by the GetConfigurationInfo service.

The GetConfigurationInfo service returns information from the PC Card's CIS including the device ID, function ID, and manufacturing ID. This information provides a way for the enabler to quickly determine whether or not it should attempt to configure the card.

Table 20-7. Information Returned by the GetConfigurationInfo Service

Information Returned	Description
Logical socket/function number	This field contains the logical socket and function number specified.
Attribute Bits	Indicates whether the PC Card has been previously configured and if exclusively owned. Also provides miscellaneous information regarding the configuration of the card.
Vcc setting	The values returned in these fields are those that the
Vpp1 setting	configuring client driver passed to card services during
Vpp2 setting	RequestConfiguration call. If the card/function has not
Interface type	been configured, these values are invalid.
Config. register base address	
Status register settings	The values returned in these fields are the values that
Pin replacement register settings	were written to the configuration registers by the enabler
Socket and copy register settings	when it called the RequestConfiguration service. These
Config. option register settings	values are invalid if the card/function is not configured.
Config. Registers implemented	This values is obtained from the information passed to card services during the RequestConfiguration call.
First device type	This value is taken from the DEVICE tuple.
Function code	These values are taken from the Function ID tuple.
System initialization byte	
Manufacturers code	These values are taken from the Manufacturers ID tuple.
Manufacturers Information	
Card values	This field is a bit map that indicates which configuration register were written with valid values.
Assigned IRQ	These fields contain the values specified when the
IRQ attributes	RequestIRQ service was called for this function/card.
Base ports 1	These fields are derived from the information specified
Number of ports	when the RequestIO function was called. If the Request-
Attributes 1	IO function has not been called the number of ports
Base ports 2	fields will contain 00h.
Number of ports	
Attributes 2	
I/O address lines	
Extended Status	Contains the value written to the extended status register when the RequestConfiguration call was made.
DMA Attributes	Defines the DREQ# pin assignments and DMA width.
Assigned Channel	Specifies the DMA channel requested during configuration.
Number of I/O windows	Specifies the number of I/O windows in use for this socket and function.
Number of memory windows	Specifies the number of memory windows in use for this socket and function.

Additionally, the GetConfigurationInfo function provides specific configuration information about a socket and card that has already been configured. If the card has been previously configured, then card services returns the client handle (in handle argument, DX register) of the enabler that has already configured the card, along with the primary configuration settings. If the card has not been configured then the client handle and configuration settings returned by the service are invalid.

Note that support for multiple function cards has been added. An enabler can specify the logical socket and a function within the PC Card that it wishes to get information about.

Scanning the CIS (GetFirstTuple, GetNextTuple, GetTuple Data)

When the client driver must determine the specific configuration requirements of the PC Card, it reads the configuration table within the PC Card's CIS. The client driver can use the GetFirstTuple function to specifically request the tuple containing the information it needs. For example, if a client driver wishes to find the first Configuration Table Entry within the CIS, it passes the socket number and the desired tuple code (1Bh for the configuration table entry tuple) to card services and calls the GetFirstTuple function. Card services will scan the card's CIS looking for the first instance of the tuple code that was specified in the call.

The GetTupleData function can be called next to obtain the data within the tuple. When the data is returned, the client driver interprets the data to determine the system resources required by the PC Card. The client then attempts to obtain these resources from card services and, if successful, no further tuple processing is necessary. However, if the system resources specified in the first configuration table entry are not available, then the client must continue processing the CIS by calling the GetNextTuple function, which finds the next occurrence within the CIS of the indicated tuple type. This process continues until the resources specified by a Configuration Table Entry are determined to be available. If no more tuples of the type specified exist within the CIS when the GetNextTuple is called, card services returns a code indicating that no more items are available.

Note that the GetFirstTuple, GetNextTuple, and GetTupleData functions use the same argument packet format. This simplifies calling these utility functions (since the argument packet returned by one function can be used when calling the other).

Simplifying CIS Processing for Memory and MTD Clients (GetFirstPartition, GetNextPartition, GetFirstRegion, GetNextRegion)

Some client drivers may need to obtain information describing partitions and regions within memory cards. Since obtaining the necessary information requires reading multiple tuples, the GetFirst/NextRegion and GetFirst/NextPartition functions can be used by clients to get the required information without having to process the tuples individually.

Resource Management Services (Assigning Resources)

Card Services maintains a database of resources available within the system. Client drivers can call card services to verify availability of resources needed by their PC Card. Configuring a PC Card and programming the HBA is a two step process.

1. The client driver must acquire each resource from the resource table one at a time. If any of the resources required are not all available, this particular combination of resources cannot be satisfied and another group must tried.
2. Once all resources required by the PC Card have been successfully allocated, the actual configuration (allocation of these resources to the HBA and PC Card) occurs.

The resource management functions allow the client driver to verify the availability of and to allocate resources required by the PC Card. These functions are listed in table 20-8. The services in the shaded boxes were added by the PC Card 95 standard. Refer to the card services specification for details related to these functions.

Table 20-8. Resource Management Functions

Resource Management Functions	
Function Name	Description
RequestIO	Used to request I/O address ranges for the PC Card. This function can be called only once per socket, and a maximum of two I/O address ranges can be specified per card. Input parameters request the starting or base address for each range and the number of I/O address locations requested for each range, and whether a given address range is to be shared with other devices within the system. This function, if successful, assigns the specified I/O address ranges to the client and adjusts the card services resource table to indicate that the assigned ranges are no longer available.
RequestIRQ	Used to obtain a system interrupt line for the calling client. The client specifies which interrupt line or lines will satisfy its interrupt needs. Input parameters request that an interrupt be either exclusive (not shared), time-multiplexed shared (client coordinates with other clients sharing this line, using the ModifyConfiguration function to enable and disable its connection to the interrupt line) or shared dynamically through an interrupt sharing protocol supported by the system. An input parameter also specifies whether the interrupt sent from the PC Card should be pulse or level mode. This function, if successful, assigns the specified IRQ line to the client and adjusts the card services resource table to indicate that the assigned IRQ is no longer available.
RequestWindow	Allows the client to request ownership of a block of system memory addresses. The client passes the starting (base) address and the size of the memory window along with a variety of other parameter to card services. Other parameters include: type of memory window (attribute or common), window enabled or disabled, whether window can be shared with other clients (only time-multiplexed sharing is permitted), whether paging of window is enabled, and speed of the memory devices. This function assigns the address ranges (if available) to the client and adjusts the resource table to indicate that they are no longer available. Note that this same block of addresses can be assigned to another client if the shared parameter is set. This function can be called multiple times per socket, up to the maximum number of memory windows supported by the HBA. Card services passes a window handle back to the client to be used when calling other functions pertaining to this window.
RequestDMA	Requests the use of a desired DMA channel for a given PC Card. One of 16 DMA channels can be specified (numbered zero through fifteen). Also specifies whether the DMA channel is to be shared and if so by which method, which PC Card pin is used for DREQ#, and what the DMA channel size is.
ReleaseIO	Adjusts the resource table by releasing the I/O address range(s) acquired by a client with the RequestIO service.
ReleaseIRQ	Adjusts the resource table by releasing the IRQ acquired by a client with the RequestIRQ service.
ReleaseWindow	Adjusts the resource table by releasing the block of memory address locations acquired by a client with the Request Window function. The window handle is passed to card services to specify the window to be released.

Table 20-8. Resource Management Functions (Continued)

Resource Management Functions	
ReleaseDMA	Adjusts the resource table by releasing the DMA channel acquired by a client with the RequestDMA service.
GetFirstWindow	This service returns the window handle and information associated with the first memory or I/O window (i.e. base address, size, and related attributes) of the specified socket and function.
GetNextWindow	This service is called following the GetFirstWindow call to obtain information associated with the next window used by the specified socket.
GetMemPage	This service return information for the specified page within the requested memory window. The window is specified by the window handle returned by the GetFirstWindow or GetNextWindow services.
ModifyWindow	Allows parameters assigned to a given block of memory addresses acquired with the RequestWindow function to be modified. These parameters include memory device speed, window type (attribute or memory) and window enabled or disabled. The window handle is passed to card services to specify the window to be modified.
MapMemPage	Selects a 16KB memory block within the PC Card to be mapped into a 16KB page within system memory. The 16KB memory block within the PC Card is identified by the client with an absolute offset value from the beginning of the PC Card's memory array.
RequestSocketMask	Selects the status change events that the client wishes the PC Card to generate. The client specifies which status change events it wants to be generated at the socket. A bit-map of the events masks each status change event that should not be reported by the HBA from the specified card. Note that during the RegisterClient function, the client driver indicates which status change events it wishes to be notified of, setting a global event mask.
ReleaseSocketMask	Releases the status change events mask, so that no status change events are reported by the PC Card residing in this specified socket.
ModifyConfiguration	Allows the configuration established by the Request Configuration function to be modified. Note that IRQ routing and the I/O address range assigned cannot be modified with this function. These parameters can only be changed by first releasing the configuration and then performing the requests for those resources again.
RequestConfiguration	Used to establish the configuration for an I/O interface. The I/O address ranges and system interrupt previously acquired are established at the hardware level (HBA and PC Card). Other configurable items are also specified based on the values indicated by the selected Configuration Table Entry, including: Vcc, Vpp1, Vpp2, interface type (memory only or memory/IO) and setting for the configuration registers, if present.
ReleaseConfiguration	This function releases the configuration information set previously using the RequestConfiguration function. This function returns the interface to a memory-only interface and power is removed from the socket (if no memory client indicates its use of the PC Card). The IRQ and I/O resources must be released separately to adjust the resource table.

Requesting a Resource

A client driver may use three types of request functions to determine if the resources that its PC Card requires is available. These functions include:

- RequestIO—used to request a range of I/O address locations
- RequestIRQ—used to request a system interrupt line
- RequestWindow—used to request a range of memory address locations
- RequestDMA—used to request a DMA channel.

A client driver whose PC Card requires one or more of these system resources calls card services to determine their availability. The client passes its handle to card services along with a pointer to the memory buffer containing the input argument packet. The argument packet passed to card services specifies parameters identifying the resource being requested. Card services checks the allocation table to determine if the requested resource is available. If available, card services updates its resource table, indicating that the resource is no longer available and returns "success" along with the argument packet, verifying that the resource parameters that have been granted.

Once all of the resources required by a PC Card have been acquired with the request functions, the actual task of programming the HBA and configuring the card can then occur. See the chapter entitled, "Client Drivers".

Card services has no way of knowing what resources are available for a PC Card to use. As a result, platform-specific utility programs have been written to probe the system and build a data base of available resources. This data base is passed to card services to manage.

Requesting Resource Combinations

Consider the example of a serial port that typically requires a range of I/O addresses and an IRQ. In a PC-DOS environment, a serial port is typically configured either as COM1 (I/O locations 3F8h-3FFh & IRQ4), COM2 (2F8h-2FFh & IRQ3), COM3 (3E8h-3EFh & IRQ4) or COM4 (2E8h-2EFh & IRQ3). The client driver for a serial port must ensure that both the RequestIO and the RequestIRQ functions return success before configuring the PC Card and HBA.

Assume that the client attempts to configure the serial port as COM1. If the RequestIO function returns "success", then I/O locations 3F8h-3FFh are allocated to the client driver and the resource table is updated to indicate these I/O addresses are no longer available. Next, the client driver calls RequestIRQ to obtain IRQ4, but card services returns BAD_IRQ to the client, indicating that IRQ4 is not available. If the client simply moved to the next configuration option (COM2), the I/O address range 3F8h-3FFh would remain allocated and other clients requesting an address within that range will not be successful, even though the addresses are not being used.

To avoid this problem, the client must release resources that have been granted but will not be used. The ReleaseIO function would be used in this instance before moving on to the next configuration option. Similarly, the ReleaseIRQ and ReleaseWindow are used to release interrupts and memory address ranges, respectively.

Configuring the HBA and PC Card (RequestConfiguration)

When the client driver has obtained from card services all of the resources needed by the card, then the actual configuration can take place. Prior to this time the resources have been granted to the client driver for assignment to its PC Card, but neither the HBA nor the PC Card have yet been configured to use these resources.

The card services client uses the RequestConfiguration function to complete the configuration process. When the RequestConfiguration function is called, card services makes the appropriate calls to socket services to set the specified values into the window registers and IRQ steering registers. Also, the index number of the Configuration Table Entry whose configuration options were successfully allocated is written to the card's Configuration Option Register, located in attribute memory.

The client must ensure that it is ready to perform all of the functions associated with a fully-operational card before calling the RequestConfiguration function. Once the function call completes, the PC Card and HBA are configured and the PC Card is now "on line". For example, in an x86 environment, if interrupts are used by a given PC Card, the client driver must ensure that the pointer to the device's interrupt service routine has been installed in the interrupt table prior to configuring the card. It will then be prepared to handle the card's interrupt requests.

Bulk Memory Services

Bulk memory services primarily relate to memory clients, utility programs, execute-in-place (XIP) managers, and other clients requiring access to memory cards. These clients can use bulk memory functions to access memory devices without knowing the details of the various memory technologies used by PC Cards. The functions within the bulk memory services group support RAM devices, but not devices such as flash memory.

Table 20-9. Bulk Memory Functions

Bulk Memory Services Functions	
OpenMemory	This function opens an area of common memory within a PC Card that is to be accessed some time in the future (i.e. read, write, copy or erase operation). A memory handle is returned that identifies this memory range when performing one of the operations mentioned above.
ReadMemory	This functions reads data from an area of common memory specified by a given memory handle (obtained from the OpenMemory function). The calling MTD passes a pointer during the call specifying a system memory buffer to which data is to be returned.
WriteMemory	This function writes data to a common memory area identified with a memory handle obtained via the OpenMemory function. The calling MTD passes a pointer to a system memory buffer that contains the data to be written.
CopyMemory	This function reads data from a source location and writes it to a destination within the same common memory region that is identified by a memory handle obtained via the OpenMemory function.
CloseMemory	This function closes an area of common memory that was previously opened with the OpenMemory function. The calling MTD passes the memory handle of the memory area to be closed along with the call.
RegisterEraseQueue	Establishes an erase queue where erase entries can be made.
CheckEraseQueue	Notifies card services that one or more erase request entries have been sent to the erase queue.
DeregisterEraseQueue	Eliminates an erase queue previously registered using the RegisterEraseQueue function. This function fails if erase entries within the queue are still pending completion.

Since flash memory devices require particular erase and write algorithms, PCMCIA chose not to attempt embedding the code necessary to support all potential variations into card services. Instead, a memory device that requires a specific algorithm must supply a memory technology driver (MTD) that is designed to handle access to the card. When a client such as a memory client attempts to access memory within a flash card, card services passes the request to the flash MTD, which makes the low-level access to the memory device. Table 20-9 lists the bulk memory functions and provides a brief description of each.

Advanced Client Functions

Advanced client functions include miscellaneous functions that satisfy the special needs of some client drivers. Table 20-10 lists the advanced client functions and provides a brief description of each. Refer to the PCMCIA card services specification for details.

Table 20-10. Advanced Card Services Functions

Advanced Card Services Functions	
ReturnSSEntry	Provides a means of gaining access directly to socket services. Normally, access to socket services is denied by card services to ensure that it maintains synchronization with the state of the HBA. If client drivers are allowed access to socket services, the HBA setting can be modified without card services knowledge. If absolutely required, a client driver can request access to socket services via the ReturnSSEntry call. The programmer must be certain that nothing is changed at the HBA level that will affect the operation of card services.
MapLogSocket	Determines the physical adapter and socket that is assigned to a logical socket number.
MapPhySocket	Identifies the logical socket number assigned to a physical adapter and socket.
MapLogWindow	Identifies the physical adapter and window that are mapped to a given logical window handle.
MapPhyWindow	Identifies the logical window handle assigned to a given physical adapter and window.
RegisterMTD	Assigns an MTD to a region of memory. When access to the assigned region occurs, the MTD is called to handle the memory operation.
RegisterTimer	Allows a client driver to register for callback at specified time intervals. A client may register multiple times to get notification at various time intervals. Timing is based on 1ms interval. The client specifies the call-back interval based on the number of 1ms ticks specified during registration. A timer handle is returned during registration and passed to the client when the call-back occurs. This permits the client to identify the specific timer that has expired when the call-back occurs.
SetRegion	Allows a client driver of a card that does not have a CIS to specify the characteristics of a given region within the card.
ValidateCIS	Scans the CIS by reading the tuple chain contained on the PC Card. The function returns the number of valid tuples found within the chain.

Table 20-10. Advanced Card Services Functions (Continued)

Advanced Card Services Functions	
RequestExclusive	Permits a client driver to request exclusive access to a given PC Card. Card services ensures that no other client is currently using the card before granting exclusive access to this client driver. If another client driver is currently using the card and is unwilling to release control, then function will fail.
ReleaseExclusive	Releases exclusive access to a card that was previously granted via the RequestExclusive function.
GetFirstClient	Returns the client handle of the first client to register with card services.
GetNextClient	Returns the client handle of the next client to register with card services.
GetClientInfo	Provides client driver information for the client handle specified.
AddSocketServices	Allows another socket services handler to be installed to support an additional HBA.
ReplaceSocketServices	Replaces the current version of socket services with a new version.
VendorSpecific	Defined by the vendor of card services to extend functionality.
AdjustResourceInfo	Adjusts the resource database maintained by card services. This data base contains the system resources that are available for use by PC Cards. This function allows system resources to either be added or removed from the database.

The Call-Back Process

Card service makes call-backs to clients that are triggered by a wide variety of events. The type of call-back events can be categorized as:

- Card insertion/removal events
- Registration complete event
- Status Change events
- Card insertion/ejection request events
- Exclusive request/compete events
- Reset request/complete events
- Client Information request event
- Erase Complete event
- MTD Request event
- Timer event
- New socket services event

When making call-backs card services uses the call-back entry point specified by each client during registration. The specific events supported by card services are listed in figure 20-11.

Some events must be supported by all clients. During registration, the client driver specifies the individual events that it wishes to be notified of. The events that must be supported include:

- Client_Info — a client may request information about another client when calling the GetClientInfo service. Card services calls-back the specified client using the Client_Info call-back.
- Exclusive_Request — an client that has previously configured a PC Card may receive a RequestExclusive call-back, indicating that another client wishes to gain exclusive access to the PC Card. For example, a generic client driver may have enabled a modem, but a device-specific client driver may want to gain exclusive access to the same PC Card.
- Reset_Request — request by a client to reset a socket/PC Card must be granted by other clients using the same socket/PC Card. This call-back notifies a client that a ResetRequest has been made.

Identifying a Status Change Event

When a status change event occurs at one of the PCMCIA sockets, an interrupt is generated by the HBA. Card services is notified of the event via a system interrupt (called a status change or management interrupt). When the card services receives the interrupt, it must determine which socket encountered the status change event. Card services accomplishes this by calling the socket services AcknowledgeInterrupt function which returns the socket(s) that experienced the status change event. Once the socket or sockets that have experienced a status change have been identified, then card services calls the GetStatus function to determine which event caused the interrupt.

The AcknowledgeInterrupt function must be called once for each HBA in the system. The client supplies the HBA number to socket services when the AcknowledgeInterrupt function is called, and socket services returns a bit map of the sockets within the adapter that have experienced a status change. When obtaining status information from the HBA, socket services also prepares the HBA to generate another status change interrupt if another should occur.

The AcknowledgeInterrupt function only identifies the sockets that have experienced a status change. After the AcknowledgeInterrupt routine completes, card services then calls the socket services GetStatus function, HBAs typically preserve the state of the status change so that the exact status change event that caused the interrupt can be determined using the GetStatus function. If the HBA does not preserve this state information, then socket services must.

Note that the AcknowledgeInterrupt function is called by the status change interrupt service routine. Interrupts must not be re-enabled while processing a status change interrupt. This could cause nesting of status change interrupts while processing the socket service's AcknowledgeInterrupt, a situation that socket services is unprepared to manage (because the routine is non-reentrant).

The Client Call-Back

Numerous events can occur that require a call-back to client drivers. These events are listed in table 20-11. The events in the shaded boxes were added with the PC Card 95 release.

Table 20-11. Call-Back Events Defined by Card Services

Event	Code	Source	Client(s)	Registered By
BATTERY_DEAD	01h	Hardware	Socket	RequestSocketMask
BATTERY_LOW	02h	Hardware	Socket	RequestSocketMask
CARD_INSERTION	40h	Hardware	All	RegisterClient
CARD_INSERTION [A]	40h	DeregisterMTD	MTDs	RegisterClient
CARD_INSERTION [A]	40h	RegisterClient	Requester	RegisterClient
CARD_INSERTION [A]	40h	ReleaseExclusive	All	RegisterClient
CARD_INSERTION [A]	40h	RequestExclusive	Requester	RequestExclusive
CARD_INSERTION [A]	40h	RequestExclusive	All	RegisterClient
CARD_LOCK	03h	Hardware	Socket	RequestSocketMask
CARD_READY	04h	Hardware	Socket	RequestSocketMask
CARD_REMOVAL	05h	Hardware	Socket	RequestSocketMask
CARD_REMOVAL [A]	05h	ReleaseExclusive	Socket	RequestSocketMask
CARD_REMOVAL [A]	05h	RequestExclusive	All	RegisterClient
CARD_RESET	11h	ResetFunction	Socket	RequestSocketMask
CARD_UNLOCK	06h	Hardware	Socket	RequestSocketMask
CLIENT_INFO	14h	GetClientInfo	Provider	RegisterClient
EJECTION_COMPLETE	07h	Hardware	Socket	RequestSocketMask
EJECTION_REQUEST	08h	Hardware	Socket	RequestSocketMask
ERASE_COMPLETE	81h	Queued Erase	Requester	RequestEraseQueue
EXCLUSIVE_COMPLETE	0Dh	RequestExclusive	Requester	RequestExclusive
EXCLUSIVE_REQUEST	0Eh	RequestExclusive	Socket	RequestSocketMask
INSERTION_COMPLETE	09h	Hardware	Socket	RequestSocketMask
INSERTION_REQUEST	0Ah	Hardware	Socket	RequestSocketMask
MTD_REQUEST	12h	Card Services	MTD	RegisterClient
PM_RESUME	0Bh	Card Services	Socket	RequestSocketMask

Table 20-11. Call-Back Events Defined by Card Services

Event	Code	Source	Client(s)	Registered By
PM_SUSPEND	0Ch	Card Services	Socket	RequestSocketMask
REGISTRATION_COMPLETE	82h	RegisterClient	Requester	RegisterClient
REQUEST_ATTENTION	18h	Hardware	All	RegisterClient
RESET_COMPLETE	80h	ResetFunction	Requester	ResetFunction
RESET_PHYSICAL	0Fh	ResetFunction	Socket	RegisterClient
RESET_REQUEST	10h	ResetFunction	Socket	RegisterClient
SS_UPDATED	16h	Card Services	All	RegisterClient
TIMER_EXPIRED	15h	Hardware	Requester	RegisterTimer
WRITE_PROTECT	17h	Hardware	All	RegisterClient

Configuring PC Cards During POST

The previous discussions of PC Card configuration have presumed that the cards will be installed when the operating system loads or when the PC Card is inserted sometime after the operating system has loaded and the system is running. If however, the need to load the operating system from the PC Card exists, the previously discussed approaches for configuring the cards don't work.

To perform initial program load (IPL) from a PC Card, ROM-based PCMCIA initialization code must be included with the system. This code must be able to program the HBA and parse the CIS to determine if a given card should be configured during POST (Power-On Self Test). Once the HBA has been programmed, memory cards containing a boot sector can be recognized as bootable since they will contain a BIOS Parameter Block (BPB) that permits the booting from the PC Card in the same fashion as a floppy drive.

Similarly, ATA drives can be recognized by ROM code by reading the initialization byte within the Function Identification tuple. The initialization byte specifies that the device should be configured during POST. Once the ATA drive is configured, IPL can occur from the PCMCIA ATA drive like any other ATA drive.

Note that this initialization process occurs prior to card services being installed. As a result, the a client driver will not have registered to receive status change events from the PC Card. When the operating system boots, a driver for the PC Card that is performing IPL can register with card services.

Chapter 21

The Previous Chapter

The previous chapter focused on the role of card services in the PCMCIA environment. It also reviewed each of the functions defined by the PC Card specification that apply to 16-bit PC Cards, and defined the related return codes. The call back mechanism was also described and the event and call back codes were defined.

This Chapter

This chapter discusses the three basic types of enablers: point enablers, device-specific enablers, and super enablers. The chapter also discusses the jobs performed by generic memory enablers (and MTDs) and I/O device enablers.

The Next Chapter

The next chapter discusses the problems associated with loading the operating system from a PC Card. It also defines mechanisms used to determine whether a given PC Card is a bootable device, and the firmware support required to support PC Card booting.

Overview

This chapter discusses PC Card enablers. The chapter focuses primarily on client driver enablers, but also includes a brief discussion of point enablers at the end of the chapter. Note that the terms PC Card enabler, client, client driver, and device driver are all used to describe the software that is responsible for configuring a PC Card. This chapter uses the terms enabler and client driver.

Specific types of client drivers (enablers) discussed in this chapter include:

- SRAM client drivers
- Flash client drivers and Memory Technology Drivers (MTDs)
- Generic I/O client drivers

In order to configure a PC Card, enablers must first register with card services. The primary function of an enabler is to detect and configure PC Cards that it supports. As such, the enabler must be prepared to configure its card no matter when it is installed. In order to configure cards installed after power up, the enabler registers with card services to receive a call back (i.e., a card insertion call-back) each time card services detects that a PC Cards has been installed. During registration, the enabler can also request that card services generate a call-back for each PC Card already installed, thereby calling the enabler's configuration routine.

The Card Insertion Call-Back

When card services makes a card insertion call-back it specifies the type of call-back initiated, along with the logical socket that the card was inserted into. The call-back routine then attempts to configure the card. Figure 21-1 illustrates the typical process used by an enabler to configure a card. The CIS may have to be accessed several times to obtain a combination of card-required resources that can be successfully allocated to the card (i.e., resources that are not already assigned to other devices).

The configuration process begins when card services makes the card insertion call-back to the enabler. The enabler detects which event caused the call-back and obtains information supplied by card services (e.g., which logical socket the card was inserted into).

The method of configuring a card varies depending of the type of card to be configured. The next section discusses generic memory enablers, and the following section describes the operation of a generic I/O enabler.

As discussed in the previous chapter, a variety of services are available for the PC Card enablers (i.e., card services client drivers) to configure a PC Card.

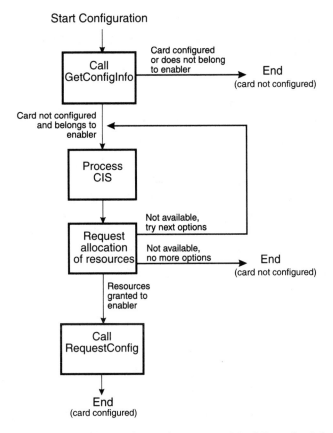

Figure 21-1. A Sample Configuration Process Used By a Card Services Client

Memory Drivers and Memory Technology Drivers

Memory client drivers provide virual disk drive support. In short, these drivers are responsible for storing and retrieving files within the memory card. The method required to access the memory card varies depending on the type of memory devices (i.e., memory technology) implemented in the card. Since memory devices (such as flash) require various programming algorithms, each memory type must have an associated memory technology driver (MTD).

Figure 21-2 illustrates the overall software architecture specified for accessing memory cards as virtual disk drives. Notice that memory client drivers receive file access requests from the file system and must access the memory card to fullfill each request. The file system might be the standard file system used by the opertating system (e.g., the DOS FAT system) or an installable system required when accessing flash memory. Card services provides bulk memory services that simplifies the memory client driver's job of accessing a specific block of memory within the memory card.

SRAM memory client drivers typically interface directly to the operating system's file manager, since there are no restrictions related to writing and reading data to or from SRAM. These client drivers are designed to access memory via the bulk memory services provided by card services. Since accessing SRAM is uniform and quite simple (byte read/write capability), the memory technology driver is incorporated into card services.

Flash memory client drivers interface directly to a flash file system. A special file system is required for flash devices due to the special requirements associated with writing to flash memory. Two major factors are:

- Write operations require first erasing a specified block of memory followed by the block write, and may take several seconds to complete.
- Flash memory also has a limited write-cycle life. That is, repetitive erasures and writes to the same memory block destroys the chips ability to retain data within that block. The maximum number of erasures and writes are specified by the manufacturer (e.g., a flash device may specify as life of as few as 10,000 writes).

Knowing the restrictions associated with accessing flash memory, the flash file system is designed specifically to provide compatible access to flash memory. For example, the flash file system distributes writes to flash memory to minimize the effects of repetitive write ware and accomodates the slow erase time.

Memory enablers (client drivers) have a formidable task to perform since a wide variety of memory card implementations exist. The enabler must also acquire a drive letter from the operating system to allocate to each card slots that a memory card might be inserted into. The following sections describe the jobs performed by SRAM and flash client drivers.

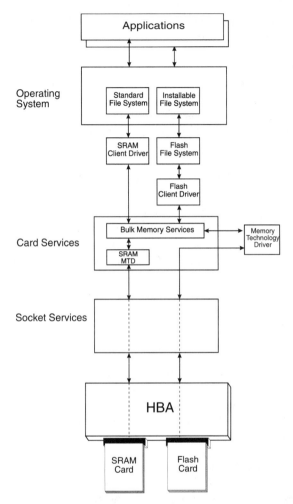

Figure 21-2. Memory Client Driver Software Environment

SRAM Client Drivers

SRAM client drivers typically load as installable device drivers via the config.sys file or equivalent mechanism. One of the tasks performed by the device driver is to detect the presence of card services by calling the GetCSInfo service. If the call returns the ASCII string "CS," then SRAM client driver recognizes that card services are installed. Note that if card services is not installed, the SRAM driver typically reports the error condition and terminates without remaining resident in memory. When card services is detected, the driver then registers with card services.

The driver must also obtain logical drive letters needed to perform the disk emulation. Note that the drive letter is acquired when the device driver installs even though a memory card may not be installed in the system. In this case, an attempt to access files associated with the drive letter assigned to the socket will result in a drive not ready error.

SRAM Client Driver Registers with Card Services

The client driver performs the registration process by calling the RegisterClient service. The SRAM client identifies itself as a memory client, registers to receive relevant call-back events, and passes a pointer to its call-back routine. The client may also request that card services generate a card insertion call-back for each PC Card already installed in the system. The memory client receives a handle value from card services when it returns from the call. Once registered, the memory client awaits call-backs from card servcies, notifying it when a PC card is inserted or removed.

The SRAM Client Driver Call-Back

When card services generates the card insertion call-back, it also passes the logical socket number that the PC Card was inserted into. The memory client then attempts to configure the PC Card.

The memory client must first determine if it should attempt to configure the PC Card by determining the card type. Memory clients can use the bulk memory services to access a specific region within the PC card. To access memory, the client first calls the OpenMemory service by specifying an offset within the card's attribute or common memory address space. Card services then returns a memory handle to the client that it can use when accessing memory relative to the offset specified in the OpenMemory service. Note that if card services does not support bulk memory services, the memory client must use the RequestWindow service to specify the host system address space that it wishes to use to access PC Card memory.

Reading from or writing to PC Card memory is accomplished by calling the ReadMemory or WriteMemory services. The memory client passes the memory handle it received from the OpenMemory service and specifies the memory offset and range of addresses it wishes to access. The call will likely specify location zero within the attribute memory address space. When the data is returned to the memory client it evaluates the DEVICE tuple to determine if the card contains SRAM.

Note that determining the card type can be a complicated process for memory clients. Some memory cards implement the CIS in attribute memory (required by the PC Card standard), some implement the CIS in common memory, while others do not implement a CIS at all. To complicate matters, some CIS implementations are invalid, requiring the enabler to attempt interpretation of the faulty CIS. If the card does not contain a CIS, the enabler attempts to detect the presence of the BPB (BIOS parameter block), which contains information that specifies the logical size of the disk. The BPB if present should reside at either location 0 or 512 in common memory.

If an SRAM card is detected, the call-back routine return to card services, indicating that the card was successfully configured. If the PC Card was not an SRAM card, the client returns to card services, indicating the card was not configured by the SRAM enabler.

Flash Client Drivers

Figure 21-3 illustrates the flash client driver software environment. Three types of flash client drivers are illustrated in figure 21-3. Two of the client drivers are shown interfacing to a flash file system and the other via a file translation layer. (Each file system is discussed later in this chapter.)

The flash client drivers typically load as installable device drivers via the config.sys file or equivalent mechanism. The first task performed by the device driver is to detect the presence of card services. If card services are not installed, the flash driver typically reports the error condition and terminates without remaining resident in memory. When card services is detected, the driver then registers with card services.

Flash client drivers differ from SRAM drivers in two important ways:

- Flash client drivers interface to the flash file system
- MTD client drivers must be installed to handle calls made to bulk memory services

The MTD must register prior to the flash client driver. This is necessary because the flash client driver uses the MTD to access the flash card.

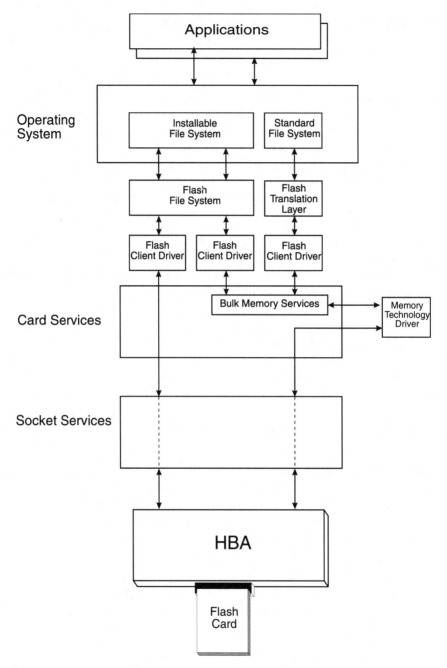

Figure 21-3. Software Environment Required for Flash Card Support

Like SRAM client drivers, flash client drivers must also obtain logical drive letters needed to perform the disk emulation. The drive letter is acquired when the device driver installs even though a memory card may not be installed in the system. In this case, an attempt to access files associated with the drive letter assigned to the socket will result in a drive not ready error.

The Flash File System

Two primary types of flash file system solution are provided by software vendors today. These systems are generally referred to as the flash file system (FFS) and flash translation layer (FTL) as illustrated in figure 21-3. The FFS provides file management based on variable size data blocks, while the FTL interfaces directly to the DOS file system which allocates data based on standard block sizes. The FTL system is compatible with disk utility programs such as Norton and PC Tools, whereas, the FFS-based systems are not.

MTD Registers with Card Services

The MTD registers with card services by calling the RegisterClient service. When registering the MTD specifies that it is a MTD client during , specifies relevant call-back events it want to be notified of, and passes a pointer to its call-back routine. The MTD client may also request that card services generate a card insertion call-back for each PC Card already installed in the system. The MTD client receives a handle value from card services when it returns from the call. Once registered, the MTD awaits call-backs from card servcies, notifying it when a PC card is inserted or removed.

The MTD Call-Back

When card services generates the card insertion call-back, it also passes the logical socket number that the PC Card was inserted into. The MTD client then determines if the PC Card contains any flash memory that it is designed to access. This can be accomplished by calling the GetFirstRegion and GetNextRegion services. These services return information (obtained from the CIS) about the card type, size, location, access time, and block erase details of the regions. If the MTD recognizes a regions of memory that it knows how to access, it then registers with card services to control access to that specific region of memory.

MTD Registers Memory Regions

To register a memory region with card services the MTD calls the RegisterMTD service. This notifies card services that the MTD has agreed to handle access to the memory regions specified. When a flash client driver requests access to this region via bulk memory services, card services will make an MTDRequest call-back to the MTD. The information specified in the call-back packet specifies the operation be requested.

Flash Client Driver Registers with Card Services

The client driver performs the registration process by calling the RegisterClient service. The flash client identifies itself as a memory client, during registration and specifies which call-back events it wishes to be notified of, and passes a pointer to its call-back routine. The client may also request that card services generate a card insertion call-back for each PC Card already installed in the system. The memory client receives a handle value from card services when it returns from the call. Once registered, the memory client awaits call-backs from card services, notifying it when a PC card is inserted or removed.

The Flash Client Driver Call-Back

When card services generates the card insertion call-back, it also passes the logical socket number that the PC Card was inserted into. The memory client then attempts to configure the PC Card.

The memory client must first determine if the card is the type that it is designed to enable. Memory clients can use the bulk memory services to access a specific region within the PC card. To access memory, the client first calls the OpenMemory service by specifying an offset within the card's attribute or common memory address space. Card services then returns a memory handle to the client for use when accessing memory starting at the offset specified in the OpenMemory service. Also when the OpenMemory service is called, card services recognized the region being opened is registered by the MTD. Note that if card services does not support bulk memory services, the memory client must use the RequestWindow service to specify the host system address space that it wishes to use to access PC Card memory.

Chapter 21: Client Drivers

Reading from or writing to PC Card memory is accomplished by calling the ReadMemory or WriteMemory services. In this instance, the memory client passes the memory handle it received from the OpenMemory service and specifies the memory offset and range of addresses it wishes to access. The call will likely specify location zero within the attribute memory address space. When the data is returned to the memory client it evaluates the DEVICE tuple to determine if the card contains flash memory.

If a flash card is detected the call-back routine returns to card services, indicating that the card was successfully configured. If the PC Card was not a flash card, the client returns to card services, indicating the card was not enabled by the flash client driver.

Accessing Flash Memory

Once the flash card has been enabled, access made to the flash card virtual drive will be fulfilled. The flash client driver receives the request from the flash file system and calls the appropriate bulk memory service. Card services recognizes that the call is to a region controlled by an MTD that previously register to access the specified memory region. Card services responds by making MTD call-backs to specify the operation being requested.

I/O Card Client Drivers

Two basic types of I/O client drivers are popular.

- Device-specific client drivers — drivers designed to detect and configure a specific PC Card. The client drivers are typically shipped by the manufacturer of a PC Card and are designed to configure this specific PC Card.
- Generic (Super) client drivers — drivers designed to detect and configure a wide range of I/O cards based on generic types, regardless of manufacturer.

Each type of I/O client driver install as device drivers when the config.sys file is executed during the system boot process. Figure 21-4 illustrates the primary actions taken by an generic I/O client driver when it initializes, registers with card services and attempts to configure PC Cards.

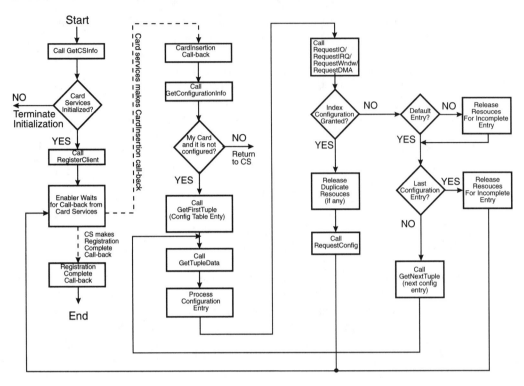

Figure 21-4. I/O Enabler Registration and PC Card Configuration Process

I/O Client Driver Registers with Card Services

The registration process begins after the client driver detects that card services has initialized. This is accomplished with the GetCardServicesInfo call. Card services returns information about card services and verifies its presence by also returning the ASCII string "CS." If card services is not initialized, the I/O client driver reports the error condition and terminates without remaining resident in memory. If card services are present the client driver calls the RegisterClient service. When the I/O client driver makes the call it:

- identifies itself as an I/O client,
- specifies which events it wants to be notified of,
- requests a card insertion call-back for each PC Card currently installed in sockets, and
- passes the entry point of it call-back routine when making the call.

Card services returns a client handle to the I/O client driver upon return from the RegisterClient service. The client driver then awaits card insertion call-backs. Card services generates a CardInsertion call-back for each PC Card already installed in a card socket (as requested by the client driver during registration). If all sockets are empty, card services generates a ConfigurationComplete call-back to signal the end of the configuration process. This example presumes that an I/O PC Card was installed when the system was powered on.

The I/O Client Driver Call-Back

Card services generates a CardInsertion call-back to the I/O client driver. The driver detects the call-back and evaluates the call-back packet to determine the socket into which the PC Card was inserted.

Identifying the PC Card

Next the GetConfigurationInfo service is called to determine if the PC Card has already been configured by another enabler. If already configured, the client driver returns to card services without configuring the PC Card. If the PC Card has not been configured, the client driver evaluates other data returned by the GetConfigurationInfo service to determine the type of function that is associated with the PC Card. If the function is one that the generic I/O enabler is designed to handle, the configuration process continues.

Determining Resources Requirements

Next, the client driver checks the first entry within the configuration table to determine the resources required by the card. This can be accomplished by and calling the GetFirstTuple service and specifying a tuple code of 1Bh (the configuration table entry tuple code). Card services scans the CIS until if finds the first instance of tuple 1Bh and returns to the client driver. The I/O driver checks the completion status and detects that card services has located the first configuration table entry. Next, the client driver calls GetTupleData and card services returns the contents of the first configuration table entry. The tuple data is evaluated to determine the resources required by the PC Card.

Requesting the Resources

As the client driver detects a configurable resource within the configuration table entry (e.g., a range of I/O address locations), it checks with card services to determine if the resource is available for the I/O card to use. The client requests a resource by calling the respective resource request service (e.g., RequestIO). When RequestIO is called Card services receives the base I/O address and range of address locations requested. It uses these values to performs a look-up within the resource management table to determine if the resource is available. Card services indicates whether or not the resource was available in the return code.

The client driver makes requests for all resources listed within the configuration table entry and determines their availability. The configurable resources that can be acquired from the system include:

- Memory address locations — via the RequestWindow service
- I/O address locations — via the RequestIO service
- Interrupt request lines — via the RequestIRQ service
- DMA channels — via the RequestDMA service

The specific actions taken when a resource is not available depends of whether the entry is a default entry of not, as discussed in the following paragraph.

If the client driver detects that the entry is tagged as a default entry, it knows that it should attempt to acquire all resources that are specified within this entry. It should retain all resource acquired from card services even if one or more of the resources requested are not available. If the entry is not a default entry, the client driver knows that the entire set of resources specified within entry must be obtained to satisfy the configuration. If any one resource is not available, then the client driver should release any individual resources that were acquired from card services by calling the respective release resource service (e.g., ReleaseIO).

If a given entry fails to satisfy the PC Card's configuration, the client driver then proceeds to the next entry by calling the GetNextTuple service. Card services finds the next configuration table entry (tuple 1B) and the client driver calls GetTupleData and starts the resource acquisition process again.

Configuring the PC Card

When all resources needed for the PC Card's configuration have been acquired from the system, the client driver configures the HBA and PC Card by calling the RequestConfiguration service. In response, card services configures the HBA and PC Card. The HBA is configured by loading the appropriate HBA registers (via socket services) that satisfy the configuration being requested. This includes reconfiguring the socket interface to memory or I/O, programming the I/O window registers, and programming the IREQ# steering logic to direct the IRQ to the appropriate system IRQ line. The PC Card is configured by writing the index number of the configuration table entry (the entry that satisfied the configuration) into the configuration option register (COR) within the card's attribute memory address space.

Point Enablers

Point enablers are dedicated enablers that bypass card and socket services. These enablers are popular in environments such as DOS where limited memory address space is available for application programs. Card and socket services take a considerable amount of memory when they install. Added to this is the space required by the enabler(s) and any TSR (terminate and stay resident programs) that might be used. As a result, too little memory is left for many application programs to run.

One solution used to relieve this memory shortage, is to remove card and socket services from the system, thereby freeing up memory that is needed to run the application program. Eliminating the card and socket services prevents PC Card client drivers from performing their functions, thus PC Card are never enabled and cannot be used. In order to use PC Cards point enablers are needed to configure the PC Cards.

In the absence of card and socket services, point enablers must communicate directly with the HBA to load the appropriate registers necessary to gain access to the PC Card. The card's CIS must be read and interpreted to identify the PC Card. If the point enabler recognizes the PC Card, it attempts to configure the card by loading the appropriate registers within the HBA to satisfy the configuration, and by writing to the configuration registers to configure the PC Card. Note that the resources used to configure the PC Card must be specified manually by the user (typically via software switches).

Chapter 22

The Previous Chapter

The previous chapter discussed the three basic types of enablers: point enablers, device-specific enablers, and generic (super) enablers. The chapter also discussed the jobs performed by generic memory enablers (and MTDs) and I/O device enablers.

This Chapter

This chapter discusses the problems associated with loading the operating system from a PC Card. It also defines mechanisms used to determine whether a given PC Card is a bootable device, and the firmware support required to support PC Card booting.

The Next Chapter

The next chapter introduces execute-in-place (XIP) support defined by the PC Card standard. The major components of an XIP environments are specified and the XIP mechanism is described.

Configuring PC Cards During POST

The previous discussions of PC Card configuration have presumed that PC Cards will be initialized either as the operating system loads or when the PC Card is inserted into a socket sometime after the operating system has loaded and the system is running. If however, the need to load the operating system from a PC Card exists, the previously discussed approaches for configuring the cards don't work.

The Problem

The normal method used in the PC environment to configure and initialize bootable devices (i.e., hard drive, video controller, and LAN adapters that support remote boot from the network) requires that the bootable device contain initialization code in a device-specific ROM. The system initialization code contained within system ROM scans the region of memory address space from location C0000h-DFFFFh to detect the presence of a device ROMs (i.e., a bootable devices). If a device ROM is detected, the system calls the initialization routine within the device ROM which is responsible for configuring the device. In this way, the bootable device is configured and can participate in loading the operating system.

To perform initial program load (IPL) from a PC Card, it too must be configured prior to beginning the boot operation. The standard method of configuring PC Cards requires the use of socket services, card services, and the PC Card's client driver. This software doesn't initialize until the operating system loads, making it unavailable for configuring a PC Card that must be used to load the operation system. Even if the PC Card contains a device ROM it cannot be detected by the system firmware during the ROM scan (because a memory window must first be programmed within the HBA to gain access to PC Card memory).

The Solution

ROM-based PCMCIA initialization code must be included with the system to support IPL from PC Cards. This firmware code must be able to program the HBA to open an attribute memory window to permit access to the CIS. Then the CIS can be evaluated to determine if the PC card is bootable, and therefore, should be configured during the POST (Power-On Self Test) sequence.

Bootable Memory Cards

The PCMCIA initialization firmware detects the presence of memory cards and configure them by opening a common memory window to provide access to the PC Cards memory array (i.e., virtual drive). The boot code being PC Card aware attempts to load the operating system from the memory card. If the memory card has been formatted and the system files reside within the memory card, the firmware will recognize the boot sector and load the operating system from the memory card.

Note that once the operating system loads, the memory cards will no longer be accessible unless the memory card contains a config.sys file that lists all of the PCMCIA relevant drivers. In this case, the socket services, card services, and the associated client drivers are loaded, thereby, providing access to the PC Cards after the operating system has loaded.

Bootable ATA Devices

PCMCIA initialization firmware recognizes ATA PC Cards by evaluating the function identification tuple within the CIS (table 22-1). The function identification tuple indicates the device type as shown in table 22-2. The shaded area identifies the value used by the ATA PC Card.

Table 22-1. Format of the Function Identification Tuple

Byte	Function Identification Tuple Format	
0	TPL_CODE	CISTPL_FUNCID (21H)
1	TPL_LINK	Link to next tuple (at least 2)
2	TPLFID_FUNCTION	PC Card function code
3	TPLFID_SYSINIT	System initialization bit mask

Note that function extension tuple will follow the function identification tuple that identify specific features associated with the ATA card (Refer to the chapter entitled, "An ATA PC Card Example"). The function identification tuple also includes an initialization byte that specifies whether the device should be configured during POST and whether the ATA card contains a device ROM. (See table 22-3.)

If the initialization byte indicates that the ATA card should be configured during POST but that it does not contain a device ROM, then the firmware is responsible for configuring the ATA card. Once the ATA card is configured, the operating system can boot directly from the drive.

Table 22-2. Contents of the Function Identification Byte

Code	Name	Meaning
0h	Multi-Function	PC Card has multiple functions. Examine the following function identification tuples that follow for individual functions.
1h	Memory	Memory Card (RAM, ROM, EPROM, flash, etc.).
2h	Serial Port	Serial I/O port, includes modem cards.
3h	Parallel Port	Parallel printer port, may be bi-directional.
4h	Fixed Disk	Fixed drive, may be silicon may be removable.
5h	Video Adapter	Video interface, extension tuples (type and resolutions supported).
6h	Network LAN Adapter	Local Area Network adapter.
7h	AIMS	Auto-Incrementing Mass Storage card.
8..FFh	Reserved	Unused in this release. Reserved by PCMCIA for future use.

Table 22-3. Contents of the Initialization Byte

7	6	5	4	3	2	1	0
Reserved for future use, must be set to zero (0)						ROM	POST

If the ATA drive also contains a device ROM, then firmware can map the ROM into the ROM scan region (C0000h-DFFFFh) and the standard initialization process will detect the device ROM. The ATA device ROM containing the ATA enabler and driver will be called by PCMCIA firmware. The ATA's device ROM performs the configuration process and returns to the system firmware. Once the drive is configured, IPL can occur from the PCMCIA ATA drive like any other ATA drive.

Chapter 23

The Previous Chapter

The last chapter discussed the problems associated with loading the operating system from a PC Card. It also defined mechanisms used to determine whether a given PC Card is a bootable device, and the firmware support required to support booting from PC Cards.

This Chapter

This chapter discusses the Execute-In-Place mechanism defined by PCMCIA that allows code to be executed directly from the card rather than copying files to and executing from system memory.

The Next Chapter

The next chapter introduces the ExCA (QuickSwap) specification that defines a required set of hardware and software support that is intended to improve PC Card interoperability across platforms based on the Intel X86 architecture.

The XIP Goals

Execute-In-Place (XIP) provides a mechanism for application programs to execute directly from PC Card memory. This eliminates the need to copy code from the PC Card into host memory before being executed, reducing the amount of system memory address space needed to load and execute a large application program. This is a particular concern in the DOS operating environment where memory address space is at a premium. Application programs written to support XIP could be supplied on a ROM-based PC Card or could be loaded from disk to a memory card (such as flash) and be executed directly from the PC Card.

Similar techniques, including the popular expanded memory specification (EMS), allow an application to reside in memory outside the memory address range that is addressable by DOS. Small portions (16KB pages) of these remote memory ranges are mapped into areas addressable by DOS, permitting them to be accessed. The EMS protocol defined in the Lotus/Intel/Microsoft (LIM) specification is supported by XIP and is called LXIP. Additionally, XIP defines support for applications designed to use extended memory (address space beyond 1MB) using Intel 80386 compatible addressing modes. This form of XIP is termed EXIP. A new type of XIP called SXIP (Simple XIP) is defined for systems with very limited paging mechanisms and small address space. The execution and read-only data images require no more than 64KB of address space.

The XIP Software Hierarchy

The functions performed by XIP software includes:

- Setting up XIP partitions in PC Card memory.
- Establishing directories within PC Card memory.
- Copying XIP applications into the XIP partitions.
- Mapping the application within the processor's addressable space.
- Starting the XIP application execution.
- Providing services for the XIP application so that it can manage program execution.

XIP File Management

XIP applications do not use the normal DOS File Allocation Table (FAT) or Flash File System (FFS). Instead, XIP applications use a dedicated software interface consisting of XIP utilities, XIP management software and socket services to map the PC Card memory into an XIP partition. The XIP software can only execute an XIP application from an XIP partition. An XIP partition can be set up in PC Card memory by utility programs. The PCMCIA specification details the organization and data structures required for partitions and directory entries.

The XIP Loader

Once the dedicated XIP partition exists then an XIP application can be loaded into the PC Card's common memory address space within an XIP partition. The XIP directory also contained within PC Card memory is then updated to reflect the application's presence. An XIP application from the user perspective begins execution in the same way that a DOS application does (by typing the name of the executable file). In this case, however, an XIP loader is invoked when an executable XIP file is called. The XIP loader's task is to find the XIP application that resides within an XIP partition in PC Card memory. The loader searches for the application within the XIP directory, maps the application into system address space and starts the application.

The XIP Device Drivers (API and Hardware Manipulation)

Once started, the application manages program execution by making the necessary calls to the XIP driver. The PCMCIA specification defines all of the functions needed by the application. The XIP device-driver functionality is split between a high-level driver (XIP.SYS) and a low-level driver (PCMCIA.SYS). The high-level driver is implemented as an installable device driver and provides all the services needed by the XIP application. This provides the XIP application's API. The low-level driver provide services for the high-level driver when it needs to access the memory-mapping hardware within the HBA. It can be installed as an installable device driver or included in the system's BIOS routines.

The intent of the split driver approach is to remove the details of the hardware interface from the high-level driver, making it easy to implement a generic XIP driver that can be used with any XIP-capable system. The system manufacturer then need only concentrate on developing the low-level driver used to manipulate the hardware (the same as the related socket service functions).

LXIP

LXIP is compatible with the LIM 4.0 specification. This protocol requires that four separate 16KB blocks of contiguous memory address space, called page frames, be mapped into the processor's memory address space. Each of these four page frames must permit access within the PC Card's XIP application, which is also organized into 16KB blocks, called pages. An LXIP application is aware of this organization and interacts with the LXIP manager to access PC Card memory via the page frames.

A PCMCIA host bus adapter designed to support the LXIP capability must have the ability to map these four 16KB address ranges independently. The LXIP manager accepts requests from the XIP application and sets up access to PC Card memory via the socket services interface and the HBA.

EXIP

EXIP specifies the ability of applications to execute directly from PC Card memory when the memory card is mapped into the processor's extended address space (above 1MB). The EXIP manager determines where PC Card memory will be allocated in extended memory and programs the HBA to map the card into extended memory.

SXIP

SXIP applications are quite small and cannot exceed more than 64KB of address space. In this respect they are similar to .com programs that execute in a single x86 memory segment. The entire program image is directly mapped into the processor's address space and no remapping or paging is performed.

Part Five

ExCA(QuickSwap)

Chapter 24

The Previous Chapter

The previous chapter described the Execute-In-Place (XIP) functionality provided by PCMCIA that allows code to be executed directly from files stored on PC Cards. Three types of XIP were defined: one for small applications (SXIP), one based on expanded memory concepts (LXIP) and the other for applications using extended memory (EXIP).

This Chapter

This chapter introduces the ExCA (QuickSwap) specification that defines a required set of hardware and software support, intended to improve PC Card interoperability across platforms based on Intel x86 architecture.

The Next Chapter

The next chapter provides a sample PCMCIA host bus adapter. The adapter documented is the Cirrus Logic PD6722 designed for use in x86 PC-based systems.

The ExCA Goal

The Intel ExCA (Exchangeable Card Architecture) specification provides specific HBA, PC Card, and software requirements for systems implementing DOS-based Intel x86 compatible systems. By defining minimum hardware and software requirements for these systems, Intel hopes to ensure PC Card compatibility across x86 systems implementing the ExCA standard.

The need for such a standard stems from the flexibility incorporated into the PCMCIA specification. The standard was designed to provide latitude for designers who are developing PCMCIA solutions over a wide range of PC and non-PC platforms. However, this latitude, while achieving its goal, also creates a greater possibility of compatibility problems.

ExCA Scope

In most respects, the ExCA specification defines a subset of the features within the PCMCIA standards, narrowing down the implementation possibilities and reducing the risk of PC Cards and systems being developed that are incompatible with one another. Additionally, ExCA defines some system characteristics not specified in the PCMCIA standard. The ExCA specification describes the minimum capabilities of the following items:

- The ExCA Host Bus Adapter
- Socket Services
- Card Services
- PC Cards (both memory-only and memory and I/O)

ExCA also encompasses a three phase compliance test, including socket hardware functional testing, system software functional testing and system integration testing.

This chapter highlights the ExCA specification's features. Refer to the ExCA specification for complete details.

ExCA Host Bus Adapter Requirements

Host bus adapter requirements fall into the following categories:

- Address Mapping (memory and I/O)
- Interrupt Support
- System Power
- PC Card Insertion and Removal
- Event WakeUp (i.e. ring indicate when system is in sleep mode)

Address Mapping (memory and I/O)

Specific requirements exist for ExCA compliant host bus adapters to ensure that address windowing capability provides the features needed in DOS-based operating environments. Address mapping features are described for

ExCA compliant sockets for both memory sockets and Memory or I/O sockets.

Memory Address Mapping

Each socket must include a minimum of four memory windows that can be acquired and used by a socket. This requirement provides support for expanded memory (L-XIP) in which four separate 16KB address ranges must be acquired from system memory and mapped to the PC Card. Support must also exist for each socket to provide a fifth window, thereby allowing access to attribute memory when necessary.

Each memory window must support system address capabilities for both real mode (within the first 1MB of memory address space) and protected mode (above 1MB of memory address space) operation. Furthermore each ExCA memory address window must have the following capabilities and characteristics:

- windows are mappable anywhere between 256KB to 16MB (in host space)
- minimum window size of 4KB
- maximum window size of 256KB (real mode)
- maximum window size of 8MB (protected mode)
- window size can be any 4KB increment (4, 8, 12, 16, 20 KB .....) or may be a power of two size (4, 8, 16, 32, 64 KB ......)

Consistent with the PCMCIA specification, memory windows are not allowed to overlap in system address space, unless use of the address range is time multiplexed.

I/O Address Mapping

ExCA requires that at least two I/O windows be implemented per socket. Characteristics of ExCA I/O windows include:

- minimum window size of 1 byte
- maximum windows size of 256 bytes
- window size must be power of two (1, 2, 4, 8, 16, 32 .... bytes)

Note that no remapping of the system I/O address is required. Addresses are directly mapped from system address locations to the same locations on the PC Card.

ExCA does not support overlapping I/O windows without time multiplexing them, as is required for overlapping memory windows. This means that no support need exist for the INPACK# signal on ExCA compliant adapters.

Interrupt Support

ExCA adapters generate a status change interrupt for all card status change events defined in the PCMCIA specification and they redirect or steer PC Card interrupts to system IRQ lines as required.

Status Change Interrupt

ExCA adapters generate a single status change interrupt for card events from all adapter sockets. Software must have the ability to globally select which type of card events generate a status change interrupt. Additionally, individual events can be masked at the socket, providing selection of specific events that generate a status change interrupt on a per socket basis. Support must also exist for enabling and disabling the status change interrupt under software control.

The adapter captures all status change events reported by each socket so that software can determine which socket encountered the status change event. The actual state of the status change signals from each socket can also be read directly from the adapter.

Status change events from I/O cards are reported when an I/O card asserts its status change pin. Status change information must be read directly from the I/O card's configuration register (pin replacement register).

PC Card Interrupts

A PC Card interrupt must be steerable to any available system interrupt. Availability depends on the host system implementation as listed in table 24-1.

ExCA compliant systems must ensure that at least one interrupt is available for standard communications and local area networks (LANs). In other words, the system must supply at least one interrupt request line from each bullet list that follows.

Chapter 24: ExCA (QuickSwap)

Table 24-1. Interrupts Potentially Available For Use By PC Cards

Systems with One Interrupt Controller	Systems with Two Interrupt Controllers	
IRQ 2	IRQ 2/9	IRQ 10
IRQ 3	IRQ 3	IRQ 11
IRQ 4	IRQ 4	IRQ 12
IRQ 5	IRQ 5	IRQ 14
IRQ 7	IRQ 7	IRQ 15

Standard Communications Interrupts (Serial Port)

- IRQ 3
- IRQ 4

Standard LAN Interrupts

- IRQ 5
- IRQ 7
- IRQ 10
- IRQ 11
- IRQ 15

Note that ExCA recommends that all interrupts listed in table 24-1 be supported by the adapter. However, a given implementation may choose to use only a subset since the system design likely uses some of the interrupts.

Interrupt sharing support is system dependent. Systems based on ISA host buses do not support interrupt sharing, while systems based on Micro Channel and EISA can share interrupts. Micro Channel and EISA devices use level sensitive interrupt triggering to support sharing, thus cards that support only the PCMCIA specified pulse-mode interrupts will not behave according to the level sensitive triggering protocol. ExCA compliant adapters must support level-mode interrupts from the PC Card, while pulse-mode support is optional.

System Power Requirements

ExCA systems must supply minimum power requirements as indicated in the ExCA specification. PCMCIA compliant PC Cards requiring more power than specified by the ExCA specification may not operate correctly when installed in sockets that are ExCA compliant. Additionally, ExCA compliant systems need not provide separate programmable voltages for Vpp1 and Vpp2. Refer to the ExCA specification for actual power requirements. The voltage supply combinations that must be provided at the socket include those listed in table 24-2.

Table 24-2. ExCA Voltage Requirements

	Vcc	Vpp1	Vpp2
required	0v	0v	0v
required	5v	5v	5v
required	5v	12v	12v
optional	5v	0v	0v

PC Card Insertion/Removal

The ExCA specification defines the sequence of events, interface signal status, Vcc and Vpp levels and critical timing delays for PC Card insertion and removal. The ExCA specification supports both cold socket insertion (recommended) and warm insertion (not recommended). Hot socket insertion of PC Cards is not supported by the ExCA. Table 24-3 defines the difference between cold, warm and hot PCMCIA sockets.

Table 24-3. State of Socket When PC Card is Inserted

Socket State	Vcc and Vpp	Address State at Signal Contact	Data State at Signal Contact	Control Signal State at Signal Contact
Cold Socket	Off	High Z or 0v	High Z or 0v	High Z or 0v
Warm Socket	On	High Z or 0v	High Z or 0v	High Z or 0v
Hot Socket	On	Driven Active	Driven Active	Driven Active

Card Insertion

The ExCA specification defines the sequence of events and minimum time duration for these events when a card is inserted into a socket. The sequence of events is listed below.

1. Card inserted into socket (both CD1# and CD2# asserted)
2. Adapter applies Vcc
3. Adapter asserts reset to PC Card
4. Adapter removes reset and PC Card begins initialization
5. Initialization completes within 20 ms or else deasserts READY
6. Client driver polls READY to detect when PC Card is ready to be accessed.

Card Removal

The ExCA specification also defines the sequence of events that are recommended when the PC Card is removed from the socket as listed below. Note that when a PC Card is removed from the system, the socket interface may be active.

1. Adapter detects card removal (CD1# and/or CD2# deasserted)
2. Adapter ceases to drive active signals to the interface (address, data and control signals go to high impedance state or 0v)
3. Vcc removed from the socket (not required if warm socket insertion is supported)

Note that the adapter detects that a card is being removed before any of the other interface or power pins lose contact with the socket (because the Card Detect pins are shortest). Next, the adapter releases the interface by tri-stating the address, data and control lines, (which are the intermediate length signal pins), and finally removes power to the Vcc pins (which are the longest pins). As the PC Card is removed it is still in contact with the signals pins and power pins long after they are disabled by the adapter.

ExCA Socket Services

The ExCA specification defines a minimum subset of socket services functions that are required for ExCA compliance. Table 24-4 lists the socket services functions and notes those that are required versus optional.

*Table 24-4. Socket Services Functions Required/Optional
for ExCA Compliant Systems*

Function	Required ?
GET_ADP_CNT	Yes
GET_SS_INFO	Yes
INQ_ADAPTER	Yes
GET_ADAPTER	Yes
SET_ADAPTER	Yes
INQ_WINDOW	Yes
GET_WINDOW	Yes
SET_WINDOW	Yes
GET_PAGE	Yes
SET_PAGE	Yes
INQ_SOCKET	Yes
GET_SOCKET	Yes
SET_SOCKET	Yes
GET_STATUS	Yes
RESET_SOCKET	Yes
INQ_EDC	No
GET_EDC	No
SET_EDC	No
START_EDC	No
PAUSE_EDC	No
RESUME_EDC	No
STOP_EDC	No
READ_EDC	No
GET_VENDOR_INFO	No
ACK_INTERRUPT	Yes
PRIOR_HANDLER	No
SS_ADDR	No
ACCESS_OFFSETS	No
VEND_SPECIFIC	No
CARD_SERVICES	Yes

Note that the EDC and vendor specific functions are optional for ExCA compliant socket services. The implementation and definition of the required socket services functions are compliant with the PCMCIA socket services standard.

ExCA Card Services

ExCA compliant systems must support card services; but, like socket services not every card services function is required. Table 24-5 lists the card services functions that are required.

Table 24-5. Card Services Functions Required/Optional For ExCA Compliance

Function	Required ?	Function	Required ?
Client Services Functions		DeregisterEraseQueue	No
GetCardServicesInfo	Partial	CloseMemory	No
RegisterClient	Yes	**Client Utilities Functions**	
DeregisterClient	Yes	GetFirstTuple	Yes
GetStatus	Yes	GetNextTuple	Yes
ResetCard	Yes	GetTupleData	Yes
SetEvenMask	Yes	GetFirstRegion	No
GetEvenMask	Yes	GetNextRegion	No
Resource Management Functions		GetFirstPartition	No
RequestIO	Yes	GetNextPartition	No
ReleaseIO	Yes	**Advanced Client Services Functions**	
RequestIRQ	Yes	ReturnSSEntry	Yes
ReleaseIRQ	Yes	MapLogSocket	Yes
RequestWindow	Yes	MapPhySocket	Yes
ReleaseWindow	Yes	MapLogWindow	Yes
ModifyWindow	Yes	MapPhyWindow	Yes
MapMemPage	Yes	RegisterMTD	No
RequestSocketMask	Yes	RegisterTimer	Yes
ReleaseSocketMask	Yes	SetRegion	No
RequestConfiguration	Yes	ValidateCIS	Yes
GetConfigurationInfo	Yes	RequestExclusive	Yes
ModifyConfiguration	Yes	ReleaseExclusive	Yes
ReleaseConfiguration	Yes	GetFirstClient	Yes
Bulk Memory Services Functions		GetNextClient	Yes
OpenMemory	No	GetClientInfo	Yes
ReadMemory	No	AddSocketServices	No
WriteMemory	No	ReplaceSocket Services	No
CopyMemory	No	VendorSpecific	No
RegisterEraseQueue	No	AdjustResourceInfo	Yes
CheckEraseQueue	No	AccessConfigurationRegister	No

PCMCIA System Architecture

ExCA PC Cards

ExCA recommends which tuples an ExCA compliant PC Card should implement. Table 24-6 below lists the recommended tuples for memory and I/O PC Cards. The lower portion of the table lists three tuples that might contain information needed by system initialization code or peripheral installation software for determining if a PC Card should be installed and configured during POST (Power-On Self Test) prior to loading the operating system. This capability is needed primarily for those devices that must be used to load and install the operating system.

Table 24-6. Tuples Recommended by the ExCA Specification

Tuples Recommended by ExCA	Memory Cards ?	I/O Cards ?
Device Information	Yes	Yes
Level 1 Version/Product Information	Yes	Yes
Configuration	Yes	Yes
Configuration Table Entry	Yes	Yes
JEDEC Device ID	Yes	No
Device Geometry Information (flash)	Yes	No
Recommended for bootable PC Cards		
Card Manufacturer ID	Yes	Yes
Function ID	Yes	Yes
Function Extension	Yes	Yes

PC Card Event WakeUp

Systems implementing power conservation modes, such as suspend or sleep, may want to wake the system up if some critical event occurs at the PC Card. Events, such as a call to a modem, could be used to wake the system up and return to normal full power operation so that the event can be processed. Currently the PCMCIA specification (release 2.1) does not define an event wakeup procedure, and in its absence, ExCA defines the following optional definition for event wakeup.

Two events can cause event wakeup in an ExCA compliant system:

- Ring Indication from a modem or fax
- remote power up from a LAN card

Chapter 24: ExCA (QuickSwap)

ExCA compliant HBAs and PC Cards use socket pin 63 (Status Change) for event wakeup, replacing either the READY, Write Protect or Battery Voltage Change status change indication on the PC Card. The PC Card indicates its support of event wakeup via the CIS.

The Configuration Table Entry tuple identifies the card's capability for using event wakeup via pin 63. The configuration entry tuple contains a miscellaneous features field that can be used to specify which status change indicators are supported by the card and is used to indicated which status change event that the event wakeup mechanism uses. The host bus adapter is programmed to direct the status change indication to the power management interrupt, which requests that the system return to full power operation.

Part Six

An Example HBA

Chapter 25

The Previous Chapter

The previous chapter introduces the ExCA (QuickSwap) specification that defines a required set of hardware and software support, intended to improve PC Card interoperability across platforms based on Intel x86 architecture.

This Chapter

This chapter provides an overview of a sample PCMCIA host bus adapter (The Cirrus Logic CL-PD6722) used in Intel x86 implementations for either an original PC or ISA compatible host bus.

Introduction to the CL-PD6722

This chapter is intended as a brief look at an actual PCMCIA host bus adapter. The Cirrus Logic CL-PD6722 was chosen as the example adapter for several reasons. First, the Intel 82365 PCMCIA adapter chip is currently implemented in more systems that any other, and the CL-PD6722 is register compatible with the Intel chip, with a few minor exceptions. The second reason is that it includes considerably more functionality than the Intel chip.

The CL-PD6722 controls two PCMCIA sockets via a single 208-pin PQFP. Features of the CL-PD6722 include the following:

- PCMCIA 2.1 and JEIDA 4.1 Compliant
- Intel 82365SL (Step A) compatible register set, ExCA compliant
- ISA host bus interface
- Dual socket interface
- Automatic Low-Power Dynamic Mode
- Programmable Suspend Mode for power conservation
- Five programmable memory windows per socket
- Two programmable I/O windows per socket
- 8-bit or 16-bit host bus interface

- ATA disk interface support for small form-factor drives
- DMA support
- Mixed-Voltage operation (3.3v or 5v) operation

Socket Power Control

The CL-PD6722 uses the PowerGood signal from the system's power supply as its reset. When PowerGood transitions from low to high the CL-PD6722 leaves the reset state and begins operation. Power to the socket is controlled by chip outputs that go to power switching devices. As shown in figure 25-1, the CL-PC6722 has four output signals per socket that control power to the socket as follows:

- Vcc_5 - when asserted 5v is applied to socket Vcc
- Vcc_3 - when asserted 3.3v is applied to socket Vcc
- Vpp_Vcc when asserted Vcc is applied to socket Vpp1.
- Vpp_PGM when asserted the programming voltage (12v) is applied to socket Vpp1.

Internal registers determine which of these signals will be asserted and when.

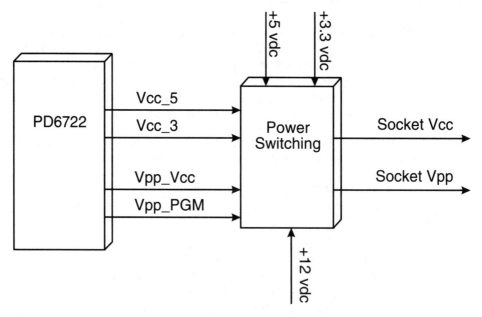

Figure 25-1. CL-PD6722 Socket Power Control Signals

Vcc Control

In PCMCIA 2.1 compliant systems, Vcc to the socket must always be 5v, but can be switched to 3.3v if the PC Card indicates the ability to operate at 3.3v via the CIS. If 3.3v operation is supported, software will write to Miscellaneous Control 1 register, specifying that Vcc should be switched to 3.3v. (Note that the CL-PD6722 provides limited support for Vcc sensing and can be used in new designs that incorporate the low voltage connectors. Contact Cirrus Logic for details.)

The CL-PD6722 supports two methods of applying Vcc to the socket:

- Vcc control via the client driver, card service and socket services software chain when a card is detected.
- Automatic Vcc control via the CL-PD6722 controller

When a card is inserted into the socket, the -CD pins are asserted and the adapter detects the card's presence. When autopower mode is not selected, the adapter waits to be commanded by the software before applying Vcc to the socket. Software must set bit four in the Power Control register (Refer to figure 25-2) to enable power to the socket. The adapter responds by asserting the Vcc_5 signal.

If bit five is set during system initialization, the adapter automatically supplies Vcc to the adapter (asserts Vcc_5) when it detects the presence of a card. Vcc is automatically removed from the card when the card is removed. Note that power is removed based on timing parameters specified in the ExCA specification.

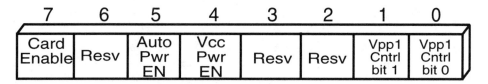

Figure 25-2. The Power Control Register

Vpp1 Control

Bits zero and one of the Power Control register determine whether Vcc (5v or 3.3 v), 12v, or zero volts is applied to the Vpp1 pin. (Refer to table 25-1)

Table 25-1. Socket Vpp Control

Bit 1	Bit 0	VPP_PGM	VPP_VCC	Socket Vpp1
0	0	Deasserted	Deasserted	zero volts
0	1	Deasserted	Asserted	selected Vcc (3.3v or 5v)
1	0	Asserted	Deasserted	+12v
1	1	Deasserted	Deasserted	zero volts

PC Card Data Transfers

The adapter monitors ISA host bus activity to see if the bus cycle is intended for it or a PC Card installed in one of its sockets. Figure 25-3 shows the signals and functional blocks involved in transferring bus cycles to the target PC Card. Note that figure 25-3 shows a single socket interface to simplify the illustration. In reality, the socket signals shown are duplicated for the second socket.

The adapter must decode the address when an ISA bus cycle is run to determine if either a local access is being made to one of its registers or whether the access is to a PC Card. PC Card accesses are determined via the window address registers. If an ISA access is made to an address location that falls within the address window programmed for a the PC Card, then the adapter knows that the PC Card is being accessed and starts a data transfer either to or from the card depending on the state of the ISA read/write command lines. In essence, the HBA decodes addresses like other ISA adapters. The HBA performs the decode to determine if the transaction is for it (an HBA register) or one of its sockets.

The CL-PD6722 uses a First In First Out serial memory (FIFO) to store up to four write operations. When a write occurs from the host ISA bus, the CL-PD6722 stores the write in the FIFO and completes the operation in zero ISA wait states. The adapter then runs the socket access to the target PC Card to complete the write transfer. In this way, write operations to PC Cards always complete at zero waits states until the FIFO fills up. Note that the FIFO is bypassed on read transfers.

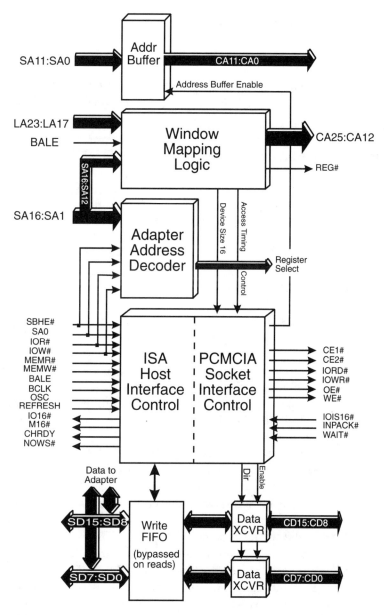

Figure 25-3. Basic Functional Blocks Used During Data Transfers

PCMCIA System Architecture

The CL-PD6722 contains two timing register sets each consisting of three registers that control transfer timing:

- Setup Timing register
- Command Timing register
- Recovery Timing register

These registers provide very flexible transaction timing when accessing PC Cards. Refer to the CL-PD6722 data book for details regarding these registers.

Address Window Mapping

The CL-PD6722 has seven window address registers for each socket: Five memory window registers and two I/O window register. Associated with each register is the transfer speed of the devices that respond within the window.

Memory Interface

The memory window register is comprised of six 8-bit registers containing the following information (refer to figure 25-4):

- **Lower byte of window start address** (LA19:LA17; SA16:SA12). Note that address line 12 is the smallest address used to define a memory address window. This supports the ExCA's requirement that windows start on 4KB boundaries. The lower 12-bits of the address (SA11:SA0) go directly to the socket via a buffer.
- **Upper portion of window start address** (LA23:LA20). The window start address reflects the maximum address capability of the ISA host bus (16MB).
- **Lower byte of window stop (end) address** (LA19:LA17; SA16:SA12). Note that memory windows must also end on even 4KB boundaries, making the smallest memory window 4KB.
- **Upper portion of window stop (end) address** (LA23:LA20)
- **Lower byte of window offset** (CA19:CA12). Note that the offset is comprised of the Card Address value that is added to the ISA address, permitting the card address to appear anywhere within the PC Card's 64MB of address space.
- **Upper portion of window offset** (CA25:CA20).

The address register also contains bits that determine characteristics about the specified range of addresses. These characteristics include:

- **Data Size** - Specifies whether access should be made to devices based on 8-bit or 16-bit addressing mode (depends on host bus size).
- **Access Time** (Timer Select) - The CL-PD6722 incorporates two timing register sets that determine the cycle time of the devices that are mapped into the address window.
- **Type of Window** (-REG) - Determines whether the window is used to access attribute memory or common memory.
- **Write Protect** (WP) - specifies whether the memory within the window address range should be write protected. Writes to address within the window are inhibited if WP is set.

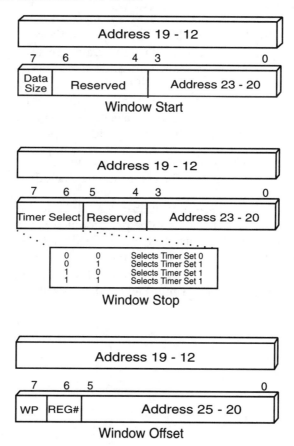

Figure 25-4. Registers Comprising a Single Memory Address Window

I/O Interface

I/O devices are mapped through the I/O window address registers. Each socket contains two I/O window registers each comprised of seven one byte registers as follows (refer to figure 25-5):

- **Upper byte of window start address** (SA15:SA8)
- **Lower byte of window start address** (SA7:SA0)
- **Upper byte of window stop (end) address** (SA15:SA8)
- **Lower byte of window start address** (SA7:SA0)
- **Upper byte of window offset register** (CA15:CA8)
- **Lower byte of window offset register** (CA7:CA1)
- **Control bits for both I/O windows**

Note that the I/O start address can begin and end on any byte boundary and can be any length. ExCA specifies constraints regarding I/O address window size and start addresses that compliant software should observe. Since the ISA host bus supports a maximum of 64KB of I/O address space, only 15 address bit are used. The offset capability allows software to map two devices at the same system address space and offset or remap the system addresses to separate locations with the PC Cards I/O address space.

Note that the characteristics of both I/O windows is controlled via the I/O window control register. The characteristics include:

- Data Size (data size and -IOIS16) - An I/O device can be either an 8-bit or 16-bit device. The size can be programmed via the data size bit or can be dynamically determined by the PC Card via the -IOIS16 signal.
- Cycle Timing (Timing Select) - the access timing of the devices responding within the window is determined by the value of a timing register set. The timing select bit determines which timer set should be used.

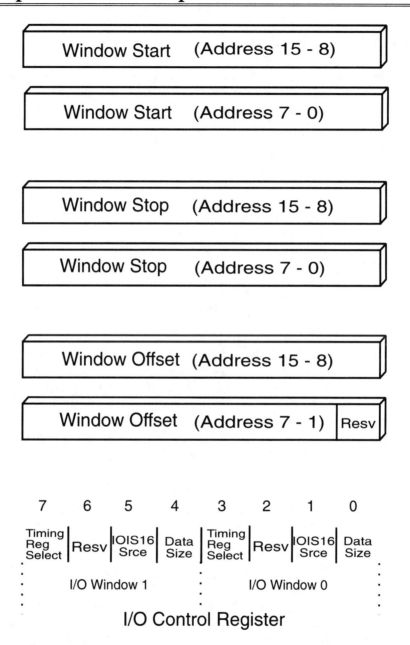

Figure 25-5. Register Comprising a Single I/O Address Window

Status Change Reporting

Status change interrupts are typically reported via a system interrupt whenever a status change event occurs. A single status change interrupt is used to report status changes for all sockets. Status change events that can result in a status change interrupt include:

For Memory Cards:

- Battery Dead Detection
- Battery Low Warning
- Change in Ready/Busy status
- Card Detect Change

For I/O Cards:

- Status Change Pin is asserted - The I/O card's configuration registers must be read to determine which of the previously mentioned status changes have occurred.

The CL-PD6722 reports a status change (also called management) interrupt over the one of the system IRQ lines specified in the Management Interrupt Configuration register (refer to figure 25-6). The upper four bits of the register determine which IRQ line the status change should be reported over, while the lower four bits determine which of the status change events should result in an interrupt being reported. These lower four bits act as a global mask to eliminate one or more of the status change events from being reported by the adapter.

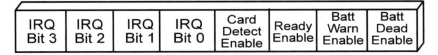

| IRQ Bit 3 | IRQ Bit 2 | IRQ Bit 1 | IRQ Bit 0 | Card Detect Enable | Ready Enable | Batt Warn Enable | Batt Dead Enable |

Figure 25-6. Management Interrupt Configuration Register

System software having been notified of a status change must determine which status change caused the interrupt. The Card Status Change register indicates the source of the status change. (Refer to figure 25-7.)

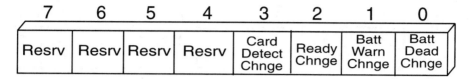

Figure 25-7. Card Status Change Register

The actual state of the socket interface pins can also be observed by software on a socket by socket basis when a memory interface is used. The interface status register provides the capability as shown in figure 25-8. When an I/O interface is defined, the PC Card must be interrogated directly to determine the state of status change indictors.

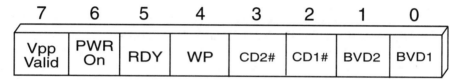

Figure 25-8. Interface Status Register

Interrupt Steering

When a card interrupt occurs, the adapter generates an IRQ to the system. The IRQ line to which the card interrupt is directed is controlled via the interrupt and general control register. (Refer to figure 25-9.) The lower four bits determine which IRQ line the interrupt is steered to. Note that this register is also used to enable management interrupt generation via bit four, and if the card uses interrupts the card type bit (five) will indicate an I/O card type.

Bit six of the register is set and reset to control reset to the PC Card. Bit seven is used when the I/O device is either a FAX, Modem, or network interface card (NIC). This pin is set when the status change pin from the PC Card is used to wake the system up due to external activity that requires system attention. The bit is defined as Ring Indicate (RI) since it is commonly used by FAX or modem cards to notify the system of an incoming call.

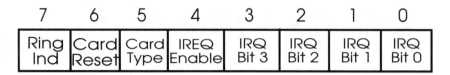

7	6	5	4	3	2	1	0
Ring Ind	Card Reset	Card Type	IREQ Enable	IRQ Bit 3	IRQ Bit 2	IRQ Bit 1	IRQ Bit 0

Figure 25-9. Interrupt and General Control Register

Refer to the CL-PD6722 data book for additional details regarding which interrupt pins are supported and how interrupts are reported.

The ATA Socket Interface

Figure 25-10 illustrates the socket interface when configured for ATA. Many of the signals used by the memory and I/O interfaces are no connections (NC) when the socket is configured for ATA. This interface is intended for manufacturers that want to use a PCMCIA socket to support their internal IDE drives. When used as an imbedded connector, the CL-PD6722 can be programmed to operate in the ATA mode, making the socket compatible with the ATA interface. This interface also provides a slight increase in performance when compared to the standard I/O interface approach described in chapter nine.

ATA Registers

The PCMCIA host bus adapter accesses ATA devices using two register groups. The groups are defined as:

- Command Block Registers - used to send commands to the drive, transfer data between the host and drive and return drive status to the host.
- Control Block Registers - used for drive control and returning alternate status information to the host.

The ATA host bus adapter accesses registers within each group by asserting the -CS0 and -CS1 signals. These signals identify which register block is being accessed, while address lines A2, A1 and A0 select the target register within the block. The binary value of A2:A0 should not be thought of as consecutive byte accesses, but rather as a binary code allowing selection of either 8-bit or 16-bit registers. For example, when CS0 is asserted the command register block is selected and address lines A2:A0 determine which of the eight register is being accessed. Register zero is the 16-bit data register selected with a binary code of zero. The next register is the 8-bit error/feature register. (Refer to table 25-2). It is beyond the scope of this book to discuss the definition and use of the ATA registers. Refer to the ANSI ATA specification and the ATA standard within the PCMCIA specification for details regarding register definition and commands.

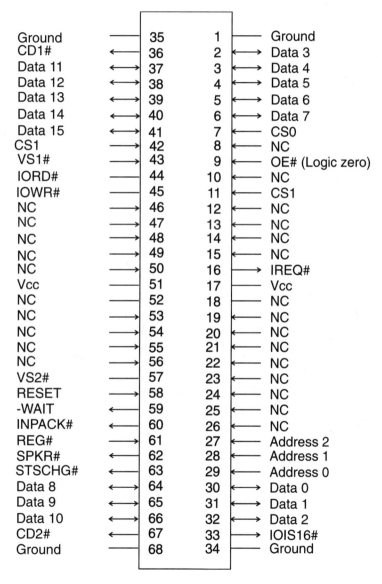

Ground	———	35	1	——— Ground
CD1#	←——	36	2	←—→ Data 3
Data 11	←—→	37	3	←—→ Data 4
Data 12	←—→	38	4	←—→ Data 5
Data 13	←—→	39	5	←—→ Data 6
Data 14	←—→	40	6	←—→ Data 7
Data 15	←—→	41	7	←—— CS0
CS1	——→	42	8	←—— NC
VS1#	——→	43	9	←—— OE# (Logic zero)
IORD#	———	44	10	←—— NC
IOWR#	———	45	11	←—— CS1
NC	——→	46	12	←—— NC
NC	——→	47	13	←—— NC
NC	——→	48	14	←—— NC
NC	——→	49	15	←—— NC
NC	——→	50	16	——→ IREQ#
Vcc	———	51	17	——— Vcc
NC	———	52	18	——— NC
NC	——→	53	19	←—— NC
NC	——→	54	20	←—— NC
NC	——→	55	21	←—— NC
NC	——→	56	22	←—— NC
VS2#	———	57	23	←—— NC
RESET	——→	58	24	←—— NC
-WAIT	←——	59	25	←—— NC
INPACK#	←——	60	26	←—— NC
REG#	——→	61	27	←—— Address 2
SPKR#	←——	62	28	←—— Address 1
STSCHG#	←——	63	29	←—— Address 0
Data 8	←—→	64	30	←—→ Data 0
Data 9	←—→	65	31	←—→ Data 1
Data 10	←—→	66	32	←—→ Data 2
CD2#	←——	67	33	——→ IOIS16#
Ground	———	68	34	——— Ground

Figure 25-10. ATA Socket Interface

Table 25-2. Example Addressing Scheme Used by ATA Cards

ATA Command Register Block (-CS1 asserted)		
Register # (A2:A0)	Read Function (-IORD asserted)	Write Function (-IOWR asserted)
0	Data Register (16-bit register)	Data Register (16-bit register)
1	Error Register (8 bits)	Features (8 bits)
2	Sector Count (8 bits)	Sector Count (8 bits)
3	Sector Number (8 bits)	Sector Number (8 bits)
4	Cylinder Low (8 bits)	Cylinder Low (8 bits)
5	Cylinder High (4 bits)	Cylinder High (4 bits)
6	Head Number (3 bits)	Head Number (3 bits)
7	Status Information (8 bits)	Command Register (8 bits)

DMA Support

The CL-PD6722 also supports DMA transfers between an I/O Card and memory. This capability is achieved through a special DMA-type PCMCIA interface cycle. This cycle is defined such that conflicts with standard PCMCIA memory or I/O cycles is avoided. These cycles are distinguished from normal I/O cycles by the -REG signal being high during an I/O cycle. This is an undefined condition in the PCMCIA 2.1 specification.

A register within the adapter controls the DMA function. The signal used by the PC Card to request a DMA transfer is programmable. When the controller sees the DMA request from the PC Card, it then requests a DMA transfer from the ISA bus's DMA controller by asserting a DMA request on the ISA bus. The CL-PD6722 uses the IRQ 9 and 10 lines to report a DMA request. If configured for DMA these IRQ lines cannot be used. Refer to the CL-PD6722 data book for details.

Appendices

Appendix A: SRAM CIS Example

The following example is the attribute memory address map showing the CIS tuples implemented within a typical SRAM card. This listing includes page number where the tuple description can be found.

Offset/Adr (hex)	Data (hex)	Description and interpretation	Page Ref
0/0	01	Device Info Tuple	353
1/2	03	Link to next tuple	353
2/4	61	Device type = 6 (SRAM) Device Speed=1 (250ns)	353
3/6	7C	Unit Size=128K Number of Units=16 Total size = 2MB	355
4/8	FF	Termination Byte	353
5/A	15	Level 1 Version/Product Information Tuple	355
6/C	20	Link to next tuple	356
7/E	04	Major Version number=4	356
8/10	01	Minor Version number=0 (PC Card 95 release)	356
9/12	58	X (The remaining entries within the tuple are ASCII codes)	356
A/14	59	Y	356
B/16	5A	Z	356
C/18	00	End Manufacturing ID	356
D/1A	32	2	356
E/1C	4D	M	356
F/1E	42	B	356
10/20	20	.	356

Offset/Adr (hex)	Data (hex)	Description and interpretation	Page Ref
11/22	53	S	356
12/24	52	R	356
13/26	41	A	356
14/28	4D	M	356
15/2A	00	End Card Description Information	356
16/2C	53	S	356
17/2E	52	R	356
18/30	30	0	356
19/32	30	0	356
1A/34	30	0	356
1B/36	30	0	356
1C/38	31	1	356
1D/3A	00	End Model Information 1	356
1E/3C	53	S	356
1F/3E	52	R	356
20/40	30	0	356
21/42	30	0	356
22/44	30	0	356
23/46	30	0	356
24/48	32	2	356
25/4A	00	End Model Information 2	356
26/4C	FF	Termination Byte	356
27/4E	10	Checksum Tuple	356
28/50	05	Link to next tuple	357
29/52	D9	Offset fm Checksum tuple (27h) to checksum start address. D9 (low byte); FFh (high byte)=FFD9h + 0027h (tuple address)=0000h	
2A/54	FF		357
2B/56	27	Number of CIS locations to be checksummed from start address = 27h (low byte);	
2C/58	00	00h (high byte)=0027h	357
2D/5A	DE	Checksum Value=DEh	357
2E/5C	FF	Termination Tuple	357

Device Information Tuple

Table -1 shows the format of the device information tuple. Shaded areas show portions of the tuple definition used by the SRAM card in the example.

The SRAM CIS listing includes a link value of 03h, indicating only two bytes are used for device info, followed by the termination byte.

Table A -1. Device Information Tuple Format

Byte	Device Information Tuple Format	
0	TPL_CODE	CISTPL_DEVICE (01h)
1	TPL_LINK	Link to next tuple (03h)
		Device Info 1 (2 or more bytes)
		Device Info 2 (2 or more bytes)
...		Device Info n (2 or more bytes)
m		FFH termination byte (marks end of device info field)

The SRAM's device information tuple contains information for a single block of memory, therefore, only one device info block (Device Info 1) is defined. Device info 1 is comprised of two bytes in this example:
- Device Type and Speed Byte
- Device Size Byte

Device Type and Speed Byte

Refer to table -2. The first byte describes the device speed, whether the write protect switch affects this address range, and the device type. Note that the device type code is only used to describe devices that use a fixed memory address range, and not for dynamically relocatable devices. Relocatable devices use the configuration entry tuples to describe the memory address ranges supported.

The device type and speed byte contains a 61h value, equating to the values shown below. Note that extended speed information can be used in lieu of the standard speed definitions. This capability permits speed definitions that might be supported by host bus adapters capable of supporting a wide range of programmable transfer rates.

Table A -2. Memory Device Type and Speed Information

Byte	7	6	5	4	3	2	1	0
0	Device Type Code = 6				WPS=0	Device Speed Codes = 1		
1	Extended Device Speed (if Device Speed Code equals 7h, otherwise omitted)							
2 .. m-1	Additional Extended Device Speed (if bit 7 of Extended Device Speed is 1, otherwise omitted)							
m .. n	Extended Device Type (if Device Type Code equals Eh, otherwise omitted)							

Table A -3. Device Speed Codes

Code	Name	Meaning
0H	DSPEED_NULL	Use when device type = null
1h	DSPEED_250NS	250 nsec
2h	DSPEED_200NS	200 nsec
3h	DSPEED_150NS	150 nsec
4h	DSPEED_100NS	100 nsec
5h-6h		(Reserved)
7h	DSPEED_EXT	Use extended speed byte.

Table A -4. Device Type Codes

Code	Name	Meaning
0	DTYPE_NULL	No device. Generally used to designate a hole in the address space. If used, speed field should be set to 0H
1	DTYPE_ROM	Masked ROM
2	DTYPE_OTPROM	One-time programmable PROM
3	DTYPE_EPROM	UV EPROM
4	DTYPE_EEPROM	EEPROM
5	DTYPE_FLASH	Flash EPROM
6	DTYPE_SRAM	Static RAM (JEIDA has Nonvolatile RAM)
7	DTYPE_DRAM	Dynamic RAM (JEIDA has Volatile RAM)
8-Ch		Reserved
Dh	DTYPE_FUNCSPEC*	Function-specific memory address range. Includes memory-mapped I/O registers, dual-ported memory, communication buffers, etc., not intended to be used as general-purpose memory.
Eh	DTYPE_EXTEND	Extended type follows.
Fh		Reserved

Device Size Byte

The SRAM's device size byte entry contains 7Ch. This represents a three bit "unit size code" of 4h, and the number of address units value of 0Fh. One is added to the number of address units value to obtain the actual number of units. Refer to table -5 for byte format.

Table A -5. Device Size Definition

7	6	5	4	3	2	1	0
# of address units(Fh) + 1= 10h (16d)					Unit Size Code = 4h		

(16 units x 128KB unit size = 2MB)

Code	Unit Size	Max Size
0	512 bytes	16 K
1	2 K	64 K
2	8 K	256 K
3	32 K	1 M
4	128 K	4 M
5	512 K	16 M
6	2 M	64 M
7	Reserved	Reserved

Level 1 Version / Product Information Tuple

Table -6 shows the format and contents of the Level 1 Version/Product Information tuple. This tuple provides the PCMCIA compliance level supported by the PC Card and includes manufacturer defined product information. The tuple includes three fields:

- The major version byte indicating PCMCIA version information.
- The minor version byte indicating compliance with a given PCMCIA release.
- A variable length field comprised of one or more strings of ASCII characters specified by the manufacturer. A value of 00h demarks each ASCII string.

Table A -6. Level 1 Version/ Product Information Tuple Format

Byte	Level 1 Version/Product Information Tuple Format	
0	TPL_CODE	CISTPL_VERS_1 (15h).
1	TPL_LINK	Link to next tuple (20h).
2	TPLLV1_MAJOR	Major version number (04h).
3	TPLLV1_MINOR	Minor version number (01h) for Release 2.0 and 2.01
4	TPLLV1_INFO	Product information string: name of the manufacturer, terminated by 00h.
		Additional product information, in text; terminated by 00H. Suggested use: lot number.
		Additional product information, in text; terminated by 00h. Suggested use: define special programming conditions.
n		FFh: termination byte (marks end of list).

Checksum Tuple

The Checksum tuple is included with this particular SRAM card for additional reliability. In this example, the CIS checksum region is defined as offset 0 (beginning of CIS) and the number of bytes included in the checksum is 27 (byte 0 to 26). Refer to table -7 for the tuple format. Note that this tuple contains three fields:

- Relative start address of the memory block within the CIS to be checked. The relative address is specified as an offset value (contents of this field) added to the offset of the checksum tuple code (the address/2). In this example the beginning of the CIS. (FFD9h + 0027 = 0000h)
- Length of the block to be checked. The length is specified as an offset value. The checksum is performed by summing the even bytes in the address range. The last location in the range can be expressed as "target address + 2 * length - 1".
- Checksum value to be tested.

Table A -7. Checksum Tuple Format

Byte	CheckSum Tuple Format	
0	TPL_CODE	CISTPL_VERS_1 (15h).
1	TPL_LINK	Link to next tuple (05h).
2 .. 3	TPLCKS_ADDR	Offset to region to be checked ,LSB first. (FFD9h)
4.. 5	TPLCKS_LEN	Length of region to be checked, LSB first. (0027h)
6	TPLCKS_CS	Checksum value of the region

Termination Tuple

The Termination tuple identifies the end of the current tuple list. The termination tuple consists only of the tuple code FFh. This tuple should be the last tuple in a linked list, but does not necessarily indicate the end of the entire string of tuples within the PC Card. Whether processing software stops or continues processing tuples upon encountering the termination tuple depends on the absence or presence of other link-specific tuples in the string as stated below:

- If a no-link tuple is contained in the tuple list, then this is the only tuple list and tuple processing ends.
- If a long-link tuple is contained in the tuple list, then process the secondary tuple list beginning at the address specified by the long-link tuple.
- When processing a secondary tuple list, if no long-link tuple is contained in the tuple list, then no more tuples exist.
- If there is no link-specific tuple contained in the primary CIS tuple list, then tuple processing should continue at location zero in common memory. In other words, a long-link tuple to common memory is implied when there is no link tuple in the primary CIS.

In this example, link-specific tuples were not included, causing parsing software to continue tuple processing at location zero within common memory address space.

Appendix B: Flash Memory CIS Example

The following is an example of a flash memory tuple chain. The reference page number indicates where the tuple description can be found.

Offset/Adr (HEX)	Data (HEX)	Description and Interpretation	Page Ref
0/0	01	Device Info Tuple	361
1/2	03	Link to next tuple	362
2/4	53	Device type = 5 (FLASH); Device Speed = 3 (150ns)	362
3/6	26	Unit Size = 2MB, Number of Units = 5, Total size = 10MB	364
4/8	FF	Tuple Termination Byte	362
5/A	1E	Device Geometry Tuple	364
6/C	06	Link to next tuple	365
7/E	02	Internal bus width of card = 2 bytes (release 1.0 and 2.0 cards)	366
8/10	11	Erase geometry block size $(2^{(n-1)}) = 2^{(11h-1)} = 2^{(16)} = $ 64K	366
9/12	01	Read geometry block size $(2^{(n-1)}) = 2^{(1h-1)} = 2^{(0)} = 1$	366
A/14	01	Write geometry block size $(2^{(n-1)}) = 2^{(1h-1)} = 2^{(0)} = 1$	366
B/16	03	Partition size$(2^{(p-1)}) = 2^{(3h-1)} = 2^{(2)} = 4$	366
C/18	01	Interleave size$(2^{(q-1)}) = 2^{(1h-1)} = 2^{(0)} = 1$	366

Offset/Adr (HEX)	Data (HEX)	Description and Interpretation	Page Ref
D/1A	18	JEDEC Identifier tuple	367
E/1C	02	Link to next tuple	367
F/1E	98	Flash Designs JEDEC-ID	
10/20	B9	46F006 JEDEC-ID	
11/22	15	Level 1 Version/Product Information Tuple	367
12/24	26	Link to next tuple	368
13/26	04	Major Version number = 4	368
14/28	01	Minor Version number = 1 (Release 2.0 or 2.1)	368
15/2A	46	F (ASCII string "FLASH DESIGNS")	368
16/2C	76	L	368
17/2E	41	A	368
18/30	53	S	368
19/32	48	H	368
1A/34	20	SPACE	368
1B/36	44	D	368
1C/38	45	E	368
1D/3A	53	S	368
1E/3C	49	I	368
1F/3E	47	G	368
20/40	4E	N	368
21/42	53	S	368
22/44	00	<end manufacturer name>	368
23/46	31	1 (ASCII string "10MB FLASH")	368
24/48	30	0	368
25/4A	4D	M	368
26/4C	42	B	368
27/4E	20	space	368
28/50	46	F	368
29/52	4C	L	368

Appendix B: Flash Memory CIS Example

Offset/Adr (HEX)	Data (HEX)	Description and Interpretation	Page Ref
2A/54	41	A	368
2B/56	53	S	368
2C/58	48	H	368
2D/5A	56	V (ASCII string "VERSION 02")	368
2E/5C	45	E	368
2F/5E	52	R	368
30/60	53	S	368
31/62	49	I	368
32/64	4F	O	368
33/66	4E	N	368
34/68	20	space	368
35/6A	30	0	368
36/6C	32	2	368
37/6E	00	<end version information>	368
38/70	FF	Tuple termination byte	368
39/72	1A	Configuration Tuple	368
3A/74	06	Link to next tuple	369
3B/76	01	Size of fields	369
3C/78	00	Index of last configuration entry within configuration table	370
3D/7A	00	Attribute memory address where configuration registers are mapped (location 4000h)	370
3E/7C	40		
3F/7E	03	Configuration register presence mask (configuration option & status registers)	371
40/80	FF	Tuple termination byte	368
41/82	FF	Termination Tuple (End of tuple string)	371

PCMCIA System Architecture

Device Information Tuple

Table B-1 shows the format of the Device Information tuple. Shaded areas show portions of the tuple definition used by the flash card in the example.

The flash CIS listing includes a link value of 03h, indicating only two bytes are used for device info, followed by the termination byte.

Table B-1. Device Information Tuple Format

Byte	Device Information Tuple Format
0	TPL_CODE CISTPL_DEVICE (01h)
1	TPL_LINK Link to next tuple
	Device Info 1 (2 or more bytes)
	Device Info 2 (2 or more bytes)
...	Device Info n (2 or more bytes)
n	FFh termination byte (marks end of device info tuple)

The Flash's device information tuple contains information for a single block of memory, therefore only one device info block (Device Info 1) is defined. Device info 1 is comprised of two bytes in this example:

- Device Type and Speed Byte (53h)
- Device Size Byte (26h)

Device Type and Speed Byte

Refer to table B-2. The first byte describes the device speed, whether the write protect switch affects this address range, and the device type. Note that the device type code is only used to describe devices that use a fixed memory address range, and not for dynamically relocatable devices. Relocatable devices use the configuration entry tuples to describe the memory address ranges supported.

The device type and speed byte contains a 53h, equating to the values shown in table B-2. Note that extended speed information can be used in lieu of the standard speed definitions. This capability permits speed

Appendix B: Flash Memory CIS Example

definitions that might be supported by host bus adapters capable of supporting a wide range of programmable transfer rates.

The device speed information contained in the tuple is specified as a code. Refer to table B-3

Table B-2. Device Information Entry

Byte	7	6	5	4	3	2	1	0
0	Device Type Code = 5				WPS=0	Device Speed Codes = 3		
1	Extended Device Speed (if Device Speed Code equals 7h, otherwise omitted)							
2 .. m-1	Additional Extended Device Speed (only if bit 7 of Extended Device Speed=1)							
m .. n	Extended Device Type (if Device Type Code equals Eh, otherwise omitted)							

Table B-3. Device Speed Codes

Code	Name	Meaning
0h	DSPEED_NULL	Use when device type = null
1h	DSPEED_250NS	250 nsec
2h	DSPEED_200NS	200 nsec
3h	DSPEED_150NS	150 nsec
4h	DSPEED_100NS	100 nsec
5h-6h		(Reserved)
7h	DSPEED_EXT	Use extended speed byte.

Table B-4. Device Type Codes

Code	Name	Meaning
0	DTYPE_NULL	No device. Generally used to designate a hole in the address space. If used, speed field should be set to 0h.
1	DTYPE_ROM	Masked ROM
2	DTYPE_OTPROM	One-time programmable PROM
3	DTYPE_EPROM	UV EPROM
4	DTYPE_EEPROM	EEPROM
5	DTYPE_FLASH	Flash EPROM
6	DTYPE_SRAM	Static RAM (JEIDA has Nonvolatile RAM)
7	DTYPE_DRAM	Dynamic RAM (JEIDA has Volatile RAM)
8-Ch		Reserved
Dh	DTYPE_FUNCSPEC*	Function-specific memory address range. Includes memory-mapped I/O registers, dual-ported memory, communication buffers, etc., that are not intended to be used as general-purpose memory.
Eh	DTYPE_EXTEND	Extended type follows.
Fh		Reserved

Device Size Byte

The flash's device size byte entry contains 26h. This represents a three bit "unit size code" of 6h, and the number of address units value of 04h. One is added to the number of address units value to obtain the actual number of units. This equates to a unit size of 2MB times 5 unit, or 10MB. Refer to table B-5.

Table B-5. Device Information Size Byte Format

Bits	7	6	5	4	3	2	1	0
Data Value	0	0	1	0	0	1	1	0
Interpretation	# of address units (04h) + 1= 05h (5d)					Unit Size Code = 6h		

(5 units x 2MB unit size = 10MB)

Table B-6. Unit Size Codes

Code	Unit Size	Max Size (32 units)
0	512 bytes	16 K
1	2 K	64 K
2	8 K	256 K
3	32 K	1 M
4	128 K	4 M
5	512 K	16 M
6	2 M	64 M
7	Reserved	Reserved

Device Geometry Tuple

The device geometry tuple provides the erase, read, and write characteristics of the flash device. This tuple consists of multiple entries for each device identified in the device information tuple. Refer to table B-7. In this example, a single device (a 150ns, 10MB flash card) was defined in the device information tuple. Therefore, a single device geometry field is defined within the device geometry tuple (as indicated by the shaded area in the table).

Note that for multiple device cards (i.e. SRAM/Flash card), multiple device information entries are continued within the device information tuple. The device geometry tuple must contain a device information

Appendix B: Flash Memory CIS Example

entry corresponding to each device information entry in the device information tuple. Device geometry entries must exist even if the device geometry information is not relevant (as in the case of SRAM).

Byte	Device Geometry Tuple Format	
0	TPL_CODE	CISTPL_DEVICEGEO (1EH)
1	TPL_LINK	Link to next tuple (6H)
2 .. 7	Device geometry for first device info entry (6 bytes)	
8 .. D	Device geometry for second device info entry (6 bytes)	
..	Device geometry for remain device info entries (6 bytes)	

Device Geometry Information

The device geometry information consists of six fields that define the characteristics of the memory array or arrays within the memory card. These entries include:

- Internal data bus width within the card.
- Minimum erase block size.
- Minimum read block size.
- Minimum write block size
- Hardware interleaving factor used by the card.

Table B-8 defines how each of these values are expressed in each of the one byte fields. Table B-9 shows the resultant characteristics of the example flash card. Note that the erase, read and write block size must be multiplied by the bus size value and interleave factor to obtain the overall geometric characteristics of the card.

Table B-8. Device Geometry Information Fields Definition

Byte	Device Geometry Fields Definition	
1	DGTPL_BUS	Internal card data bus width. This entry = n, where the bus width is $2^{(n-1)}$ bytes. n=2 for release 1.0 & 2.0 cards.
2	DGTPL_EBS	Minimum Erase Block Size of memory arrays. This entry=n, where the minimum EBS is $2^{(n-1)}$ address increments for bus-width accesses.
3	DGTPL_RBS	Minimum Read Block Size of memory arrays or segments. This entry=n, where the minimum RBS is $2^{(n-1)}$ address increments for bus-width accesses.
4	DGTPL_WBS	Minimum Write Block Size of memory array segments. This entry=n, where the minimum WBS is $2^{(n-1)}$ address increments for bus-width accesses.
5	DGTPL_PART	Minimum size or granularity into which memory array segments can be partitioned. This entry=p, where the minimum partition granularity is $2^{(p-1)}$ erase blocks. P=1 where array partitioning on erase block boundaries is allowed.
6	DGTPL_HWIL	Value = q, where card architectures employ a multiple of $2^{(q-1)}$ times interleaving of the entire memory array or subsystems with the above characteristics. Non-interleaved cards have values of q=1. The value q = 00h is not allowed.

Table B-9. Interpretation of the Device Geometry Information Fields for Sample Flash Card

Device Geometry Field Description	Calculated Value from Field Entry	Data Bus Width	Interleave Factor	Resultant Geometry
Bus Width	2 bytes	NA	NA	NA
Hardware Interleave	1	NA	NA	NA
Erase Geometry	64k x	2 bytes x	1 =	128 kb
Read Geometry	1 x	2 bytes x	1 =	2 bytes
Write Geometry	1 x	2 bytes x	1 =	2 bytes

Appendix B: Flash Memory CIS Example

JEDEC Identifier Tuple

The JEDEC Identifier tuple is an optional tuple used by programmable devices. This tuple must have a JEDEC identifier entry for each device specified in the device information tuple, whether or not a given device is programmable. In this way, a one-to-one correspondence is maintained between the device information tuples and the JEDEC identifier entries. If a given device is not programmable, then the corresponding JEDEC identifier entry for that device will contain 00h.

The basic structure of the JEDEC Identifier tuple is shown in table B-10. Only the shaded fields are used for the flash card example. Refer to table B-11 for a description of the contents of each JEDEC identifier.

Table B-10. JEDEC Identifier Tuple Format

Byte	JEDEC Identifier Tuple Format	
0	TPL_CODE	CISTPL_JEDEC_C (18H)
1	TPL_LINK	Link to next tuple (2H)
2 .. 7	JEDEC identifier for first device info entry (2 bytes)	
8 .. D	JEDEC identifier for second device info entry (2 bytes)	
..	JEDEC identifier for remaining device info entries (2 bytes)	

Table B-11. JEDEC Identifier Entry Definition

Byte	7	6	5	4	3	2	1	0
0	parity	Device manufacturer ID assigned by JEDEC (odd parity)						
1	Manufacturer-specific data specifying device type, programming info, etc.							

Level 1 Version / Product Information Tuple

Table B-12 illustrates the format and contents of the level 1 version/product information tuple. This tuple provides the PCMCIA compliance level supported by the PC Card and includes manufacturer defined product information. The tuple includes three data fields:

- The major version byte indicating PCMCIA version information.
- The minor version byte indicating compliance with a given PCMCIA release.

- A variable length field comprised of one or more strings of ASCII characters specified by the manufacturer. A value of 00h demarks each ASCII string. The tuple is terminated by FFh.

Table B-12. Level 1 Version/Product Information Tuple Format

Byte	Level 1 Version/Product Information Tuple Format	
0	TPL_CODE	CISTPL_VERS_1 (15H)
1	TPL_LINK	Link to next tuple
2	TPLLV1_MAJOR	Major version number (04H)
3	TPLLV1_MINOR	Minor version number (01h) for Release 2.0 and 2.01
4	TPLLV1_INFO	Product information string: name of the manufacturer, terminated by 00h. Additional product information, in text; terminated by 00h. Suggested use: lot number. Additional product information, in text; terminated by 00h. Suggested use: programming conditions.
n		FFH: termination byte (marks end of list).

Configuration Tuple

The configuration tuple identifies the number of configuration registers implemented and their location in attribute memory. The configuration tuple consists of six data entries. Table B-13 shows the actual format of the configuration tuple. Note that the entries used in the flash example are shaded.

- Size of fields—specifies the number of bytes in the "configuration registers base address" field, in the "configuration presence mask" field, and in the "reserved field."
- Index number of the last entry in the configuration table.
- Configuration registers base address in attribute memory.
- Configuration presence mask—identifies the configuration registers that are implemented.
- Reserved Field.
- Subtuple information—containing additional card configuration information.

Appendix B: Flash Memory CIS Example

Table B-13. Configuration Tuple Format

Byte	Configuration Tuple Format	
0	TPL_CODE	Configuration tuple code (CISTPL_CONFIG, 1Aн)
1	TPL_LINK	Link to next tuple (n-1; minimum 1)
2	TPCC_SZ	Size of Fields Byte
3	TPCC_LAST	Index Number of the last entry in the Card Configuration Table
4..	TPCC_RADR	Configuration Registers Base Address in attribute memory space. 1,2,3, or 4 bytes depending upon the size field in TPCC_LAST
..	TPCC_RMSK	Configuration Registers Presence Mask. 1 to 16 bytes as indicated by the count in TPCC_SZ.
..	TPCC_RSVD	Reserved area 0 - 3 bytes. Must be 0 bytes until defined.
q+1..r	TPCC_SBTPL	The rest of the tuple is reserved for subtuples containing optional information related to the card 's configuration.

Size of fields

The size of fields entry describes the number of bytes used in the TPCC_RADR, TPCC_RMSK and TPCC_RFSZ fields as shown in table B-14. In the flash card example, the size of fields entry has a value of 01h, indicating the following values:

- TPCC_RASZ — a one must be added to the hex value in this field to determine the number of bytes in TPCC_RADR used to specify the configuration registers base address. In this example, the TPCC_RADR entry consists of two bytes.

- TPCC_RMSZ — a one must be added to the hex value in this field to determine the number of bytes in TPCC_RMSK used to indicate which of the option registers have been implemented. In this example, the TPCC_RMSK entry consists of one byte.

- TPCC_RFSZ — the number of bytes reserved for future use (either 0,1,2 or 3). Must be zero for release 2.0 compliance.

Table B-14. Size of Fields Byte

Bits	7	6	5	4	3	2	1	0
Data Value	0	0	0	0	0	0	0	1
Field Definition	TPCC_RFSZ (RESR Size=0)		TPCC_RMSZ (Size of TPCC_RMSK=0)			TPCC_RASZ (Size of TPCC_RADR=1)		

Index Number of Last Configuration Entry

This entry contains the index number of the last configuration entry of the card's configuration table and a reserved field as shown in table B-15. Since no configuration table is used in this example, the "last index" value is zero. Bits six and seven are reserved future use and must be set to zero.

Table B-15. Last Configuration Index

Bits	7	6	5	4	3	2	1	0
Data Value	0	0	0	0	0	0	0	1
Field Definition	Reserved for future use (Resr bits=0)		The index number of the final entry in the Card Configuration Table when scanning the CIS from address zero (Last Index = 0)					

Configuration Registers Base Address Entry

The entry consists of either 1,2,3 or 4 bytes as specified by the "TPCC_RASZ" field of the "Size of Fields" entry. In this example, the "TPCC_RASZ" field indicates this entry consists of two bytes as shown in the shaded area of table B-16. The resulting address is attribute memory location 4000h (or 32,768d).

Table B-16. Configuration Register Base Address Entry

Bits	Configuration Register Base Address Entry
Field	Base Address Bits 7:0 (00H)
Definition	Base Address Bits 15:8 (40H)
	Base Address Bits 23:16
	Base Address Bits 25:24

Appendix B: Flash Memory CIS Example

Configuration Presence Mask

The presence mask entry consists of a variable number of fields as determined by the TPCC_RMSZ field within the size of fields tuple entry. The presence mask is a bit map of configuration registers that can be implemented. The presence mask entry can contain a maximum of sixteen one byte fields (TPCC_RMSZ = 4 bits), and the eight bits in each field represents a configuration register; therefore, 128 configuration registers can be identified. The format of the presence mask fields is shown in figure B-17. In this example, the presence mask entry consists of a single byte (indicated by shading).

Currently, only four registers are specified by the PCMCIA standard. Each of these registers is numbered as follows:

Register 0 = Configuration Option Register
Register 1 = Card Configuration and Status Register
Register 2 = Pin Replacement Register
Register 3 = Socket and Copy Register

The value 03h specified in the flash card example indicates that the "configuration option register" and "card configuration and status register" have been implemented in this card. Refer to Table B-17.

Table B-17. Configuration Register Presence Mask Entry Format

Bits	Configuration Register Presence Mask Entry Format
Field Definition	Configuration Registers 7:0 (03H)
	Configuration Registers 15:8
	Configuration Registers 23:16
	Configuration Registers 31:24
	Configuration Registers 39:32
	Configuration Registers 47:40
	Configuration Registers 55:48
	....
	Configuration Registers 127:120

Termination Tuple

The termination tuple consists only of the tuple code FFh. This tuple should be the last tuple in the linked list. The action taken when encountering an end of list tuple depends on which form of link tuple, if any, was previously encountered in the tuple:

- If a no-link tuple is contained in the tuple list, then this is the only tuple list.
- If a long-link tuple is contained in the tuple list, then process the secondary tuple list beginning at the address specified by the long-link.
- when processing a secondary tuple list, If no long-link tuple is contained in the tuple list, then no more tuples exist.
- If no link-specific tuples are contained in the primary CIS tuple list, then tuple processing should continue at location zero in common memory. In other words, a long-link tuple to common memory is implied when there is no link-specific tuple in the primary CIS. Tuple processing continues only if the link-target tuple is found at location zero in common memory.

Appendix C: FAX/Modem Tuple Example

Offset/Addr (hex)	Data	Description and interpretation	Page Ref
0/0	01	Device Info Tuple	379
1/2	02	Link = 2h	379
2/4	00	Not a memory device	379
3/6	FF	Termination byte	379
4/8	15	Level 1 Version/Product Information Tuple	379
5/A	24	Link = 24h	380
6/C	04	Major Version number = 4	380
7/E	01	Minor Version number = 1 (Release 2.0 or 2.1)	380
8/10	58	X (The remaining entries within the tuple are ASCII codes)	380
9/12	59	Y	380
A/14	5A	Z	380
B/16	00	<End manufacturers name>	380
C/18	32	2	380
D/1A	2E	.	380
E/1C	34	4	380
F/1E	2F	/	380
10/20	39	9	380
11/22	2E	.	380
12/24	36	6	380
13/26	20		380
14/28	44	D	380

Offset/Addr (hex)	Data	Description and interpretation	Page Ref
15/2A	41	A	380
16/2C	54	T	380
17/2E	41	A	380
18/30	2F	/	380
19/32	46	F	380
1A/34	41	A	380
1B/36	58	X	380
1C/38	20		380
1D/3A	4D	M	380
1E/3C	4F	O	380
1F/3E	44	D	380
20/40	45	E	380
21/42	4D	M	380
22/44	00	<End product name>	380
23/46	30	0	380
24/48	30	0	380
25/4A	31	1	380
26/4C	00	<End lot number>	380
27/4E	41	A	380
28/50	00	<End version information>	380
29/52	FF	Termination byte (End tuple)	380
2A/54	20	Manufacturer Identification Tuple	380
2B/56	04	Link to next tuple	381
2C/58	AA	Manufacturer AAh (low byte); 00 (high byte) = AA00h	381
2D5A	00		
2E/5C	96	Product code = 96h	381
2F/5E	00	Revision Information = 0	381
30/60	21	Function Identification Tuple	381
31/62	02	Link to next tuple	382
32/64	02	Function code 2 = serial interface	382
33/66	00	Initialization byte = no init during POST and no ROM	382
34/68	22	Function extension tuple	383
35/6A	04	Link to next tuple	384
36/6C	00	Tuple function extension type = 0	385

Appendix C: FAX/Modem Tuple Example

Offset/Addr (hex)	Data	Description and interpretation	Page Ref
37/6E	01	UART type = 1 (16450 UART)	385
38/70	0F	UART capabilities = even, odd parity; mark, space, 1	
39/72	1C	stop and 7 bit characters	385
3A/74	22	Modem function extension tuple	385
3B/76	09	Link to next tuple	385
3C/78	05	Tuple function extension type = 5	385
3D/7A	1F	Flow control methods = 31 Trans, RTS/CTS, XON/XOFF	385
3E/7C	3F	DCE command buffer size = 63	385
3F/7E	00	DCE to DTE buffer size = 000300h (768d)	385
40/80	03		
41/82	00		
42/84	00	DTE to DCE buffer size = 000300h (768d)	385
43/86	03		
44/88	00		
45/8A	22	Modem function extension tuple	385
46/8C	09	Link to next tuple	385
47/8E	06	Tuple function extension type = 6	385
48/90	1F	Flow control methods = 31 Trans, RTS/CTS, XON/XOFF	385
49/92	3F	DCE command buffer size = 63	385
4A/94	00	DCE to DTE buffer size = 000400h (16384d)	385
4B/96	40		
4C/98	00		
4D/9A	00	DTE to DCE buffer size = 000400h (16384d)	385
4E/9C	04		
4F/9E	00		
50/A0	22	Modem function extension tuple	385
51/A2	0D	Link to next tuple	385
52/A4	02	Tuple function extension type = 2	385
53/A6	01	Max DTE to UART BPS (v 75) = 256	385
54/A8	00		
55/AA	3F	Modulation Standards = 003Fh (V.22BIS, V.22, Bell212A, V23,	

Offset/Addr (hex)	Data	Description and interpretation	Page Ref
56/AC	00	V21 and Bell 103)	385
57/AE	03	Error Correction Detection protocols = 03h (V.42 MNP)	385
58/B0	03	Data compression protocols = 03h (MNP5, V.42BIS)	385
59/B2	1F	Command protocols = 1Fh (V.25BIS, MNP AT, AT 3-1)	385
5A/B4	07	Escape mechanisms = 7	385
5B/B6	00	Data encryption = 0	385
5C/B8	01	Misc. features = 1 (caller ID)	385
5D/BA	B5	Country Code = 181	385
5E/BC	FF	Country Code = 255	385
5F/BE	22	Modem function extension tuple	385
60/C0	08	Link to next tuple	385
61/C2	13	Tuple function extension type = 13	385
62/C4	01	Max. DTE to UARTBPS (v/75) = 256	385
63/C6	00		
64/C8	07	Modulations Standards supported = V.29, V.27ter, V.21	385
65/CA	00	Data encryption = 0	385
66/CC	00	FAX feature selection = 0	385
67/CE	00		
68/D0	B5	Country Code = 181	385
69/D2	22	Modem function extension tuple	385
6A/D4	08	Link to next tuple	385
6B/D6	23	Tuple function extension type	385
6C/D8	01	Max. DTE to UART BPS (v/7 5) = 256	385
6D/DA	00		
6E/DC	07	Modulation standards supported = v.29, V.27ter, V.21	385
6F/DE	00	Data encryption = 0	385
70/E0	00	FAX feature selection = 0	385
71/E2	00		
72/E4	B5	Country Code = 181	385
73/E6	1A	Configuration Table Tuple	385
74/E8	05	Link to next tuple	386
75/EA	01	2-byte base address register; 1-byte configuration mask	386
76/EC	24	Index number of last configuration table entry = 24h	387

Offset/Addr (hex)	Data	Description and interpretation	Page Ref
77/EE	00	base address of configuration registers = 0200h	18
78/F0	02		
79/F2	17	Configuration mask = Config Option, Status and Pin Replacement	388
7A/F4	1B	Configuration Table Entry Tuple	389
7B/F6	11	Link to next tuple	390
7C/F8	E0	Config Index = E0h (Interface byte used, default entry, Index = 20h)	390
7D/FA	41	Interface description byte = Mem/IO interface, READY active, BVD inactive, WP inactive, MWait inactive.	391
7E/FC	9D	Feature selection byte = (Power, timing, I/O, INTR, Misc. defined)	393
7F/FE	78	Power description byte (Istatic, Iavg, Ipeak, Ipwrdn)	395
80/100	75	Istatic = 80ma	397
81/102	7D	Iavg = 90ma	397
82/104	06	Ipeak = 100ma	397
83/106	15	Ipwrdn = 13ma	397
84/108	E7	Timing description byte (READY scaling factor=10d, no wait timing, and no reserved speed)	398
85/10A	5F	5.0(mantissa) * 10ms (exponent) * 10 (scaling factor) = 500 ms max READY Delay	399
86/10C	AA	I/O description byte (10 address lines, 8-bit device, includes range)	400
87/10E	60	Length size descriptor = 1 address and 1 length	402
88/110	F8	Start address = 03F8h	
89/112	03		403
8A/114	07	Length of address block = 0-7 (8 bytes)	403
8B/116	24	Interrupt descriptor byte = IRQ4, level mode	403
8C/118	28	Misc. description byte = Audio Feedback present	403
8D/11A	1B	Configuration Table Entry	404
8E/11C	08	Link to next tuple	404
8F/11E	21	Configuration Index = 21h, no interface description byte	404
90/110	18	Feature selection byte	404

Offset/Addr (hex)	Data	Description and interpretation	Page Ref
91/122	AA	I/O description byte (10 address lines, 8 bit device, includes range)	404
92/124	60	Length size descriptor = 1 address and 1 length	404
93/126	F8	Start address = 02F8h	404
94/128	02		404
95/12A	07	Length of address block = 0-7 (8 bytes)	404
96/12C	23	Interrupt description byte = IRQ3, level mode	404
97/12E	1B	Configuration Table Entry	404
98/130	08	Link to next tuple	404
99/132	22	Configuration Index = 22h, no interface description byte	404
9A/134	18	Feature selection byte	404
9B/136	AA	I/O description byte (10 address lines, 8 bit device, includes range)	404
9C/138	60	Length size descriptor = 1 address and 1 length	404
9D/13A	E8	Start address = 03E8h	404
9E/13C	03		404
9F/13E	07	Length of address block = 0-7 (8 bytes)	404
A0/140	24	Interrupt description byte = IRQ4, level mode	404
A1/142	1B	Configuration Table Entry	404
A2/144	08	Link to next tuple	404
A3/146	23	Configuration Index = 23h, no interface description byte	404
A4/148	18	Feature selection byte	404
A5/14A	AA	I/O description byte (10 address lines, 8 bit device, includes range)	404
A6/14C	60	Length size descriptor = 1 address and 1 length	404
A7/14E	E8	Start address = 02E8h	404
A8/150	02		
A9/152	07	Length of address block = 0-7 (8 bytes)	404
AA/154	23	Interrupt description byte = IRQ3, level mode	404
AB/156	1B	Configuration Table Entry	404
AC/158	06	Link to next tuple	404

Offset/Addr (hex)	Data	Description and interpretation	Page Ref
AD/15A	24	Configuration Index = 24h, no interface description byte	404
AE/15C	18	Feature selection byte	404
AF/15E	23	I/O description byte (3 address lines, no range)	404
B0/160	30	Interrupt description byte (use IRQ mask)	404
B1/162	BC	Permissible IRQ lines = IRQ2, 3, 4, 5, 7, 9, 10 or 15	
B2/164	86		404
B3/166	14	No Link Tuple	404
B4/168	00	Link to next tuple	404
B5/16A	FF	Termination Tuple (end of tuple list)	404

Device Information Tuple

The device information tuple must be the first tuple of any release 2.0 compliant system and must be located at attribute memory address location zero. Device information provided in this tuple applies only to memory devices. When an I/O only card is used, the device information field will be only one byte long and contain a zero. Table C-1 shows the format of the device information tuple. Shaded area show portions of the tuple definition used by the FAX/modem card in this example.

The FAX/modem CIS listing includes a link value of 02h, indicating only one byte for device information, followed by the termination byte.

Table C-1. Device Information Tuple Format

Byte	Device Information Tuple Format	
0	TPL_CODE	CISTPL_DEVICE (01h)
1	TPL_LINK	Link to next tuple (02h)
		Device Info 1 (00h = null – not a memory device)
		Device Info 2 (2 or more bytes)
...		Device Info n (2 or more bytes)
n		FFh termination byte (marks end of device info field)

Level 1 Version / Product Information Tuple

Table C-2 shows the format and contents of the level 1 version/product information tuple. This tuple provides the PCMCIA compliance level supported by the PC Card and includes manufacturer defined product information. The tuple includes three fields:

- The major version byte indicating PCMCIA version information.
- The minor version byte indicating compliance with a given PCMCIA release.
- A variable length field comprised of one or more strings of ASCII characters specified by the manufacturer. A value of 00h demarks each ASCII string.

Table C-2. Level 1 Version/Product Information Tuple Format

Byte		Level 1 Version/Product Information Tuple Format
0	TPL_CODE	CISTPL_VERS_1 (15h).
1	TPL_LINK	Link to next tuple (24h).
2	TPLLV1_MAJOR	Major version number (04h).
3	TPLLV1_MINOR	Minor version number (01h) for Release 2.0 and 2.01
4	TPLLV1_INFO	Product information string: name of the manufacturer, terminated by 00h. Additional product information, in text; terminated by 00h. In this example: • Product name • Lot number • Version
n		FFh termination byte (marks end of list).

Manufacturer Identification Tuple

This tuple provides information about the PC Card manufacturer and consists of two fields:

- Manufacturer ID
- Manufacturer specific card ID information

The format of the Manufacturer Identification tuple is shown in Table C-3.

Appendix C: FAX/Modem Tuple Example

Table C-3. Manufacturer Identification Tuple

Byte	Manufacturer Identification Tuple	
0	TPL_CODE	CISTPL_MANFID (20h)
1	TPL_LINK	Link to next tuple (04h)
2..3	TPLMID_MANF	PCMCIA PC Card manufacturer code
4..5	TPLMID_CARD	Manufacturer information (Card Number and/or Revision)

Manufacturer ID Field (TPLMID_MANF)

The value stored in this two-byte field is assigned by PCMCIA with ID codes starting at 0100h and ending at FFFFh. The first 256 codes, 0000h to 00FFh, are reserved for manufacturers that already have an eight-bit JEDEC ID code from the Electronics Industry Association (EIA). This eight-bit ID code may be used as part of the PCMCIA ID. In this case, the JEDEC ID is used as the least-significant eight bits of the PCMCIA code, with the most significant eight bits all zeros.

Manufacturer Card ID Field (TPLMIC_CARD)

This two-byte field is designated for manufacturer information regarding the PC Card. The first byte is typically used to identify the card and the second byte for card revision information. The FAX/modem listing defines the first byte as a product code (28h) and the second as revision information (00h).

Function Identification Tuple

This tuple identifies individual functions within the PC Card and specifies whether the function should be automatically configured during system initialization. The tuple contains two fields:

- Function Code byte
- System Initialization Bit Mask

If a PC Card contains multiple functions, this tuple must be repeated for each function. In this case, an initial function identification tuple must be used to specify the PC Card as a multifunction card, followed by a separate function identification tuple for each function. For a given function, if additional function-specific information is available, function extension tuples will follow the function identification tuple for that function. Refer to table C-4 for the tuple's basic format.

Table C-4. Function Identification Tuple Format

Byte	Function Identification Tuple Format	
0	TPL_CODE	CISTPL_FUNCID (21h)
1	TPL_LINK	Link to next tuple (02h)
2	TPLFID_FUNCTION	PC Card function code (02h)
3	TPLFID_SYSINIT	System initialization bit mask (00h)

Function Code Byte (TPLFID_FUNCTION)

This field contains a code that identifies the basic function of the PC Card. In this example, the FAX/modem is a serial device (code 02h). Table C-5 lists the functions supported by PCMCIA.

Table C-5. PC Card Function Codes

Code	Name	Meaning
0	Multi-Function	PC card has multiple functions. Function identification tuples for each individual function must follow this tuple.
1	Memory	Memory card (RAM, ROM, EPROM, flash, etc.).
2	Serial Port	Serial I/O port (includes modem cards).
3	Parallel Port	Parallel printer port (may be bi-directional).
4	Fixed Disk	Fixed drive (may be silicon or removable).
5	Video Adapter	Video interface extension tuples (type and resolutions).
6	NetworkLAN Adapter	Local Area Network adapter.
7	AIMS	Auto-Incrementing Mass Storage card.
8..FFh	Reserved	Unused in release 2.x. Reserved by PCMCIA for future use.

Appendix C: FAX/Modem Tuple Example

System Initialization Byte (TPLFID_SYSINIT)

This field contains two bits that permits a PC Card to perform initial program load (IPL):

- POST bit — specifies whether a given function should be configured during system initialization
- ROM bit — indicates whether the PC Card contains an expansion ROM

The format of the system initialization byte is shown in table C-6. Note that for the FAX/modem both bits are zero, indicating no requirement for configuration during system initialization and no expansion ROM is included on the card.

Table C-6. Initialization Byte Format

7	6	5	4	3	2	1	0
Reserved for future use, must be set to zero (0)						ROM	POST

Function Extension Tuple

Not all classes of devices have function extension tuples defined. Working groups within PCMCIA that are concerned with specific PC card functions define function extensions. Relevant to the FAX/modem example, the function extensions for the serial port have been defined by PCMCIA. These extensions include support for the serial port itself (UART), data modems, facsimile modems, and voice modems.

The extension tuples for modem support include the features normally seen in application software. The extension tuples provide information for use by application software and play no role in the PC Card's configuration. The types of information included in the extensions include the various features supported by the modem such as: communication protocols, error correction, command support, and data compression support.

Table C-7 shows the common format of the function extension tuples. Each function extension tuple has the same tuple code (22h), a link field and two function-specific fields:

- Function Extension Type Code Field — this field identifies the specific function extension defined by this tuple.
- Function-specific information — this field contains data that is specific to a given extension type.

Table C-7. Function Extension Tuple Format

Byte	Function Extension Tuple Format	
0	TPL_CODE	CISTPL_FUNCE (22H)
1	TPL_LINK	Link to next tuple
2	TPL_TYPE	Function Extension Type Code (see table C-8)
3..n	TPLFE_DATA	Function-specific information

Function Extension Type Code (TPL_TYPE)

A separate function extension tuple is used for each type of extension defined. The particular type of function extension is defined in the function extension type code entry (TPL_TYPE). TPL_TYPE consists of two fields:

- Subfunction ID — this is the function extension type ID code
- Subfunction Descriptor — this identifies the EIA/TIA modem service class

Table C-8 lists the modem extensions and their associated function codes. This example includes serial port, data modem and facsimile modem extensions (those used in the example are shown in the shaded areas). The subfunction descriptor specifies a numeric value related to the EIA/TIA class of service supported by the modem. The FAX/modem in this example specifies a subfunction descriptor for the facsimile modem for class 1 and class 2 support.

Table C-8. Modem Function Extensions

7	6	5	4	3	2	1	0
Subfunction Descriptor				Subfunction ID			
Code	Extension Descriptor			Code	Extension Function		
1-15	Describes the EIA/TIA Service Class specified in the numeric value of the code			0	Describes serial port interface. (UART)		

• The extension descriptor is used in conjunction with the FAX modem services function (code 3h).

• In addition to the FAX modem services, the descriptor code adds the following:

    13h = class 1 fax command support

    23h = class 2 fax command support

Note: The sequence of function extension tuples in the FAX/Modem example is as follows:

Code 0 - Modem Interface Description. (Default for Data & FAX, 8 & 9 not used)

Code 5, 6 - Data & FAX modem inter-face capabilities.

Code 2, 3, 3 - Data Modem Services & FAX Modem Services (class 1 & class 2)

Code	Extension Function
1	Describes capabilities of the modem interface common to all modem services.
2	Describes data modem services.
3	Describes facsimile modem services.
4	Describes voice encoding services
5	Describes capabilities of the data modem interface.
6	Describes capabilities of the facsimile modem interface.
7	Describes capabilities of the voice modem interface.
8	Describes serial port interface for data modem services.
9	Describes serial port interface for facsimile modem services.
10	Describes serial port interface for voice modem services.
11-15	Reserved for future standardization, set to zero.

Function-Specific Data (TPLFE_DATA)

Definition of the function-specific data depends on the subfunction ID or mode extension type. The structure of these data fields are detailed in the PCMCIA specification and are not repeated here. A review of the tuple list gives a good idea of the information specified in each type of function extension tuples.

Configuration Tuple

The Configuration tuple identifies the number of configuration registers implemented and their location in attribute memory. The configuration tuple consists of six data entries. Table C-9 shows the actual format of the configuration tuple. Note that the data entries used in the FAX/Modem example are shaded.

- Size of fields—specifies the number of bytes in the configuration registers base address field, in the configuration presence mask field, and in the reserved field.
- Index number of the last entry in the configuration table.
- Configuration registers base address in attribute memory.
- Configuration presence mask—identifies the configuration registers implemented.
- Reserved Field.
- Subtuple information—containing additional card configuration information.

Table C-9. Configuration Tuple Format

Byte	7	6	5	4	3	2	1	0
0	TPL_CODE		Configuration tuple code (CISTPL_CONFIG, 1Ah)					
1	TPL_LINK		Link to next tuple (05h)					
2	TPCC_SZ		Size of Fields Byte (01h)					
3	TPCC_LAST		Index Number of the last entry in the Card Configuration Table (24h)					
4..	TPCC_RADR		Configuration Registers Base Address in Reg Space. 1,2,3, or 4 bytes depending upon the size field in TPCC_LAST (0200h)					
..	TPCC_RMSK		Configuration Registers Present Mask. 1 to 16 bytes as indicated by the count in TPCC_SZ. (17h)					
..	TPCC_RSVD		Reserved area 0-3 bytes. Must be 0 bytes until defined.					
q+1..r	TPCC_SBTPL		The rest of the tuple is reserved for subtuples containing standardized optional additional information related to the Card Configuration.					

Size of fields

The size of fields entry describes the number of bytes used in the TPCC_RADR, TPCC_RMSK and TPCC_RFSZ fields as shown in table C-10. In the Flash card example, the size of fields entry has a value of 01h, resulting in the following values:

Appendix C: FAX/Modem Tuple Example

- TPCC_RASZ — a one must be added to the hex value in this field to determine the number of bytes in TPCC_RADR used to specify the configuration registers base address. In this example, the TPCC_RADR entry consists of two bytes.
- TPCC_RMSZ — a one must be added to the hex value in this field to determine the number of bytes in TPCC_RMSK used to indicate which of the option registers have been implemented. In this example, the TPCC_RMSK entry consists of one byte.
- TPCC_RFSZ — the number of bytes reserved for future use (either 0,1,2 or 3). Must be zero for release 2.0 compliance.

Table C-10. Size of Fields Byte

Bits	7	6	5	4	3	2	1	0
Data Value	0	0	0	0	0	0	0	1
Field Definition	TPCC_RFSZ (RESR Size=0)		TPCC_RMSZ (Size of TPCC_RMSK=0)			TPCC_RASZ (Size of TPCC_RADR=1)		

Index Number of Last Configuration Entry

This entry contains the index number of the last configuration entry of the card's configuration table and a reserved field as shown in table C-11. The value contained in the "last index" field in this example is 24h. Bits six and seven are reserved future use and must be set to zero.

Table C-11. Last Configuration Index

Bytes/Bits	7	6	5	4	3	2	1	0
Data Value	0	0	1	0	0	1	0	0
Field Definition	Reserved for future use (Resr bits=0)		The index number of the final entry in the Card Configuration Table when scanning the CIS from address zero (Last Index = 24h)					

Configuration Registers Base Address Entry

This entry consists of either 1,2,3 or 4 bytes as specified by the "TPCC_RASZ" field of the "Size of Fields" entry. In this example, the "TPCC_RASZ" field indicates this entry consists of two bytes as shown in the shaded area of table C-11. The resulting address is attribute memory location 0200h (or 512d).

Table C-12. Configuration Register Base Address

Bytes/Bits	7	6	5	4	3	2	1	0
Field	Base Address Bits 7:0 (00H)							
Definition	Base Address Bits 15:8 (02H)							
	Base Address Bits 23:16							
	Base Address Bits 25:24							

Configuration Presence Mask

The "presence mask" entry consists of a variable number of fields as determined by the TPCC_RMSZ field within the "size of fields" tuple entry. The presence mask is a bit map of configuration registers that can be implemented. The presence mask entry can contain a maximum of sixteen one byte fields (TPCC_RMSZ = 4 bits), and the eight bits in each field represents a configuration register; therefore, 128 configuration registers can be identified. The format of the presence mask fields is shown in table C-13. In this example, the presence mask entry consists of a single byte (indicated by shading).

Currently, only four registers are specified by the PCMCIA standard. Each of these registers is numbered as follows:

Register 0 = Configuration Option Register
Register 1 = Card Configuration and Status Register
Register 2 = Pin Replacement Register
Register 3 = Socket and Copy Register

The value 17h specified in the FAX/Modem card example means that the configuration option register, card configuration, and status register, pin replacement register and a manufacturer specific register 4 have been implemented in this card.

Appendix C: FAX/Modem Tuple Example

Table C-13. Configuration Register Mask

Bytes/Bits	7	6	5	4	3	2	1	0
Field	Configuration Registers 7:0 (17H)							
Definition	Configuration Registers 15:8							
	Configuration Registers 23:16							
	Configuration Registers 31:24							
	Configuration Registers 39:32							
	Configuration Registers 47:40							
	....							
	Configuration Registers 127:120							

Configuration Table Entry Tuple

Configuration table entry tuples comprise the configuration table within the CIS. This table provides the configuration options available for the PC Card, with each configuration table entry containing a different combination of options. These configuration table entries are scanned in sequence by PC Card enabling software in an attempt to find a configuration that can be satisfied with available system resources.

Enabling software reads the configuration table entries one at a time to determine the configurable resources that the card requires. After each configuration table entry is read, the enabling software checks available system resources to see if the resources requested are available. If available, enabling software configures the host bus adapter and PC Card. If, however, the configuration cannot be satisfied, enabling software proceeds to the next configuration table entry to obtain alternate configuration options. This process continues until the PC Card's configuration is satisfied. If the configuration cannot be satisfied will available resources, the card cannot be enabled by the enabling software.

Typically, the first configuration entry tuple within the configuration table is specified as the default. This tuple details the desired configuration for the PC Card. Since this tuple is the default, any configuration parameters that are successfully acquired from card services will be retained. Subsequent configuration entries include other permissible configuration combinations.

Refer to table C-14 for the following discussion. The configuration table entry tuple contains up to twelve entries. The number of entries depends on the number of configuration parameters that must be specified for the additional PC Card options the designer needs to specify. The shaded areas of table C-14 show the entries used by the FAX/Modem in the first configuration table entry tuple. Note that in this example, the link value is 11h. The other entries are detailed below.

Table C-14. Configuration Table Entry Tuple

Byte	7	6	5	4	3	2	1	0
	TPL_CODE		Configuration Entry tuple code (CISTPL_CFTABLE_ENTRY, 1BH)					
1	TPL_LINK		Link to next tuple					
2	TPCE_INDX		Configuration Table Index Byte					
..	TPCE_IF		Interface-definition byte (This field is present only when the interface bit of the Configuration-Table Index Byte is set)					
..	TPCE_FS		Feature-selection field indicates which optional fields are present					
..	TPCE_PD		Power-description structure					
..	TPCE_TD		Timing-description structure					
..	TPCE_IO		I/O-description structure					
..	TPCE_IR		Interrupt-request-description structure					
..	TPCE_MS		Memory-space-description structure					
..	TPCE_MI		Miscellaneous-information structure					
..n	TPCE_ST		Additional information about the configuration in subtuple format					

Configuration Table Index Byte

Refer to table C-15. The index byte consists of three fields:

- Configuration Index
- Default bit
- Interface bit

Table C-15. Configuration Index Entry

7	6	5	4	3	2	1	0
Interface	Default	Configuration Entry Number (Index)					

Configuration Index

Each configuration table entry contains a unique index number for identification purposes. The index number of the configuration table entry tuple that satisfies the configuration tells the PC Card which configuration options were selected during the configuration process. To enable the configuration described in the tuple, the index number is written to the configuration option register .

Default Bit

This bit specifies whether or not this particular configuration table entry provides default values. In the FAX/Modem example, the first entry is a default entry. If the enabler is able to acquire all configuration parameters specified by a default entry (i.e. obtain the resources required by the card) then the card is configured with the based on the system resources specified within the entry. In the event that some, but not all resources were successfully acquired from the system, the enabler retains those that were granted. The enabler then proceeds to the next entry and attempts to complete the configuration based on alternative parameters specified in the next entry.

When the default bit of the entry is not set, the default conditions are those specified by the last entry encountered that had its default bit set. If one or more of the resources specified by a non-default entry, then the enabler must release all resources specified by the non-default entry. Note that all entries in the FAX/Modem example are non-default entries, except the first entry.

Interface Bit

The interface bit is set in the first entry of this example, specifying that an interface configuration byte follows this byte. If this bit is a zero, then the interface configuration byte is not present within the tuple. (All subsequent entries have the interface bit cleared.) When no interface byte exists, the interface is presumed to be a standard memory only interface, with no requirement to support the wait signal.

Interface Description Byte

This byte describes the type of interface the card requires and specifies some associated features. Refer to table C-16. The fields within the Interface-definition byte are:

- The interface type field
- The card status reporting fields, consisting of:
- - Battery Voltage Detection Active field
- - Write Protect Active field
- - Ready/Busy Active field
- Memory Cycle Wait signal required field

Table C-16. Entry Interface Description Field

Bits	7	6	5	4	3	2	1	0
Value	0	1	0	0	0	0	0	1
Function	M Wait not Re-q'd	RdyBsy Active	WP Inactive	BVDs Inactive	Interface Type			

The Interface Type Field

The four-bit interface type field defines the PC Card's interface type. Notice that the FAX/Modem has an interface type field value of 1h. The 16 possible values and their associated meanings are:

0h	Memory Only Interface — The status reporting bit fields are not valid for this interface type.
1h	Memory or I/O Interface — All other bits within this entry are meaningless when this interface is selected.
2h-3h	Reserved for future standardization.
4h-7h	Custom Interfaces (0-3) corresponding to the definition of the CCSTPL_CIF subtuples in the Configuration Tuple. The custom interface number is the relative position of the CCSTPL_CIF subtuple used by this configuration in the set of CCSTPL_CIF subtuples within the Configuration Tuple for this card.
8h-Fh	Reserved for future standardization.

The Card Status Reporting Fields

When an I/O device such as the FAX/Modem is used the status reporting signals, which are part of the memory interface pinout, are not available when the memory or I/O interface is used. These status signals are:

- Battery Voltage Detection
- Write-Protect switch position
- Ready/Busy status

Since the FAX/Modem reports ready/busy status, the I/O device must report status via the Pin Replacement Register within the CIS in lieu of the signal pins. The Rdy/Bsy Active bit is set to indicate that the Pin Replacement Register is used to report ready/busy status.

Memory Cycle Wait Signal Required Field

This single bit field specifies that the PC Card requires wait support for the memory device accesses.

Feature-selection field

This byte indicates which additional fields are present within the tuple. The FAX/Modem has a value of 9Dh in the feature selection byte as shown in table C-17. Definition of each of the feature selection byte's fields is detailed in table C-18. Note the definition used by the FAX/Modem is indicated by shading.

Table C-17. Feature Selection Byte

Bits	7	6	5	4	3	2	1	0
Value= 9d	1	0	0	1	1	1	0	1
Option Fields	Misc	Mem Space		IRQ	IO Space	Timing	Power	

Table C-18. Feature Selection Byte Field Definition

Power	The power supply requirements and load characteristics for this configuration are indicated. There may be 0,1,2, or 3 fields following representing Vcc, Vpp, or both Vpp1 and Vpp2 in that order. The coding is as follows:	
	Code	Description
	0	No power-description structures. Use the default
	1	Vcc power-description-structure only.
	2	Vcc and Vpp (Vpp1=Vpp2) power-description-structures.
	3	Vcc, Vpp1 and Vpp2 power-description-structures.
Timing	0	When the default bit is set in this tuple, or no configuration entry tuple has been scanned with its default bit set, then no timing is specified. RDY/BSY may indicate busy indefinitely. WAIT will be active from 0 to 12 microseconds.
	1	A timing description structure is present following the power description structure.
IO Space	0	When the default bit is set in the tuple, or no configuration-entry tuple has been scanned with its default bit set, then no I/O space is used. Otherwise, the I/O space requirement is specified by the most-recently scanned configuration entry tuple with its default bet set.
	1	An I/O description structure is present following the timing-description structure.
IRQ	0	When the default bit is set in this tuple, or no configuration-entry tuple has been scanned with its default bit set, then no Interrupt is used. Otherwise, the Interrupt request requirement is specified by the most recent scanned configuration entry tuple with its default bit set.
	1	An Interrupt request description structure is present following the I/O space description structure.

Table C-18. Feature Selection Byte Field Definition (Continued)

MemSpace	Memory address space mapping requirements for this configuration. There may be 0,2,4, or n bytes of information following the interrupt request structure. The coding follows:	
	Code	Description
	0	When the default bit is set in this tuple, or no configuration entry tuple has been scanned with its default bit set, then no configuration dependent, memory address space is used. Otherwise, the memory address space requirement is specified by the most recently scanned configuration entry tuple with its default bit set.
	1	Single 2-byte length specified.
	2	Length (2 bytes) and card address (2 bytes) specified.
	3	A memory space selection byte followed by table memory space descriptors (length determined by selection byte)
Misc	0	When the default bit is set in this tuple, or no Configuration-Entry tuple has been scanned with its default bit set, then the miscellaneous fields are interpreted to be all zero. Otherwise, the miscellaneous fields are specified by the most-recently scanned configuration entry tuple with its default bit set.
	1	A miscellaneous-fields structure is present following the memory space description structure.

Power-Description Structure

The feature selection byte determines which power structure(s) will be defined within the configuration table entry tuple (only a Vcc power description structure in this example). Additionally, each power-description structure defines a variable number of power parameters that will be specified. The power description structure consists of:

- A Power Parameter Selection byte
- Power Parameter Definition byte(s)

Power Parameter Selection byte

The power parameter selection byte specifies which parameters are to be described within the power-description structure. Table C-19 lists the power parameters specified by the FAX/Modem (78h). Note that current parameters but no voltage parameters are defined. Definition of the parameter selection fields is stated in Table C-20.

Table C-19. Power Description Structure Parameter Selection Byte

	7	6	5	4	3	2	1	0
value	0	1	1	1	1	0	0	0
Power Def.	RFU (0)	PDwn I	Peak I	Avg I	Static I	Max V	Min V	Nom V

Table C-20. Power Selection Parameter Definition

Nom V	Nominal operating supply voltage. In the absence of other information the nominal operating voltage has a tolerance of ± 5%.
Min V	Minimum operating supply voltage.
Max V	Maximum operating supply voltage.
Static I	Continuous supply current required.
Avg I	Maximum current required averaged over 1 second.
Peak I	Maximum current required averaged over 10 milliseconds.
PDwn I	Power-down supply current required.
RFU	Reserved for future standardization.

Power Parameter Definition Bytes

Values for each of the power parameters is determined by codes placed in the mantissa and exponent fields of the power parameter definition byte. Table C-21 shows each of the definition bytes along with the corresponding values for each of the four parameters specified by the power parameter selection byte. The actual values are calculated by multiplying the mantissa and exponent together. The values for the mantissa are given in table C-22 and values for the exponent are given in table C-23.

Appendix C: FAX/Modem Tuple Example

Note that bit seven in each of the parameter definition bytes indicates whether power parameter extension bytes will follow each of the definition bytes. The FAX/Modem card does not implement power extensions. However, for reference purposes table C-24 shows the values and definition provided by the extensions.

Table 3-21. Power Parameter Definition for FAX/Modem

Byte	7	6	5	4	3	2	1	0
1	0	1	1	1	0	1	0	1
Istatic	EXT	Mantissa = Eh (8)				Exponent = 5h (10ma)		
2	0	1	1	1	1	1	0	1
Iavg	EXT	Mantissa = Fh (9)				Exponent = 5h (10ma)		
3	0	0	0	0	0	1	1	0
Ipeak	EXT	Mantissa = 0h (1)				Exponent = 6h (100ma)		
4	0	0	0	1	0	1	0	1
Ipwrdn	EXT	Mantissa = 2h (1.3)				Exponent = 5h (10ma)		

* The extension bytes may be continued indefinitely until the first byte which contains a 0 or 7, which is the final byte of the extension

Table C-22. Mantissa Values for Power Definition

The Mantissa Values (hex)	
Mantissa	Value
0	1
1*	1.2
2*	1.3
3*	1.5
4	2
5*	2.5
6	3
7*	3.5
8	4
9*	4.5
A	5
B*	5.5
C	6
D	7
E	8
F	9

* These values are not permitted when the EXT bit is set.

Table C-23. Exponent Values for Power Definition

The Exponent of the Current and Voltage Values are given below:		
Exponent	Current Scale	Voltage Scale
0	100 nA	10 µV
1	1 µA	100 µV
2	10 µA	1 mV
3	100 µA	10 mV
4	1 mA	100 mV
5	10 mA	1 V
6	100 mA	10 V
7	1 A	100 V

Table C-24. Power Descriptor Extension Byte

Extension (Bit 7)	Extension Values and Definition (Bits 6:0)	
	0..63h	Binary value for the next two decimal digits to the right of the current value.
	64..7Ch	Reserved
	7Dh	No connection (i.e. high impedance) permitted during sleep or power-down only (Must be last extension byte).
	7Eh	Zero value required (must be only extension byte).
	7Fh	No connection (i.e. high impedance) is required (must be only extension byte).
	Extension bytes may be concatenated indefinitely. The final extension byte contains a 0 in bit 7.	

Timing Description Structure

The Timing Description structure allows the card designer to specify:

- maximum time interval the wait signal will be asserted
- maximum time interval that the card will remain in the busy state
- reserved-time definition

The timing description structure defines up to four bytes used to define the timing parameters. Refer to table C-25. The first byte (byte 0), called the timing scale factor byte, has two purposes: to determine which of the timing parameters are to be defined and if so, what scaling factor is to be applied to the timing descriptor for that parameter. The three bytes that follow the timing scale factor byte are the actual timing descriptors for the three parameters. Only the Ready/Busy timing parameter is implemented by FAX/Modem (the bytes used are shaded).

Appendix C: FAX/Modem Tuple Example

Table C-25. Timing Parameters

Byte	7	6	5	4	3	2	1	0
0	Reserved Scale = 7h (no reserved speed)			Ready/Busy Scale = 1h (scaling factor of 10d)			Wait Scale = 3h (no wait used)	
1	Wait Signal Timing Descriptor							
2	Ready/Busy Timing Descriptor (5Fh)							
3	Reserved-Speed Timing Descriptor							

Timing Scale Factor Byte

Each field within the timing scale factor byte defines how the timing parameter values that follow are to be interpreted. Refer to table C-26.

Table C-26. Timing Scale Factors

WAIT Scale	This field is the power of 10 scaling factor to be applied to the MAX WAIT timing parameter byte which follows. The value 3 indicates that the WAIT signal is not used and the MAX WAIT Speed is not present following this byte.
RdyBsy Scale	This field is the power of 10 scaling factor to be applied to the MAX time the card will be in the Busy State. A value of 7 indicates that Ready/Busy is not used and no maximum time is present.
Res'd Scale	This field is the power 10 scaling factor which is to be applied to a reserved-time definition. A value of 7 indicates that no reserved-speed bytes follows.

Ready/Busy Timing Description Byte

The FAX/Modem has a value of 5Fh in the ready/busy timing description byte. The format of the timing description byte is shown in table C-27. The mantissa and exponent values are speed codes, referring to the values in table C-28. The ready/busy timing parameter is calculated as follows:

5.0 (mantissa) * 10ms (exponent) * 10 (scaling factor) = 500 ms

Table C-27. Timing Description Byte

Byte	7	6	5	4	3	2	1	0
1	0	1	0	1	1	1	1	1
Istatic	NA	Mantissa = Bh (5.0d)				Exponent = 7h (10ms)		

Table C-28. Extended Device Speed Codes

Mantissa		Exponent	
Code	Meaning	Code	Meaning
0h	Reserved	0h	1 ns
1h	1.0	1h	10 ns
2h	1.2	2h	100 ns
3h	1.3	3h	1 μs
4h	1.5	4h	10 μs
5h	2.0	5h	100 μs
6h	2.5	6h	1 ms
7h	3.0	7h	10 ms
8h	3.5		
9h	4.0		
Ah	4.5		
Bh	5.0		
Ch	5.5		
Dh	6.0		
Eh	7.0		
Fh	8.0		

I/O-Description Structure

The I/O-description structure consists of the following entries as shown in table C-29:

- I/O Address Decode Requirements byte
- I/O Address Range Descriptor Byte (defines the number of address ranges included within the structure, and characterizes the number of bytes used to define each of the I/O address ranges that follow)
- Address Range Descriptions (up to 16 entries, each defining a range of I/O addresses that the card uses)

Appendix C: FAX/Modem Tuple Example

Table C-29. I/O Description Structure

Byte	7	6	5	4	3	2	1	0
0	I/O Address Decode Requirements Byte							
1	I/O Address Range Descriptor Byte							
2..n	Address Range Description (number of bytes specified by I/O Address Range Descriptor Byte)							
....	Address Range Description (Up to 16 address range descriptions can be defined.)							

I/O Address Decode Requirements Byte

This byte contains four fields as shown in table C-30. The table also provides a definition for each field. The FAX/Modem contains a value of AAh in this field, representing the following:

- Ten I/O Address lines are used by the card's address decoder.
- The card is an 8-bit device.
- One I/O address range (followed by one I/O address descriptor).

I/O Address Range Descriptor Byte

This byte determines the number of address ranges that the card requires and determines the number of bytes used in each address range description that follows. Three fields specify this information:

- Number of I/O Address Ranges field - specifies the number of I/O address blocks that the card requires. For each range specified, an address range description entry follows.
- Address Size field - specifies the number of bytes used in the I/O address descriptions to specify the starting address range.
- Length Size field - specifies the number of bytes used in the I/O address descriptions to specify the length of the address range.

The FAX/Modem contains a value of 60h in this field, telling software responsible for reading the card's I/O address requirements how to interpret the address range descriptions. Refer to table C-31. The number of I/O address ranges is one, so only one I/O address range description follows this byte. Within this I/O address description, the starting address is specified by two bytes, while a single byte specifies the length of the range.

Table C-30. I/O Address Decode Description

Bits	7	6	5	4	3	2	1	0
value (AAh)	1	0	1	0	1	0	1	0
Def.	Range	Bus16	Bus 8	I/O Address Lines = 10				

	I/O Address Lines Field (Total number of address lines used by card decoder)
0	When the I/OAddress Lines field is zero, the card will respond to all addresses presented to it. The system is entirely responsible for when the card is selected, and at what addresses the card is selected. The system must assign to the card a portion of the address space which is at least as large as the number of bytes indicated in the length field of the following range entry. The Base Address for the I/O space (assigned to the card by the system) must begin on a 2*n address boundary such that 2*n is greater than the number of bytes indicated in the length field.
1-26	When IOAddrLines is non-zero, the card performs address decoding to determine when it is selected. In this case, the card and the system share the determination of when a card is actually selected. The card must indicate in IOAddrLines the highest address line (plus 1) which it decodes to determine when it has been selected. The card provides a list of ranges of addresses for which it is selected within the I/O space that it decodes. The system and the card then share the task of determining when the card is selected. The system controls when the CE# pins are asserted during I/O cycles, and the card determines to which addresses it will respond when it is enabled by those CE# signals. The card returns the INPACK# signal to the system whenever the card can recognizes the I/O address on the bus.
27-31	Reserved

Bus16	Bus8	Description
0	0	Reserved
0	1	Card registers accessible over data lines D7:D0 only.
1	0	16-bit registers accessible over data lines D15:D0 only (no 8-bit accesses to 16-bit registers are supported) 8-bit card registers accessible to odd bytes may take place over D15:D8 or D7:D0.
1	1	Same as previous combination except 8-bit access are supported to 16-bit registers.

Range	When this bit is a "one", the range of addresses to which the card responds follows this byte, in the "I/O address range descriptor byte". If this bit is a "zero", the card responds to all addresses and uses all I/O address lines to distinguish among its I/O ports. In this case, the amount of address space which should be allocated to the card is indicated by the number of address lines decoded by the card (e.g. 4 lines means 16 addresses). No I/O address range descriptor byte follows.

Appendix C: FAX/Modem Tuple Example

Table C-31. I/O Address Requirements

Byte	7	6	5	4	3	2	1	0
Value	0	1	1	0	0	0	0	0
1	Length Size (1 byte)		Address Size (2 bytes)		Number of I/O Address Ranges (value +1= 1 address range)			

Address Range Description

The actual I/O addresses specified by the FAX/Modem for the first configuration table entry are 3F8-3FFh as indicated in table C-32.

Table C-32. I/O Address Range Description

Start of I/O Address (3F8h) — This field is 0, 1, 2 or 4 bytes long (2 bytes in this example). Address bits in bytes which are not present are zeros								
Data	7	6	5	4	3	2	1	0
F8h	1	1	1	1	1	0	0	0
03h	0	0	0	0	0	0	1	1
Length of I/O Address (field value + 1) — This field is 1, 2 or 4 bytes long (1 byte in this example) Length bits in bytes which are not present are zeros								
Data	7	6	5	4	3	2	1	0
07h+1	0	0	0	0	0	1	1	1

Interrupt Request Description Structure

The interrupt request description consists of either a single byte or three bytes depending on the value of bit 4 (mask) in the first byte. In the FAX/Modem example, the mask bit is a zero, meaning that the mask registers (bytes 1 & 2) will not be used. Refer to table C-33. The shaded area shows the values used in this example.

Table C-33. Interrupt Request Description Structure

Byte	7	6	5	4	3	2	1	0
0	Share 0	Pulse 0	Level 1	Mask 0	IRQn Line 0-15 (4h)			
1	IRQ7	IRQ6	IRQ5	IRQ4	IRQ3	IRQ2	IRQ1	IRQ0
2	IRQ15	IRQ14	IRQ13	IRQ12	IRQ11	IRQ10	IRQ9	IRQ8

Miscellaneous Information Structure

The miscellaneous information structure defines additional features that a given PC Card might support. These features are defined in table C-34.

Table C-34. Miscellaneous Features Field

Byte	7	6	5	4	3	2	1	0
0	EXT	Resrvd (0)	Pwr Down	Read Only	Audio	Max Twin Cards		

Max Twins	This field indicates that cards which support installation of identical cards in the system be differentiated from each other in a sequential manner. For example, first twin is card 0, second is card 1, and so on. This allows the cards to share I/O ports and interrupts in a manner consistent with some peripherals commonly used in PC computers, such as ATA drives. The max-twins field specifies the maximum number of other identical cards which can be configured identically to this card. This permits more than one card to be installed in host which responds to the identical I/O addresses. The host allows the cards to distinguish among themselves by writing their "Copy" numbers (e.g. 0, for the first card, 1 for the second, etc.) into the copy field of the Socket and Copy Register in the Card Configuration Registers.
Audio	This bit indicates that the card allows the BVD2 signal to be used as Audio Waveform for the speaker. This operation is controlled by the Audio Enable Bit in the Card Control and Status Configuration Register.
Read Only	This bit indicates that the card contains a data-storage medium which is read-only for this configuration. There may be other configurations for which the storage medium is read/write.
Pwr Down	This bit indicates that the card supports a power-down mode controlled by the power-down bit in the Control and Status Register.
Resrvd (0)	These bits are reserved for future definition and must be 0.
EXT	An extension follows this byte. A series of extension bytes, which will be defined by PCMCIA, is terminated when an extension byte is encountered which does not have the EXT bit set.

The remaining tuple entries provide options for the I/O range and IRQ lines. If these resources requested in the first configuration table entry are not available, then the next configuration table entry is checked. This continues until a resource combination is satisfied. Note that the last configuration table entry requests any 8-byte range of I/O addresses and a large variety of possible IRQ lines, thereby increasing the chances that the card can be configured.

Appendix D: ATA Disk CIS Example

The following section includes a sample CIS for an ATA PC Card. This sample CIS is from the Maxtor MobileMax 105 MB ATA Drive. Notice that the CIS includes four configuration table entry tuples to support all four addressing modes.

Offset/Addr (hex)	Data (hex)	Description and Interpretation
0/0	01	Device Info Tuple
1/2	04	Link to next tuple
2/4	DF	Device type = D (Function Specific Memory Device) Device Speed=7 (ext.)
3/6	4A	Mantissa = 9 (4.0) Exponent = 2 (100ns) - Speed = 400ns
4/8	01	Unit Size=2KB Number of Units=1 - Total size = 2KB
5/A	FF	Termination Byte
6/C	15	Level 1 Version/Product Information Tuple
7/E	11	Link to next tuple
8/10	04	Major Version number=4
9/12	01	Minor Version number=1 (Release 2.0 or 2.1)
A/14	4D	M (The remaining entries within the tuple are ASCII codes)
B/16	61	a
C/18	78	x
D/1A	74	t
E/1C	6F	o
F/1E	72	r
10/20	00	end of manufacturer name string

Offset/Addr (hex)	Data (hex)	Description and Interpretation
11/22	4D	M
12/24	78	X
13/26	4C	L
14/28	31	1
15/2A	30	0
16/2C	35	5
17/2E	00	00 End Model Information String
18/30	FF	Tuple end byte
19/32	1A	Configuration Tuple
1A/34	05	Link to next tuple
1B/36	01	Configuration register address size = 2 bytes
1C/38	03	Last configuration entry number = 3
1D/3A	00	Configuration Registers base address = 00 (LSB) 02 (MSB)
1E/3C	02	base address = 200h
1F/3E	0F	configuration registers at location 200, 202, 204, and 206
20/40	1B	Configuration Table Entry Tuple
21/42	10	Link to next tuple
22/44	C0	Config entry = 0; interface byte follows; default set
23/46	C0	Interface = memory; wait & rdy/bsy active; bvd & wp inactive
24/48	A5	Feature Selection = Power, Timing, Memory address range, misc entries
25/4A	7F	Power Description = nom v, min v, static i, avg i, peak i, and pwrdwn i
26/4C	55	nom v = 5v
27/4E	4D	min v = 4.5 v
28/50	D5	max v = 5.25v
29/52	19	
2A/54	26	static i = 400ma
2B/56	26	avg i = 400ma
2C/58	6E	peak i = 700ma
2D/5A	54	pwrdwn i = 5ma
2E/5C	FF	no extended wait, no rdy/bsy, or reserved defined
2F/5E	08	2KB memory address range starting at address 0
30/60	00	
31/62	20	Support for powerdown bit in configuration status register
32/64	1B	Configuration Table Entry tuple
33/66	12	Link to next tuple

Appendix D: ATA Disk CIS Example

Offset/Addr (hex)	Data (hex)	Description and Interpretation
34/68	C1	Configuration entry = 1; interface described; default set
35/6A	41	Interface = I/O; rdy/bsy active; wait, wp and bvd not active
36/6C	9D	Feature selection = power, timing, I/O addr range, IRQ and misc. entries
37/6E	7F	Power descrip = nom v, min v, max v, static i, avg i, peak i, & pwrdn i
38/70	55	nom v = 5v
39/72	4D	min v = 4.5 v
3A/74	D5	max v = 5.25v
3B/76	19	
3C/78	26	static i = 400ma
3D/7A	26	avg i = 400ma
3E/7C	6E	peak i = 700ma
3F/7E	54	pwrdwn i = 5ma
40/80	FF	no extended wait, no rdy/bsy, or reserved defined
41/82	64	I/O addr range = 16 contiguous bytes, 8 or 16-bit mode
42/84	F0	IRQ shared, pulse or level mode supported
43/86	FF	All IRQs supported = IRQ15: IRQ0
44/88	FF	
45/8A	20	Support for powerdown bit in configuration status register
46/8C	1B	Configuration Table Entry tuple
47/8E	0C	Link to next tuple
48/90	82	Configuration entry = 2; interface described; default not set
49/92	41	Interface = I/O; rdy/bsy active; wait, wp and bvd not active
4A/94	18	Feature selection = I/O address range and IRQ entries
4B/96	EA	10 addr lines decoded, 8 or 16 bit mode, subranges follow
4C/98	61	2 address ranges; 2 byte addresses; 1byte length
4D/9A	F0	first address range = F0 (LSB), 01 (MSB) = 01F0h
4E/9C	01	
4F/9E	07	Length of first address range = 8 bytes
50/A0	F6	Second address range = F6 (LSB), 03 (MSB) = 03F6h
51/A2	03	
52/A4	01	Length of second address range = 2 bytes
53/A6	EE	IRQ shared, pulse or level, IRQ 14
54/A8	1B	Configuration Table Entry tuple
55/AA	0C	Link to next tuple
56/AC	83	Configuration entry = 2; interface described; default not set

Offset/Addr (hex)	Data (hex)	Description and Interpretation
57/AE	41	Interface = I/O; rdy/bsy active; wait, wp and bvd not active
58/B0	18	Feature selection = I/O address range and IRQ entries
59/B2	EA	10 addr lines decoded, 8 or 16 bit mode, subranges follow
5A/B4	61	2 address ranges; 2 byte addresses; 1byte length
5B/B6	70	first address range = 70 (LSB), 01 (MSB) = 0170h
5C/B8	01	
5D/BA	07	Length of first address range = 8 bytes
5E/BC	76	Second address range = 76 (LSB), 03 (MSB) = 0376h
5F/BE	03	
60/C0	01	Length of second address range = 2 bytes
61/C2	EE	IRQ shared, pulse or level, IRQ 14
62/C4	21	Function ID Tuple
63/C6	02	Link to next tuple
64/C8	04	Device type 4= Fixed Disk Drive
65/CA	01	Initialization byte = attempt configuration at Power-On Self Test (POST)
66/CC	22	Disk Drive Function Extension Tuple
67/CE	02	Link to next tuple
68/D0	01	Disk device interface
69/D2	01	ATA interface
6A/D4	14	No-link tuple
6B/D6	00	link to next tuple
6C/D8	FF	End of Tuple String

Device Information Tuple

The device information tuple must be the first tuple of any release 2.0 compliant system and must be located at attribute memory address location zero. Device information provided in this tuple applies only to memory devices. Normally when an I/O only card is used, the device information field will be only one byte long and contain a zero. In this case, however, the PC Card supports memory-mapped I/O. Table D-1 shows the format of the device information tuple. Shaded area show portions of the tuple definition used by the ATA card in this example.

Appendix D: ATA Disk CIS Example

The CIS listing includes a link value of 04h, indicating that the extended speed byte is used.

Table D-1. Device Information Tuple Format

Byte	Device Information Tuple Format	
0	TPL_CODE	CISTPL_DEVICE (01H)
1	TPL_LINK	Link to next tuple
		Device Info 1 (00h = no valid device information)
		Device Info 2 (2 or more bytes)
...		Device Info n (2 or more bytes)
n		FFH (marks end of device info field)

The ATA card's Device Information tuple contains information for a single block of memory, therefore, only one device info block (Device Info 1) is defined. Device info 1 is comprised of three bytes in this example:

- Device Type and Speed Byte
- Extended Speed Byte
- Device Size Byte

Device Type and Speed Byte

Refer to table D-2. The first byte describes the device speed, whether the write protect switch affects this address range, and the device type. Note that the device type code is only used to describe devices that use a fixed memory address range, and not for dynamically relocatable devices. Relocatable devices use the configuration entry tuples to describe the memory address ranges supported.

The device type and speed byte contains a DFh value equating to the values shown below. Note that extended speed information is used in lieu of the standard speed definitions (refer to table D-3), since the devices being accessed within the memory address range are registers.

The extended speed byte contains a codes for a mantissa and exponent value. The ATA card's CIS in this example contains a value of 4Ah, equating to a mantissa of 4.0 and an exponent of 100ns or a device speed of 400ns.

Table D-2. Memory Device Type and Speed Information

Byte	7	6	5	4	3	2	1	0
0	Device Type Code = D				WPS=1	Device Speed Codes = 7		
1	Extended Device Speed (if Device Speed Code equals 7h, otherwise omitted)							
2 .. m-1	Additional Extended Device Speed (if bit 7 of Extended Device Speed is 1, otherwise omitted)							
m .. n	Extended Device Type (if Device Type Code equals Eh, otherwise omitted)							

Table D-3. Device Speed Codes

Code	Name	Meaning
0h	DSPEED_NULL	Use when device type = null
1h	DSPEED_250NS	250 nsec
2h	DSPEED_200NS	200 nsec
3h	DSPEED_150NS	150 nsec
4h	DSPEED_100NS	100 nsec
5h-6h		(Reserved)
7h	DSPEED_EXT	Use extended speed byte.

Table D-4. Device Type Codes

Code	Name	Meaning
0	DTYPE_NULL	No device. Generally used to designate a hole in the address space. If used, speed field should be set to 0H
1	DTYPE_ROM	Masked ROM
2	DTYPE_OTPROM	One-time programmable PROM
3	DTYPE_EPROM	UV EPROM
4	DTYPE_EEPROM	EEPROM
5	DTYPE_FLASH	Flash EPROM
6	DTYPE_SRAM	Static RAM (JEIDA has Nonvolatile RAM)
7	DTYPE_DRAM	Dynamic RAM (JEIDA has Volatile RAM)
8-Ch		Reserved
Dh	DTYPE_FUNCSPEC*	Function-specific memory address range. Includes memory-mapped I/O registers, dual-ported memory, communication buffers, etc., which are not intended to be used as general-purpose memory.
Eh	DTYPE_EXTEND	Extended type follows.
Fh		Reserved

Appendix D: ATA Disk CIS Example

Device Size Byte

The ATA device size byte entry contains 01h. This represents a three bit "unit size code" of 4h, and the number of address units value of 0Fh. One is added to the number of address units value to obtain the actual number of units. Refer to table D-5 for byte format.

Table D-5. Device Size Definition

7	6	5	4	3	2	1	0
# of address units(0h) + 1= 1h					Unit Size Code = 1h		

(1 unit x 2KB unit size = 2KB)

Code	Units	Max Size
0	512 bytes	16 K
1	2 K	64 K
2	8 K	256 K
3	32 K	1 M
4	128 K	4 M
5	512 K	16 M
6	2 M	64 M
7	Reserved	Reserved

Level 1 Version / Product Information Tuple

Table D-6 shows the format and contents of the level 1 version/product information tuple. This tuple provides the PCMCIA compliance level supported by the PC Card and includes manufacturer defined product information. The tuple includes three fields:

- The major version byte indicating PCMCIA version information.
- The minor version byte indicating compliance with a given PCMCIA release.
- A variable length field comprised of one or more strings of ASCII characters specified by the manufacturer. A value of 00h demarks each ASCII string.

Table D-6. Level 1 Version/Product Information Tuple Format

Byte	Level 1 Version/Product Information Tuple Format	
0	TPL_CODE	CISTPL_VERS_1 (15h).
1	TPL_LINK	Link to next tuple (24h).
2	TPLLV1_MAJOR	Major version number (04h).
3	TPLLV1_MINOR	Minor version number (01h) for Release 2.0 and 2.01
4	TPLLV1_INFO	Product information string: name of the manufacturer, terminated by 00h. Additional product information, in text; terminated by 00h. In this example: • Product name • Model Information
n		FFh: marks end of list.

Configuration Tuple

The Configuration tuple identifies the number of configuration registers implemented and their location in attribute memory. The configuration tuple consists of six data entries as follows. Table D-7 shows the actual format of the configuration tuple. Note that the tuples used in the ATA disk example are shaded.

- Size of fields—specifies the number of bytes in the "configuration registers base address" field, in the "configuration presence mask" field, and in the "reserved field"
- Index number of the last entry in the configuration table
- Configuration registers base address in attribute memory
- Configuration presence mask—identifies the configuration registers implemented
- Reserved Field
- Subtuple information—containing additional card configuration information

Appendix D: ATA Disk CIS Example

Table D-7. Configuration Tuple Format

Byte	7	6	5	4	3	2	1	0
0	TPL_CODE		Configuration tuple code (CISTPL_CONFIG, 1AH)					
1	TPL_LINK		Link to next tuple (n-1; minimum 1)					
2	TPCC_SZ		Size of Fields Byte					
3	TPCC_LAST		Index Number of the last entry in the Card Configuration Table					
4..	TPCC_RADR		Configuration Registers Base Address in Reg Space. 1,2,3, or 4 bytes depending upon the size field in TPCC_LAST					
..	TPCC_RMSK		Configuration Registers Present Mask. 1 to 16 bytes as indicated by the count in TPCC_SZ.					
..	TPCC_RSVD		Reserved area 0-3 bytes. Must be 0 bytes until defined.					
q+1..r	TPCC_SBTPL		The rest of the tuple is reserved for subtuples containing standardized optional additional information related to the Card Configuration.					

Size of fields

The size of fields entry describes the number of bytes used in the TPCC_RADR, TPCC_RMSK and TPCC_RFSZ fields as shown in table D-8. In the Flash card example, the size of fields entry has a value of 01h, resulting in the following values:

- TPCC_RASZ — a one must be added to the hex value in this field to determine the number of bytes in TPCC_RADR used to specify the configuration registers base address. In this example, the TPCC_RADR entry consists of two bytes.
- TPCC_RMSZ — a one must be added to the hex value in this field to determine the number of bytes in TPCC_RMSK used to indicate which of the option registers have been implemented. In this example, the TPCC_RMSK entry consists of one byte.
- TPCC_RFSZ — the number of bytes reserved for future use (either 0,1,2 or 3). Must be zero for release 2.0 compliance.

Table D-8. Size of Fields Byte

Bits	7	6	5	4	3	2	1	0
Data Value	0	0	0	0	0	0	0	1
Field Definition	TPCC_RFSZ (RESR Size=0)		TPCC_RMSZ (Size of TPCC_RMSK=0)			TPCC_RASZ (Size of TPCC_RADR=1)		

Index Number of Last Configuration Entry

This entry contains the index number of the last configuration entry of the card's configuration table and a reserved field as shown in table D-9. The value contained in the "last index" field in this example is 03h. Bits six and seven are reserved future use and must be set to zero.

Table D-9. Last Configuration Index

Bytes/Bits	7	6	5	4	3	2	1	0
Data Value	0	0	0	0	0	0	1	1
Field Definition	Reserved for future use (Resr bits=0)		The index number of the final entry in the Card Configuration Table when scanning the CIS from address zero (Last Index = 03d)					

Configuration Registers Base Address Entry

This entry consists of either 1,2,3 or 4 bytes as specified by the "TPCC_RASZ" field of the "Size of Fields" entry. In this example, the "TPCC_RASZ" field indicates this entry consists of two bytes as shown in the shaded area of table D-10. The resulting address is 0200h or attribute memory location 512d.

Table D-10. Configuration Register Base Address

Bytes/Bits	7	6	5	4	3	2	1	0
Field Definition	Base Address Bits 7:0 (00h)							
	Base Address Bits 15:8 (02h)							
	Base Address Bits 23:16							
	Base Address Bits 25:24							

Appendix D: ATA Disk CIS Example

Configuration Presence Mask

The "presence mask" entry consists of a variable number of fields as determined by the TPCC_RMSZ field within the "size of fields" tuple entry. The presence mask is a bit map of configuration registers that can be implemented. The presence mask entry can contain a maximum of eight one byte fields (TPCC_RMSZ = 3 bits), and the eight bits in each field represents a configuration register; therefore, 64 configuration registers can be identified. The format of the presence mask fields is shown in figure D-11. In this example, the presence mask entry consists of a single byte (indicated by shading).

Currently, only four registers are specified by the PCMCIA standard. Each of these registers is numbered as follows:

Register 0 = Configuration Option Register

Register 1 = Card Configuration and Status Register

Register 2 = Pin Replacement Register

Register 3 = Socket and Copy Register

The value 0Fh specified in the ATA CIS means that the "configuration option register", "card configuration and status register", "pin replacement register" and "Socket and Copy register" have been implemented in this card.

Table D-11. Configuration Register Mask

Bytes/Bits	7	6	5	4	3	2	1	0
Field	Configuration Registers 7:0 (0Fh)							
Definition	Configuration Registers 15:8							
	Configuration Registers 23:16							
	Configuration Registers 31:24							
	Configuration Registers 39:32							
	Configuration Registers 47:40							
	Configuration Registers 55:48							
	Configuration Registers 63:56							

Configuration Table

The configuration table contains four entries each of which describes a different combination of resource options required by the ATA card.

Function Identification Tuple

This tuple identifies a PC card's function and specifies whether the function should be automatically configured during system initialization. The tuple contains two fields:

- Function Code byte.
- System Initialization Bit Mask.

Refer to table D-12 for the tuple's basic format.

Table D-12. Function Identification Tuple Format

Byte	Function Identification Tuple Format	
0	TPL_CODE	CISTPL_FUNCID (21H)
1	TPL_LINK	Link to next tuple (at least 2)
2	TPLFID_FUNCTION	PC Card function code
3	TPLFID_SYSINIT	System initialization bit mask

Function Code Byte (TPLFID_FUNCTION)

This field contains a code that identifies the basic function of the PC card. In this example, the ATA card is a Fixed Disk (code 04h). Table D-13 lists the functions supported by PCMCIA.

Appendix D: ATA Disk CIS Example

Table D-13. PC Card Function Codes

Code	Name	Meaning
0h	Multi-Function	PC Card has multiple functions. Examine the following function identification tuples that follow for individual functions.
1h	Memory	Memory Card (RAM, ROM, EPROM, flash, etc.).
2h	Serial Port	Serial I/O port, includes modem cards.
3h	Parallel Port	Parallel printer port, may be bi-directional.
4h	Fixed Disk	Fixed drive, may be silicon may be removable.
5h	Video Adapter	Video interface, extension tuples (type and resolutions).
6h	Network LAN Adapter	Local Area Network adapter.
7h	AIMS	Auto-Incrementing Mass Storage card.
8..FFh	Reserved	Unused in this release. Reserved by PCMCIA for future use.

System Initialization Byte (TPLFID_SYSINIT)

This field contains two bits that permit a PC card to perform initial program load (IPL):

- POST bit — specifies whether a given function should be configured during system initialization.
- ROM bit — indicates whether the PC card contains an expansion ROM.

The format of the System Initialization byte is shown in table D-14. Note that for an ATA card, the POST bit is usually set to one, indicating the card should be configured during system initialization. A designer may or may not choose to incorporate an expansion ROM on the card.

Table D-14. Initialization Byte

7	6	5	4	3	2	1	0
Reserved for future use, must be set to zero (0)						ROM	POST

Function Extension Tuple

Two extension tuples have been defined for ATA drives. One identifies the interface type and another specifies additional PC Card ATA features. Table D-15 shows the common format of the Function Extension tuples. Each Function Extension tuple has the same tuple code (22h), a link field and two function-specific fields:

- Function Extension Type Code field — this field identifies the specific function extension defined by this tuple.
- Function-specific information — this field contains data that is specific to a given extension type.

Table D-15. Function Extension Tuple Format

Byte	Function Extension Tuple Format	
0	TPL_CODE	CISTPL_FUNCE (22H)
1	TPL_LINK	Link to next tuple
2	TPL_TYPE	Function Extension Type Code
3..n	TPLFE_DATA	Function-specific information

Appendix E: Metaformat Layers 2, 3, and 4

The following table lists and describes the tuples defined for the Layer 2: Data Recording Format, of the PC Card Metaformat.

Code	Name	Description
23h	CISTPL_SWIL	Software interleaving — This tuple allows software interleaving of data within a partition on the card. This tuple indicates the software interleaving factor.
40h	CISTPL_VERS_2	Level-2 version tuple — This tuple indicates the compliance of the level 2 tuples within the card and provides information regarding the general organization of the PC Card.
41h	CISTPL_FORMAT	Data recording format for Common Memory — This tuple provides information about how the card is organized and accessed for use as a virtual disk drive. This tuple includes information defining: • Whether access is memory-like (byte accessible) or disk-like (accessed in blocks of address space). • The error correction method employed and length. • Byte address of first data byte in this partition • Number of data bytes in this partition.
42h	CISTPL_GEOMETRY	Partition geometry — This tuple is for use by cards that have disk-like partitions. Provides instructions to the file management system that requires data be

		located based on cylinders, tracks, and sectors.
43h	CISTPL_BYTEORDER	Byte ordering for disk-like partitions — This tuple is intended for PC Cards that have a memory-like organization. That is, cards that can be read from and written to one byte at a time. This tuple specifies the order for multi-byte data, and the order in which bytes map into words (even two byte block) for 16-bit cards.
44h	CISTPL_DATE	Card Initilization date — This tuple indicates the date and time that the PC Card was last formatted.
45h	CISTPL_BATTERY	Battery replacement date — This tuple is intended for PC Cards having battery-backed storage. It indicates the date of the last battery replacement, and the date that replacement is likely to be required again.
47h	CISTPL_FORMAT_A	Data recording format for Attribute Memory — This tuple provides information about how the card is organized and accessed for use as a virtual disk drive. This tuple includes information defining: • Whether access is memory-like (byte accessible) or disk-like (accessed in blocks of address space). • The error correction method employed and length. • Byte address of first data byte in this partition • Number of data bytes in this partition.

Appendix E: Metaformat Layers 2, 3, and 4

The following table describes the tuple defined for metaformat Layer 3: Data Organization Tuples.

Code	Name	Description
46h	CISTPL_ORG	Partition organization — This tuple contains information about the organization of a partition within a PC Card. The tuple describes whether: • the partition contains a file system and specifies type and version. • the partition contains applications-specific information and specifies name and version. • the partition contains executable code images and specifies name and version of the organization scheme. • the partition uses a vendor-specific organization.

The table below describes the tuple defined for metaformat Layer 4: System-Specific Standard Tuples.

Code	Name	Description
90h	CISTPL_SPCL	Special Purpose — These tuple has meaning for DOS file systems and are used to define an interchange format for cards formatted with the DOS-FAT-based file system. Also provides a standard for executing code directly from a PC Card, called execute-in-place or XIP.
80h - 8Fh	Vendor unique tuples	

Appendix F: References

Additional references on PCMCIA:

Dipert, Brian and Levy, Markus *Designing with Flash Memory*, Annabooks, 1993.

Mori, Michael T. And Welder, W. Dean, *The PCMCIA Developer's Guide*, Second Edition, Sycard Technology, 1994-95.

PCMCIA/JEIDA, *PC Card Standard*, Volumes 1-12, February 1995
2635 North First Street, Suite 209, San Jose, CA 95131, USA, phone: (408) 433-2273.

Glossary

Access speed. The time required for a given memory or I/O device to accept or supply data when it is selected by a given bus master.

Address offset. The value (typically measured in bytes) that specifies an address location relative to a given base (or, start) address.

Address translation. The process of converting one form of address to another. Typically performed by a bridge device when passing a transactions between buses that implement different addressing protocols.

Address window speed. The cycle time associated with accessing a memory or I/O device. PCMCIA specifies the same cycle time for all devices that are mapped within the same host bus adapter address window.

Advanced client services. A category of services within card services that perform advanced functions not typically used by standard client drivers (or, enablers).

AIMS interface. Auto-Indexing Mass Storage (or, AIMS) is an extension to the PCMCIA specification that provides a simple PC Card interface used typically for storing large images.

AT. An acronym for advanced technology used by IBM when naming their 80286-based PCs (i.e. IBM PC-AT). Note that AT and ISA (Industry Standard Architecture) are commonly used terms to designate compatibility with the IBM PC-AT.

ATA. An acronym for AT attachment. An ANSI standard that defines a disk drive interface between an AT compatible bus and IDE (integrated drive electronics) disk drives.

ATA PC Card. A PC Card that conforms to the ATA standard (in most respects), providing a standard programming interface which is supported by virtually all of today's PCs.

ATA flash card. An PC Card that employs flash memory and uses an ATA interface to emulate a disk drive.

Attribute memory. PC Card address space used to store configuration information. The card's CIS and configuration registers are mapped into attribute memory address space. Only even address locations within attribute memory contain valid information.

Battery warning. Memory cards used to emulate disk drives must provide a battery to retain information, if they use volatile memory. These cards have two signals pins (BVD1 and BVD2 – battery voltage detect 1 and 2) that can be used to report a low battery warning or a dead battery indication to the system.

Bulk memory services. A category of card services used by memory client drivers to gain access and manage block memory transfers.

BVD1 and BVD2. Memory cards used to emulate disk drives must provide a battery to retain information, if they use volatile memory. These cards have two signals pins (BVD1 and BVD2 – battery voltage detect 1 and 2) that can be used to report a low battery warning or a dead battery indication to the system.

Call-back. The process used by card services to notify clients of events that they should respond to. The call-back calls a routine within the client driver used to handle the event notification.

Card detection. The process of recognizing that a PC Card has been inserted into a socket and notifying enabling software responsible for configuring the card.

Card information structure. Also called the CIS, this data structure is incorporated into PC Cards to characterize the function(s) contained within the card. The CIS consists of individual elements called tuples, each of which describes a given characteristic of the card. The CIS is typically mapped into attribute memory address space, but is sometimes implemented in common memory address space.

Card services. A collection of software functions based on the client server model that permits unified control to all PC Card sockets and related hardware. PC Card client drivers register with card services to obtain access to PC Cards and sockets.

Resource Management Services. A category of card services that used by a client driver to acquire system resources needed for configuring their card. When a client driver requests resource for their card, card services checks to verify that the requested resource is not being used by some other device within the system. Card services performs look-ups within its resource management table that contains the resources that are available for allocation to PC Cards.

Card Types. PCMCIA are defines three card types (types 1, 2, and 3). These cards have the same electrical interface and different only in height.

CD1# and CD2#. The Card Detect (CD) pins signal that a card is fully inserted into a PC Card socket. When the HBA detects these pins asserted it notifies card services via an interrupts.

CE1# and CE2#. The card enable (CE) pins specify that a PC Card is being accessed and whether one or two bytes are being requested.

CIS. See Card information structure.

Client driver. A client driver, also called an enabler, is responsible for configuring and enabling a PC Card when it is first inserted into a card socket. The client registers with and makes calls to card services provides the services necessary to fulfill the clients requests.

Client utility services. A category of card services used by client drivers to request that card services perform complex tasks that would otherwise require many low-level requests be made by the client driver.

Common memory. Address space within a PC Card used as the working memory, where files are typically stored.

Configuration process. The process involving reading and interpreting a PC Cards CIS entries to determine the type of function implemented by the PC Card and it configuration requirements.

Configuration registers. Configuration registers within a PC Card provide the ability to program it for a given configuration and obtain status information about the card.

DACK. DMA acknowledge (or, DACK) is a PC Card input for PC Card I/O functions that support DMA transfers. This signal is returned to the I/O card from the host system's DMA controller in response to a DMA request by the card. DACK signals the beginning of the DMA transfer between memory and the I/O function.

Dedicated enabler. A PC Card enabler that is designed to configure and enable a specific PC Card. Dedicated enablers are usually supplied by the PC Card manufacturer. Also called Device-specific enabler.

Device-specific enabler. See Dedicated enabler

Digital Audio Waveform. The audio information output over a PC Card's SPEAKER# (SPKR#) pin to the host system's, used to drive the host system's speaker.

DMA. Direct memory access (or, DMA) in the PC environment is the a transfer between the host system's main memory and an I/O device. The transfer is controlled by the host-resident DMA controller.

DMA Acknowledge. DMA acknowledge (or, DACK) is a PC Card input for PC Card I/O functions that support DMA transfers. This signal is returned to the I/O card from the host system's DMA controller in response to a DMA request by the card. DACK signals the beginning of the DMA transfer between memory and the I/O function.

DMA Bus Cycle. A bus cycle performed by the host system DMA controller

DMA clock. The clock used to run the Host DMA controller. 4MHz in a PC Compatible system.

DMA Request. DMA request (or, DREQ#) is a PC Card signal used by I/O cards that support DMA. The I/O card asserts DREQ# to notify the host DMA controller that it is ready to transfer data between itself and memory.

DREQ#. See DMA Request.

Dual-voltage cards. PC Cards that can operation at either 5vdc or 3.3vdc.

EMS. Expanded Memory Specification (or, EMS) defines a memory management procedure that allows additional memory to be added to a DOS-based PC that typically supports only 1MB of usable address space. EMS was defined by Lotus, Intel, and Microsoft and is also referred to as the (LIM specification). Only applications written to support EMS can access the additional system memory.

Enabler. The software responsible for detecting, configuring, and enabling a PC Card. Enablers are also called client drivers, because they interface to the PC Card environment via card services. Compare Point Enabler.

Event call-back. The mechanism used by card services to notify its clients (PC Card enablers) of specific events that have occurred at the PC Card and socket. The enablers are responsible for processing the events.

Event notification. Another term for a card services call-back. See Event call-back.

Event wakeup. An event that is external to the PC that stimulates a PC Card to perform some type of action (e.g. a remote call to a modem), when the system is in a power conservation state. The external event is used to "wake" the system so that it can respond.

ExCA. Exchangeable Card Architecture (or, ExCA) is a specification defined by Intel to promote interoperability of PC Cards between x86-based PCs. Note that ExCA has been renamed QuickSwap.

Execute-in-place. Execute-in-place (or, XIP) refers to the ability of a PC memory card that emulates a disk drive to execute code directly from memory, rather than having to copy and execute the file from host memory. Only applications written to support XIP can execute directly from PC Card memory.

EXIP. A type of XIP, called Extended XIP, that requires a 386 or later x86 compatible processor. PC Card memory in this case is mapped into host system address space above 1MB.

Expanded Memory Specification. Expanded Memory Specification (or, EMS) defines a memory management procedure that allows additional memory to be added to a DOS-based PC that typically supports only 1MB of usable address space. EMS was defined by Lotus, Intel, and Microsoft and is also referred to as the (LIM specification). Only applications written to support EMS can access the additional system memory.

FFS. See Flash file system.

Flash file system. A file system designed to manage access to PC Card flash memory that emulates a disk drive. A specific file system is required for flash memory to support the special write characteristics of flash memory. Also called FFS.

Flash translation layer. A form of flash file system that interfaces to the DOS file system, rather than implementing a specific installable file system that replaces DOS when accessing virtual flash drives. Also called FTL.

FTL. See Flash translation layer.

Generic enabler. A PC Card enabler designed to recognize and configure a wide variety of card types. Compare Dedicated enabler.

HBA. Host Bus Adapter (or, HBA) is the hardware interface between the host expansion bus and PC Card sockets. The HBA bridges, or translates transactions between the PC Card sockets and the expansion bus.

HLDA. Hold Acknowledge (or, HLDA) is an output from an x86 processor and an input to the DMA controller. HLDA is asserted by the processor when it detects its HOLD signal has been asserted by the DMA controller in response to DREQ# being asserted by the PC Card I/O device.

HOLD. Hold request (or, HOLD) is an input to an x86 processor that directs it to relinquish control of the system bus. This signal is asserted by the host DMA controller to request use of the system buses so that it can perform a DMA transfer. See also HLDA.

Host bus adapter. Host Bus Adapter (or, HBA) is the hardware interface between the host expansion bus and PC Card sockets. The HBA bridges, or translates transactions between the PC Card sockets and the expansion bus.

Hot insertion. The term used to describe the ability of PC Cards to be inserted and removed from the system after it has already been powered on.

I/O address window. A range of I/O address location programmed into the HBA that corresponds to the address locations used by an I/O card to access its internal registers. The HBA recognizes when software attempts an access to a location within the specified range and forwards the transaction to the target I/O card and socket.

I/O Read Command. A command that is asserted by the host system to indicate that an I/O read operation is being performed. A card socket signal (IORD#) is asserted when an I/O read targets a PC Card register.

I/O size is 16-bits. A socket interface signal (IOIS16#) output from an I/O card, telling the HBA the size of the register being accessed (either 8- or 16-bits).

I/O Status Change. A socket interface signal (STSCHG#) asserted by an I/O card to notify the HBA and the enabler that a status change has occurred within the PC Card

I/O Write Command. A command that is asserted by the host system to indicate that an I/O write operation is being performed. A PC Card signal (IOWR#) is asserted by the HBA when it recognizes that an I/O write operation is targeting a PC Card register.

IDE. Integrated drive electronics (or, IDE) is a type of hard drive that incorporates must of the hard drive controller logic within the drive itself. The interface between an ISA compatible bus and the IDE drive is called the ATA interface.

INPACK#. See Input port acknowledge.

Input port acknowledge. Input port acknowledge (or, INPACK#) is an output signal from an I/O card during an I/O read that accesses a PC Card register. This signal notifies the HBA that the access belongs to the PC Card.

Interrupt request. A request to the system that indicates that the I/O card needs servicing. The interrupt request ultimately calls the PC Card's interrupt service routine (or, ISR). The interrupt request is signaled via the card's IREQ# pin.

IOIS16#. I/O is 16 bits (or, IOIS16#) is a socket interface signal output from an I/O card, telling the HBA the size of the register being accessed (either 8- or 16-bits).

IORD#. The I/O read command (or, IORD#) is a signal asserted by the host system to indicate that an I/O read operation is being performed from the I/O card.

IOWR#. A command that is asserted by the host system to indicate that an I/O write operation is being performed. The PC Card signal (IOWR#) is asserted by the HBA when it recognizes that an I/O write operation is targeting a PC Card register.

IPL. Initial Program Load refers to the process of loading the operating system during the power-up sequence. Sometimes also referred to as the boot process.

IREQ# Also called IREQ#, this PC Card

JEDEC. Acronym for Joint Electronics Device Engineering Council.

JEIDA. Acronym for Japanese Electronics Industry Development Association.

Level mode interrupts. A method of signaling interrupts to the host system. A PC Card using level mode interrupts causes an interrupt to be registered, or triggered, by asserting the IREQ# pin and keeping it low until the interrupt is cleared by the ISR.

LIM 4.0. See Expanded Memory Specification.

Low voltage socket. A PC Card socket that can apply either 5vdc or 3.3vdc as the initial Vcc power to the socket. The HBA that supports a low voltage socket monitors the voltage sense pins (VS1# and VS2#) to detect the initial voltage required by the PC Card.

LXIP. A form of XIP referred to as Expanded XIP that employs an expanded memory approach to map the PC Card memory.

Management interrupts. Interrupts generated by the HBA to notify card services that a status change has occurred within the PC Card environment.

Memory address windows. A range of memory address location programmed into the HBA that corresponds to the address locations used by a memory card to access its internal memory array. The HBA recognizes when software attempts an access to a location within the specified range and forwards the transaction to the memory card and socket.

Memory enabler. PC Card software designed to recognize, configure, and enable memory cards. Also called memory client driver.

Memory-only interface. The PC Card socket interface that supports only memory cards. The socket is always configured as a memory-only socket when a PC Card is first inserted. The socket can be changed to a memory or I/O interface if the enabler detects that the PC Card contains an I/O function.

Memory or I/O interface. The PC Card socket interface that supports both memory and I/O functions. The socket is changed from a memory-only to a memory-only socket when the HBA and PC Card are configured.

Memory technology driver. A client driver employed to handle low-level access to flash memory that requires special programming algorithms. Card services calls the memory technology driver when a flash memory enabler calls the bulk memory services. Also referred to as an MTD.

Metaformat. A formatting standard defined by the PC Card standard that describes low-level formatting information.

MTD. See Memory technology driver.

OE#. Output enabler (or, OE#) is a socket interface signal that indicated that a memory read command is being performed from PC Card memory.

Offset. The value (typically measured in bytes) that specifies an address location relative to a given base (or, start) address.

PCMCIA. Acronym for Personal Computer Memory Card International Association.

Point enablers. A PC Card enabler that recognizes and configures a PC Card by accessing the HBA and PC Card directly without the support of card and socket services.

Power Management. A hardware and software solution employed to conserve power.

Pulse mode interrupts. A form of interrupt triggering used to support interrupt sharing in the ISA environment. The interrupt is triggered on the trailing edge of the PC Card's negative pulse.

READY. An output pin from a memory card that indicates that it is ready for the next transaction. If deasserted, indicates that the memory card is busy performing a command and is not ready to receive the next transaction.

REG#. The register (REG#) pin is a socket interface pin asserted by the HBA to indicate an attribute memory access (when OE# or WE# is asserted) or an I/O access (when IORD# or IOWR# is asserted).

Registration. The process used by enablers to obtain the services of card services.

Reset. A socket interface pin used to reset the PC Card.

Resource allocation. The process employed by a PC Card enabler and card services to determine if system resources are available to be assigned to the PC Card.

Socket interface. The electrical and mechanical interface for PC Cards.

Socket services. PCMCIA specific software that provides low-level routines needed to access a given implementation of HBA. Socket services consists of a collection of functions that are typically called by card services to access HBA registers.

SPKR#. The speaker signal defined by the memory or I/O socket interface. Used to carry digital audio information from the PC Card to the host speaker.

Status change events. PC card and socket events that reflect some change in the status of the PC Card. When a status change event occurs, the HBA generates an interrupt to signal card services of the event.

STSCHG#. Status change is an output signal from an I/O card to signal that a status change has occurred.

SXIP. A type of XIP, called simple XIP, that maps PC Card memory into an address range no larger than 64KB in size.

TC. An output signal from the DMA controller indicating that the transfer is complete (i.e. the DMA controller has reached the Terminal Count). This signal is an input to PC Cards that support DMA transfer.

Tuples. The name given to the elements within the CIS that describe characteristics of the PC Card.

Type 1 card. A PC Card with a maximum thickness of 3.3mm.

Type II card. A PC Card with a maximum thickness of 3.3mm.

Type III card. A PC Card with a maximum thickness of 3.3mm.

Virtual disk. A memory card that is used to emulate a hard drive.

Vpp1 and Vpp2. Programming voltage pins defined for the socket interface.

VS1# and VS2#. Voltage sense pins defined for the low-voltage socket interface. These pins determine the initial Vcc level to apply to the socket.

WAIT#. A socket interface pin used by a PC Card to force wait states into a transaction.

WP. See Write-protect.

Write-protect. Write-protect (or, WP) is a output pin from a PC memory card indicating whether the user has chosen to write-protect memory (i.e. files).

XIP. See Execute-in-place.

XIP-expanded memory. A form of XIP referred to as Expanded XIP that employs an expanded memory approach to map the PC Card memory.

XIP-extended. A type of XIP, called Extended XIP, that requires a 386 or later x86 compatible processor. PC Card memory in this case is mapped into host system address space above 1MB.

XIP-Simple. A type of XIP, called simple XIP, that maps PC Card memory into an address range no larger than 64KB in size.

Index

MindShare, Inc.
Technical Seminars

MindShare Courses

- PCI System Architecture
- PCI Software Environment
- PCMCIA System Architecture
- 80486 System Architecture
- EISA System Architecture
- CardBus System Architecture*

- Pentium System Architecture
- Plug and Play System Architecture
- ISA System Architecture
- PowerPC Hardware Architecture
- PowerPC Software Architecture
- PowerPC PREP Architecture

Public Seminars

MindShare offers public seminars on their most popular courses on a regular basis. Seminar schedules, course content, and pricing can be obtained by contacting MindShare as shown below. Periodically, seminars are held on older technologies, (e.g. ISA and EISA) based on customer demand.

On-Site Seminars

If you are interested in training at your location, please contact us with your requirements. We will tailor our courses to fit your specific needs and schedules.

Contact MindShare at:

Internet: mindshar@interserv.com
CompuServe: 72507,1054

Note: New courses are constantly under development. Please contact MindShare for the latest course offerings.

*Available summer '95